a Private Life of
Michael Foot

Carl Rollyson

University of Plymouth Press

Paperback edition first published in the United Kingdom in 2015
by University of Plymouth Press, Endsleigh Place, Drake Circus,
Plymouth, Devon, PL4 8AA, United Kingdom.

Paperback   ISBN 978-1-84102-390-8

A CIP catalogue record of this book is available from the British
Library.

Publisher: Paul Honeywill
Editor: Michelle Phillips

Typeset by University of Plymouth Press in Janson 10/14pt
Printed and bound by Edwards Brothers Malloy

PREFACE

This is not a conventional biography. I rely not on documents, but almost exclusively on recorded interviews and memories of Michael Foot constituting a raw record of conversations not smoothed over by a biographical narrative. This is a book about process. I show how I went about obtaining my story, which ostensibly concerned Jill Craigie, who married Michael Foot in 1949. Michael entered Jill's life in 1945. He was such an important source for this biography that, inevitably, I learned as much about him as about her.

Readers come to biographies to learn about the subject, not the biographer. Yet the biographer is, in a sense, half the story. Or, as Paul Murray Kendall put it in *The Art of Biography*, every biography is an autobiography. So *A Private Life of Michael Foot* is an effort to show how a biographer struggles to tell his own story, even as family and friends cherish differing narratives about that same subject. My wish is to highlight these clashes of perception rather than reconcile their discrepancies.

There is value, too, in showing the rough edges of biography, the stops and starts, in an unapologetic fashion. I wonder if there has ever been a biography that has treated a British political and literary figure in quite so revealing a fashion.

Contents

a Private Life of

Michael Foot

Carl Rollyson

March 2000

1

"Here's my library, which, I'm sorry to say, is a bit of a mess. Jill used to [huh!] reprimand me." 'The huh!' does not do justice to Michael's high-pitched wheeze, or capture the wry pleasure he took in recalling her scolding. Their Hampstead home on Pilgrim's Lane she had so beautifully refurbished had a shabby and dishevelled appearance now—rather like its surviving rumpled owner. The room was lined top to bottom with bookshelves. It even had a wall of bookshelves that could be moved like a door, opening to a smaller room congested with more books and papers. The library seemed to serve as a huge storage vault: a long table was piled high with books, books blocked up an unused fireplace and the floor supported still more heaps of books and papers.

It had been nearly five years since I had last seen Michael. Then we had talked in a cosy sitting room where we were surrounded by books, but also by lovely furnishings. I had come to discuss Rebecca West, the subject of the biography I was writing at the time and Jill was not only telling me about the writer and woman she befriended and grew to love, but also she was producing Rebecca's first scrapbook of articles. These West wrote just after she had abandoned her family name, Cicily Fairfield. Jill , pointed to Rebecca's own handwriting announcing:

Rebecca West born on 11 December 1912

Michael was a widower. I had missed Jill's memorial service because I had recently moved and Michael had sent the notice to my old address. I first met Jill just after Michael retired from Parliament in 1992. The couple were selling their cottage in Wales. Over dinner, Jill asked me if I knew anyone who might like to buy it. "A good place for a writer," she added, smiling at me. Her 'big eyes,' which both her daughter and an ex-lover, William MacQuitty, extolled, seemed to swallow me up. I wanted to buy the place on the spot, such was her charm—and Michael's. They displayed not just the good humour biographers experience during interviews that go well, but also extended an affection that amounted to a blessing.

When Michael greeted me at the entrance to their home only three months after Jill's death, his pallid complexion shocked me. I thought that I had arrived at death's door. He appeared to have aged more than a decade. I remembered that he sometimes stumbled, even with a cane, but now he was all wobble, yet his voice was as strong as ever and as engaging as it always had been.

I had come to discuss writing Jill's biography. In order to ascertain if Michael would be receptive to my overture, I had consulted my agent (Gloria Ferris) who had represented Michael's biographer, Mervyn Jones. Gloria and Mervyn thought Michael would meet me. So I wrote to Michael, simply saying that I had felt a terrible loss myself when I read Jill's obituary in *The New York Times*. Perhaps it was too soon to think about a biography, but if he should decide he wanted one, I asked him to keep me in mind. Two weeks later he called me at my home in Cape May County, New Jersey: "You are the one to do it! Jill would have approved!"

I knew that both Jill and Michael had liked my biography of Rebecca West, but just how much quite astounded me. I had kept them apprised of my progress on the book, sending them chapters for their comments. Jill could be exceptionally critical, especially on the subject of feminism and I worried that she would find my chapters on Rebecca's early years as a radical feminist wanting. But her praise was more than gratifying. Michael later touted my book in his biography of H. G. Wells. They had discussed my work often, Michael said.

Michael had published articles in praise of Rebecca West's patriotism. Unlike many others on the Left, he did not find her fierce anti-Communism troubling. Indeed, it was in accord with his own mission to develop a Socialism that would provide the world with an antidote to Soviet tyranny. Mervyn Jones told me that while researching his biography of Michael, he had been impressed with the vehemence of Michael's own anti-Communism as expressed in the hard Leftist *Tribune*, which Michael edited for several years.

Biographers are often made to feel like supplicants. But Michael's first phone call was a wooing, making me feel that as the biographer of Rebecca West, I was conferring an honour on Jill. He provided me not just with unfettered access to Jill's study: I was to live with him whenever I was in London. I was to go about the house as if it were my own. I could rifle through every drawer, cupboard, room and receptacle. I slept on a sofa bed in Michael's library. Each night before retiring, I would go through a shelf or pile of books (his only filing system) filled with letters and reviews and notes. Every night brought a new revelation. A few letters from Mary Welsh, Hemingway's fourth wife, whom Michael had known in the war, were tucked into Hemingway books. In a debunking biography of Michael's hero, Aneurin Bevan, founder of the National Heath Service, I read Michael's comment on the flyleaf, which began "read with rising anger ... "

I often thought of Boswell and Johnson during my stays with Michael Foot. In Michael's company, I was very much a Boswell, keen to get the great man to talk. I recorded everything, compiling a hundred hours of Michael reminiscing and nearly another hundred of others commenting on him. Scholars estimate that Boswell spent something like four hundred days in Samuel Johnson's company. Over a period of three years and ten trips to England, I lived for something like one hundred days with Michael. Boswell knew Johnson much longer (more than twenty years), but he did not live with his subject and see him throughout the entire course of a day and night. I was with Michael from breakfast through to dinner in the evening and everything in between and usually more talk right up until bedtime. I watched the cycle of Michael's days and became a part of them, sometimes locking up the house at night or taking messages when he was away for part of a day—and once having to rush down the stairs of his Hampstead house and into the street to pick up him when he had tripped and fallen.

Michael was a gallant man who rarely let down his guard. But with me, perhaps because I was American and because we spent so many continuous hours together, he would sometimes reveal himself. He was profoundly angry the night I had to pick him up in the street. Sitting at the kitchen table, he nearly sobbed and said, "You don't know what it is like to grow old. You don't know." His humiliation was palpable.

Our conversations—like most conversations—were circular. Michael would keep coming back to the same topics, digress, then lose his place—"I was just ... [un-huh] ... I was just ... " A soundtrack accompanied his conversations. He could not walk without making noise, groaning in different octaves and punctuating many expressions with a "whee!"

Michael wanted my biography of Jill to do what she could not do for herself: write the whole story of what it means to be a woman. Like the subjects of *Daughters of Dissent*, her never completed epic about the struggle for female suffrage, Jill saw herself as a dissident fighting for recognition.

2

Our March meeting lasted for nearly two hours. Toward the end of the interview, I brought up Michael's relationship with Julie Hamilton, Jill's daughter by her first marriage:

> [CR] Mervyn mentions that when you first married Jill, Julie wasn't happy about that.
> [MF] We've had our problems over the years, but ... anyhow you talk to her ... anyhow I don't think we had much trouble. We had some other ... you talk to Julie. You're going to see her tomorrow?

I did. Michael was never one to discuss relationships in depth. I would have to press him again and again—usually in response to what others said—to get him to open up. His pauses were blanks I had to fill in by talking to others.

Michael was not openly recalcitrant, but he would often

cut off discussion by reverting to the sort of encouragement that became a refrain in our relationship: "Anyhow, Carl, I'm very glad that you're doing it. I'm going to have a sleep now."

Even as Michael was heading off for his nap and I was backing out of Jill's study, where our first conversation about my biography of her took place, I stopped and said, "I've just got to take a quick peek in here [a drawer]. I want to see if it contains more manuscript." As I fingered photocopies and note cards, Michael said, "There's nothing to be hidden." I took him at his word.

3

"Michael's life is one long love affair. It is a love affair with the Labour Party, a love affair with Hazlitt, Swift, H. G. Wells, and my mother," Julie told me over drinks in a pub the next day.

Julie first caught sight of Michael right at the end of the war, shortly after her mother had made her film *The Way We Live*, shot in bombed-out Plymouth and featuring a cameo performance by Michael Foot who was campaigning for a parliamentary seat during what became the Labour landslide of 1945. Jill, a beauty, had had her pick of men and was then involved with a handsome suitor, her producer William MacQuitty, while at the same time conducting an affair with a good looking painter, Denis Matthews. She was also still married to her second husband, Jeffrey Dell.

Yet to Julie's amazement, Jill set out to captivate Michael early on. "He was the most revolting specimen of a man I'd ever seen," Julie recalled. "He had asthma and eczema. How could my mother touch him, let alone get in bed with him?" This shy, myopic man appealed to Jill because unlike so many of her other lovers, he talked of building a better world and took her entirely on her own terms, barely inquiring about her past. What he did know only made him prouder of his conquest. He would later brag to me about how Jill had led on so many men. He spoke of winning her. During the early days of their courtship, she had shown up at a miner's gala event in Durham with another man, "But," he chortled, "she came home with me."

Michael's brothers, by his own account, were astounded when he won Jill. Brought up as a strict Methodist, Michael never had the easygoing attitude toward sex that seemed second nature to Jill. With Jill, Julie could talk about sex freely, sharing the most intimate details of her relationships. Sex, in Michael's Plymouth home, had been unmentionable: "Don't put your hands under the covers, young man!" his mother admonished him.

"Slowly, slowly, slowly," Julie began to appreciate Michael. Although she found him reticent and difficult to have fun with, he was always there for her when she was in distress. "He took me to movies like *Ivanhoe* and *Scaramouche* I loved to see and that mother was not interested in at all." Later, as Julie developed a love of opera, she would share record albums with Michael. "He thinks he shared everything with Jill," Julie noted, adding that Jill would say, "*I'm* not the one who loves opera."

Michael's trusting nature, his absolute faith in Jill, irritated Julie. The director Ronnie Neame, who employed Jill in the 1950s to write screenplays for *The Million Pound Note* and *Windom's Way*, was, Julie recalled, "always round the house." The teenaged Julie became suspicious. As soon as Michael came home, she would say, "Ronnie's just left." Michael, never one to become jealous, would laugh and call Julie Iago. There was something wrong with a man, in Michael's view, if he wasn't in love with Jill. He scoffed at the idea of Ronnie as Jill's lover when I raised the subject with him later and Julie did the same, even though she admitted, "Michael was a loving man but no sexual athlete and my mother was a sexy woman." Jill once confessed to Julie that Michael had "many wonderful attributes, but after five years their sex life was virtually over." Michael would make the most of his romantic revivals with Jill during their many trips abroad, especially to Venice, but Jill's own journal reveals how terribly disappointed she was by his flagging sexual appetite.

"Was Jill jealous of Michael?" I asked Julie. "You can't publish this if Michael is still alive," she replied, her voice dropping. "She had cause to be." I mentioned Jill's comment in a published interview that if Michael had an affair, she did not want to know about it. "She knew about it," Julie said "and it devastated her." Julie then began to tell me in capsule form the story of Michael's affair with 'Lamia' (not her real name). "It isn't publishable," she repeated. I agreed, although in the end, I published part of the story in *To Be a Woman* after a struggle with Michael and those close to him about what was really central to the story of the Foot-Craigie marriage.

Jill stuck by Michael, "out of love," Julie believed, "but also out of a sense that he was making a contribution to society. She was the most subservient feminist ever. Intellectually, she was a feminist, but in her behaviour she was not." Recalling the marriage's dynamics in the 1970s and thereafter, Julie noted that if Michael wanted a cup of coffee and Jill was writing her book, he got his cup of coffee. She was always complaining about these interruptions. "Why not go away for six weeks and finish your book?" Julie would ask her. "But who would take care of Michael?" Jill replied. No one—not Julie, not anyone—could take care of Michael as Jill did. To Jill, Michael was "special." Then Julie added, "Excuse my language, but fuck that! He was just a man. I took issue there, *strongly.*"

"I think my mother had quite a tough time with Michael. He adored her in a cerebral way, but she had to do all the dog work." He was attentive. He brought Jill flowers and gifts, often consulting with Julie about what Jill might like best. But to Julie, Michael never put Jill first. "He did on a certain level. He only wanted to hear praise of her after she died. But that tells me that he realised he had not worshipped her as he should have done."

After listening to Julie over the course of three years, I did begin to wonder why Michael never gave Jill the space or time she gave him. I could never formulate the question in a way that would not seem accusatory, especially to a man who was still grieving. But in retrospect, I wish I had asked: "Michael, did you ever—especially after you retired from public office—just say to Jill, 'Why don't you go off and finish your book. I'll get on?'" Indeed, there were all sorts of friends and family—as I discovered—who were quite willing to coddle him. Other than complaining to others—as Jane Carlyle did about her mate—Jill never made an issue of her husband's selfishness and perhaps, for all sorts of reasons, she did not really want to finish her book, but the nagging question is why he did not do more to encourage her? He was interested in her work. He read it and made editorial suggestions (which he did not want me to mention in her biography for fear this would somehow diminish her achievement), but as far as making some significant alteration in a life built around him, he seemed incapable of proposing a plan for her book that would free her to confront the formidable task of telling the story of women's struggle for equality.

Michael was the male partner in a dance, but he did not know how to lead. Or rather, he led by default, since Jill did not challenge his authority. He simply filled a vacuum. As a political man, he would have the same problem: he had a solid group of adherents, but he could not use that base to assert his authority. He was a sort of effigy of a great man and he seems to have known it, since he became leader of the Labour Party only after considerable prodding from Jill and others. It would have looked cowardly not to accept the leadership. But Michael was a sort of hollow man, as he acknowledged with self-deprecating humour during his 1983 campaign against Margaret Thatcher: "I'm here to impersonate the leader of the Labour Party. What have I been doing the rest of the week? You might well ask."

4

"Did you see Michael yesterday" Mervyn Jones asked me before we sat down to lunch at his flat in Brighton. "People say he is so old and frail. But Jill said to me once, 'You know, Michael is as tough as old boots.'" Although they had once been close friends, Mervyn had little contact with Michael now, the result of some bad blood over his biography of Michael. I should have taken this development as a warning sign.

I asked Mervyn about Michael's pronounced limp, occasioned by surgery after a catastrophic car accident in 1963. "I haven't dared to ask him, but it's painful, isn't it, just for him to move?" I had never heard Michael complain, although his explosive grunts made me wonder. But Mervyn did not take the question seriously, simply saying Michael had stiff joints "like old people do" and this was very much the way others close to Michael saw matters. Rather than seeing the strain he was under because of his disability, more than one friend called Michael's straining "nervous energy." Michael was like some mechanism constantly agitating and lacking a muffler. He had not merely endured a severe physical injury, he had turned his crippled condition into a kind of performance—like a merry pirate with a peg leg, an Ahab without animus. There was, however, fury in his temperament and even hatred, especially for traitors to the cause like David Owen, who had split off from the Labour Party during Michael's leadership and whom Michael called a "mountebank."

Mervyn only noticed Michael's shortness of breath during walks on Hampstead Heath. Michael had been an all-day walker for much of his life, but at eighty-seven, the rises robbed him of air and he had to stop frequently to tell his anecdotes. Yet he was still taking buses and clattering along with his cane, sometimes hitting posts with it for emphasis. The walking stick had also become a prop, an animated exclamation mark. Sometimes Michael would wave it high and take my breath away, since I was certain that he would take a tumble. He would later wave the stick high while standing atop picturesque Dubrovnik and I worried whether he would topple over in an off-balance movement, plunging into the sea. Michael's word for his condition was "rickety."

5

Mervyn listened to me expatiate on my enthusiasm for doing

Jill's biography:

> **[CR]** My experience with them was as equals. When we went out to dinner, or when I was in their home, the back-and-forth between them was marvellous. I had no sense that this was simply Michael Foot's wife. I liked the whole feeling of that and when I read her obituary, I thought, "if I can work that into a biography ... "
>
> **[MJ]** Yea [I can now detect on the tape recording Mervyn's unexpressed dismay]. Well, there are problems.

I pressed Mervyn to explain.

Well, I think a certain legend is being created about Jill, which came through in my own obituary. I wouldn't stand by it. It was eulogistic —for Michael's sake, of course and so were the speeches at the memorial service.

I assured Mervyn that after writing about my previous subjects, I was prepared for problems. "That's what Gloria said. 'He knows what problems are,'" Mervyn laughed, and continued: "The legend is that she was a great feminist and I just don't think that was true. She really didn't get on with other women. ... The only person who considered Jill Michael's intellectual equal was Michael. You're going to have trouble with that." I heard echoes of Julie's criticism of her mother in Mervyn's rather harsh assessment.

Mervyn had had a rough time with Jill over Michael's biography, which she thought neglected her own role in Michael's life, mischaracterised her experience as a mother and failed to capture Michael's domestic side. To Mervyn, Jill seemed rather high handed. "When Jill said we're having dinner, it was a royal command. If you were doing something else, she would say, 'Drop it.'" This aspect of Jill did get short shrift in my biography. Michael objected to Mervyn's remarks, which I included in a draft without using Mervyn's name and I could see that unless I identified my source, neither Michael nor the reader would take the criticism seriously. Mervyn warned me that Michael would not be able to see—or admit?—that Jill had an overbearing quality.

What enchanted Michael? I asked Mervyn. "Beauty," he said, but then added:

> For a political man to have a wife with a career of
> her own and was an achiever you could be proud of
> was, at that time, unusual. Labour leader wives were
> uneducated. But most people thought of Jill as Michael
> Foot's wife. That's not what you want and that's not what
> Michael wants. That's a big hurdle in the writing of the
> biography."

If this was true, I thought, what does that say about Michael?

6

"Gloria mentioned a woman at *Tribune* who was in love with Michael. She could only remember her first name: Sheila," I told Mervyn. "That was my impression too," he answered. "Mind you, she hated Jill, presumably because she was in love with Michael." I encountered Sheila Noble on several occasions in Michael's home, where she would come for a day to help him with his correspondence. When I asked her for an interview, she just smiled and shook her head. "Sheila adored Michael. I don't believe she ever had an affair," Mervyn said.

"The other person to see is Elizabeth Thomas, Michael's personal secretary—way back, in the 1940s. Then she started working at *Tribune* and then when Michael became a minister, she was his political advisor. They were never lovers, I don't think." Mervyn was wrong on that last score, as I learned later from Michael himself in a rather trying scene. Like Sheila, Elizabeth rebuffed my request to interview her about Michael and Jill. It is apparent now that certain women formed a *cordon sanitaire* around Michael, one that Jill grew to resent.

Did Michael ever stray with other women? I asked Mervyn.[1] "I'm convinced it was a rare event," he replied.

> Actually, Elizabeth Thomas, an extremely sensible woman, told me an anecdote about Michael straying. He spent a night with another woman. He came home at breakfast time and Jill was *completely* furious and said, "I'm divorcing you." He managed to smooth it over. My respect for Elizabeth is that she had never told me the story before and she didn't want to tell me this story while I was writing a biography of Michael. If I put it in, the press would have fun with it. It would have run away with the biography, of course.

I was beginning to feel uneasy about falling into the authorised biographer's trap of becoming privy to secrets that could not be divulged. I could see that I was heading toward some kind of confrontation with Michael. The way he handled it would

---

[1] "Michael always struck me as being an exceptionally monogamous person," said his old friend Mike Bessie. "Did I think the same thing was true of Jill? I never observed in all the years of their marriage any signs that she longed for other male companionship."

be another means of assessing his character.

Talk about Michael sex's life segued into a discussion of Arthur Koestler's rape of Jill, a story that Michael himself first revealed in a review of a book about Koestler. He caused an uproar in the press and among Jill's and Michael's friends. Frederic Raphael wrote a piece questioning Jill's account, suggesting she had exaggerated or perhaps had even led Koestler on. There were other skeptics, although another woman came forward, writing a letter to the press that described Koestler's assault on her (she managed to escape being raped). Then it was revealed that Koestler had also raped one of Dick Crossman's wives.

Jill had kept the rape secret for more than 40 years— supposedly not even telling Michael —but had blurted it out late one night at a small party with her friends, many of whom I would interview on subsequent trips to England. Mervyn was skeptical about the story, although he believed Koestler quite capable of rape. Mervyn had asked Jill, "Did you tell Michael?" She hesitated and said, "Michael saw the scratches on my arm. He said, 'What's this?' I didn't tell Michael I was fully raped but that I was assaulted and that it was Arthur." It all seemed a strange story to Mervyn, especially when Jill said Michael's response was, "Well, you have to admit he's a very good writer." Mervyn thought this was an unbelievably "crass thing to say. A man has raped your wife—I couldn't believe Michael had said this."

As I pieced together the story of Jill's rape for my biography of her, I realised there was a missing element: exactly what Michael knew and what he did about it. I spoke with him many times about the rape but never came close to comprehending what, in the end, was the truth. But I also held back certain testimony, which led me to believe that Mervyn's assessment of Jill and his belief in Michael was misguided. The Koestler rape became just one of many instances when Michael did not stand by Jill. To do so, would have meant an ugly confrontation with his wife's rapist, a writer Michael would continue to rhapsodise over in our conversations.

June 2000

7

"I went to see Mervyn," I told Michael at the beginning of my second stay at Pilgrim's Lane.

> [CR] I raised the issue with him that there were things about his book that Jill didn't like. I mentioned the house and the garden. My impression is that to this day, this is something Mervyn doesn't grasp. He admired you. He admired your politics, but the domestic side did not become part of the story. Jill must have been terribly disappointed.
>
> [MF] Mervyn has quite a good artistic interest. In fact, he got on with Jill, you see, earlier. In a kind of way he was understanding Jill as well as anyone. But she did say, "Fancy him, writing the book without appreciating what this house was."

I made no comment but thought, 'How could Michael be so wrong about Mervyn?' Other than a few respectful comments about Jill's film career and her passionate commitment to nuclear disarmament, his tone was highly dismissive of her.

Michael had an aching need to show the world what Jill had not been able to display herself, much as Thomas Carlyle had done for his late wife Jane and H. G. Wells had done for his Jane after she died. These men relied on women to perform in what Martha Gellhorn liked to call "the kitchen of life."

Just then the phone rang and before Michael could heave himself into motion, his housekeeper, Emma, answered the call. "She's a great help," Michael said, "She's knows what she's up to."

"My legs are not quite properly operating and I'm having physiotherapy every Tuesday," Michael said after Emma had beaten him to the phone. I accompanied him on one of these sessions, where he had to wait like anyone else for his turn. I was amazed that he did not have someone come to the house and that the therapy was not more frequent. He could barely walk now. But he was loyal to the National Health Service, the creation of his hero Nye Bevan and avoided any appearance of seeking special treatment or assistance outside the NHS.

"Tomorrow I'm going to see Bill MacQuitty," I told Michael, who responded: "He knew Jill before I did. He was the producer of her films and a wonderful friend to her and to us. I hope he is in as full possession of his faculties as I am," Michael said, laughing. I asked him if he had read MacQuitty's memoir, *A Life to Remember*, which included passages about Jill. "I haven't, really," Michael admitted. I would continue to be surprised at how little Michael knew about Jill apart from what she herself had told him. She had been able, in fact, to fashion an image of herself for him that he could not bring himself to contest, even when I began to present him with evidence that Jill had sometimes misrepresented her life.

When I mentioned that Jill had a brief career as an actress, Michael responded, "I didn't know that. She never told that to me." In 1937, she appeared in a film, *Makeup*, written by her second husband, Jeffrey Dell. They had also collaborated on a successful stage play. "I see," Michael said, seeming to muse over this new information. "I never met Jeffrey Dell. Jill said he was very clever." That seemed to sum up all Michael knew about the man—or cared to know. Michael was not the kind of spouse to concern himself with his wife's former life. "Jill didn't talk much about Jeffrey Dell."

Just then Michael was exercised about a letter he had received from Michael Scammell, Arthur Koestler's authorised biographer, raising doubts that his subject had actually raped Jill. Certain of her friends had expressed their skepticism to Scammell, he reported. Michael pronounced Scammell's name so that it sounded to me like "Scoundrel. "I'm going to write to the fellow in a pretty fierce way." Michael revered the author of *Darkness at Noon*, a riveting exposé of Stalinist tyranny that Michael had stayed up reading all night when it was published in 1940. Michael was quite proud of his role in introducing Koestler's writing to a British audience. As editor of the *Evening Standard*, he arranged for Koestler to write a column because he "knew more about what was happening in Spain than almost anybody. He was very good to teach the bloody fool English how these things run. I knew him as well as anybody." Michael fondly remembered the pre-rape days, when he and Jill had socialised with Koestler, visiting him in France along with Richard Crossman and his wife.

Michael then retold the story of the rape. "She didn't report it to me then, and she did not report it to anybody," Michael said, "except maybe Ronald Neame. You can ask Ronnie Neame about that." I did and Neame's account would raise disturbing questions about Michael's version of events.

Scammell entered the story because a rival, David

Cesarani, had scooped him, interviewing Jill about the rape and publishing her account as part of his Koestler biography. In Michael's view, Scammell was attempting not only to discredit Cesarani but also to destroy Jill's report of the rape. I had had my own run-in with Scammell when, as American director of PEN, he had denied me access to board minutes dating from the period of Susan Sontag's presidency. As a PEN member, I had a right to see the minutes, which I wanted to consult for my biography of her, and PEN's Freedom-to-Write committee had supported my request thirteen to one (the holdout was an attorney associated with Sontag's publisher). Telling Michael about Scammell's shameful behaviour strengthened the bond between us, especially since Michael was a staunch partisan and believed in backing his friends to the hilt.

Scammell's announcement that he was the "authorised biographer" also grated on Michael. "I don't agree myself about definitive, authorised biographies. Absolute balls." He handed over Scammell's correspondence to me: "That's a terrible letter, isn't it?"

"Why hadn't Jill seen Scammell?" Scammell's letter pointed out that ten years earlier when he came calling, Michael had spoken with him but Jill had not. "She hadn't told me about the rape," Michael said. "She didn't want to ... " Michael hesitated and I added, "open the whole story." I have to wonder, given what I was later to learn about Michael, if Jill ever wanted the whole story told. Julie told me she doubted her mother wanted Michael to know exactly what happened because he would not react as a normal man would. He had too much respect for Koestler as a writer to confront him. Just after Michael spoke of his admiration for Koestler's "abilities," I decided to put the question directly:

> [CR] Michael, this is a hard question to deal with. It's
> difficult putting yourself back in that time. What do you
> suppose you would have done if Jill had told you?
> [MF] I don't know.
> [CR] It's hard to say, I'm sure.
> [MF] I think I would have written him a letter, you
> know. Something like that. It would have been a terrible
> shock to me.

Michael's response confirmed Julie's speculation that Jill
would not have confided in Michael because she knew his
response would not be visceral, but intellectual. But later,
after interviewing Elizabeth Rushdie, Salmon Rushdie's ex-
wife, I began to doubt that Michael knew as little about the
rape as his retrospective account suggested, even if Jill had
not spelled out the details.

The more Michael talked about Koestler, the warmer
his memories of the man became. Beaverbrook considered
it quite a coup to get such a writer ("starting on his fame," as
Michael put it) into a paper that was admittedly thin during
wartime. Michael believed it was important for his country
to give Koestler, an exile, a "proper reception." Koestler
appreciated Michael's efforts, Michael emphasised: "he took
an interest in my life and I took an interest in his."

"You'll find me dodging all over the bloody place in my
mind, but don't you worry about that, you make order out of
chaos," Michael directed. "I will," I replied. "I've got many
more questions to ask you, but I'm perfectly willing to listen."
He wanted me to ask him everything, he assured me "and

you must make the judgment about what you use and don't use." The dodging was oftentimes simply an expression of the gusto of a man with many stories to tell, and story-making is often a matter of digression, but there were occasions when I simply could not bring Michael to the point. I wondered whether he could not see the point —or wished to avoid it.

Michael loved to talk about books he read with Jill. The first was Wynwood Reade's *The Martyrdom of Man*. H. G. Wells had called it one of the great books of the world, Michael pointed out, and it was one of the first presents he gave Jill at the White Tower restaurant. The book was not a European-based view of the world. "It is written like a poem and beautifully shaped. It is a defence of heresies. Heresies make the world go round."

Mentioning the White Tower brought on memories of the war and Mary Welsh, then a reporter for Beaverbrook's *Daily Express*. In these pre-Jill days, Michael used to frequent the restaurant with Mary and Connie Ernst, the daughter of renowned American attorney Morris Ernst.

[MF] Mary and I invited our fellow journalists to come and have a lunch with us — chiefly ones that had just come from America or Australia — and then halfway through the lunch we'd say to them, "You know, by the way, you're paying for this meal because we're giving you so much information." We did have quite a big list of those who would come — and along came Hemingway. I'd never met him nor did she. It was a sunny day in the second year of the war and we put to him the proposition and he didn't object to that at all and indeed was enamoured of it. "Come tomorrow, if you like, and I'll take you to the Dorchester," he said. Of course he went off with Mary Welsh. Farewell to Mary.

This farewell could not have been more breezy or light-hearted. She faded from our view like a 'dissolve' in a motion picture.

The period with Mary coincided with Michael's years as editor of the *Evening Standard*. Lord Beaverbrook had hired Michael on the strength of Aneurin Bevan's recommendation after putting Michael through a kind of on-the-job simulation. Michael enjoyed retelling the story of how Beaverbrook asked him to read the morning papers and then give him an account of the news. When Michael did so without hesitation, not even pausing to look at notes, he won the press proprietor's admiration — and soon his affection. Beaverbrook enjoyed arguing with his journalists whatever their politics and Michael certainly did not keep his socialism a secret. Like Aneurin Bevan, Michael satisfied Beaverbrook's intense curiosity about what the other side was thinking. Michael enjoyed quoting bits of Beaverbrook's advice: "Don't use question marks in headlines. It implies you don't know the answer."

Later Jill fit right into Beaverbrook's circle, feeding the old man tasty bits of gossip about Labour Party personalities and sharing with him her hopes for Michael's career. Beaverbrook did not ordinarily care for his journalists' wives, so Michael was quite proud of how Jill charmed his employer.

But the Beaverbrook-Foot-Craigie attachment went much deeper. Michael was virtually a second son, adopted not merely by Beaverbrook himself but by the press baron's family. "They might have been awful with me, or jealous, but it was exactly the opposite," Michael told me. Why did Michael admire Beaverbrook so much? In part, it had to do with Beaverbrook's openness to people. "He had no kinds of prejudices such as the English people have. Of course, he hated the English aristocracy," Michael observed.

Michael and Jill were connoisseurs of personality, transcending politics. They loved Randolph Churchill, who ran two losing campaigns against Michael in Plymouth and they adored Benjamin Disraeli, Mrs. Pankhurst, Lady Astor— all of them affiliated with the Tories. Sometimes, as I would later learn, Michael would go into contorted arguments to support those he liked even when they manifestly stood for views opposite to his own.

Friendship was, I think, a deep enchantment for Michael. He built up his favourite as a nonpareil. He touted you. But if you broke the spell, he would erupt with fury and then subside in a silence that just cut you out entirely.

8

William MacQuitty, then ninety six and still handsome, had a spacious flat overlooking the Thames near the Putney Bridge underground station. A world class raconteur, his conversation ranged from his upbringing in Ulster, where he saw the Titanic launched (he later made the film classic, *A Night to Remember*), to his years as a banker in India learning about Hinduism and other world religions, to his study of psychology with Wilhelm Stekel, to his renowned collection of two hundred and fifty thousand photographs (he was a superb photographer), to his entrepreneurial start in the film industry with a self-produced documentary entitled *Simple Silage* (based on his years as a farmer). His wife Betty brought in tea, which I proceeded to serve to this ancient.

MacQuitty, Jill's producer during the war, had wanted to marry Jill—or so Michael, Julie and everyone else then on the scene except William MacQuitty--told me. When I pressed him about his feelings for Jill, he changed the subject, portraying a woman who believed in a world he could not conceive of ever coming to pass. He thought Jill and Michael were fantasists, their socialism a pipe dream.

"The dog and the duffle coat and the flowing hair. They're a lovely couple," MacQuitty said, laughing. But he believed they had no idea of what was up. He remembered one of Jill's first meetings with Michael. When Jill and Liam (as she called him) went to see Michael during the making of Jill's film *The Way We Live*, about the rebuilding of Plymouth, they were treated to an "oration," MacQuitty recalled. Michael was "inspired, talking Jill's language," MacQuitty said. "Where there is no vision, the people perish and here was a man with vision."

But where was that vision leading? Jill and Michael reminded MacQuitty of a joke. A pretty Liverpool girl wanted to get to the Far East, but she had no money. So she stowed away. A fortnight later she was discovered aboard ship. The Captain said, "You look very spruce, well fed and turned out. How come?" She said, "One of the crew took pity on me." After more questioning, she revealed that her benefactor was the second officer. "What did you give him in return?" the Captain asked. "Well," she replied, "You might say he took advantage of me." Then the Captain said, "I can confirm that. You are on the Liverpool-Birkenhead ferry."

MacQuitty was full of this kind of badinage, but he was a wary gent who kept referring me to his published memoirs.

He seemed uncomfortable with the idea of straying from his text. I would make several return visits, but I was only slightly successful in penetrating his persiflage.

9

MacQuitty's joke reminded me of Ronnie Neame's view of Michael. Before my June visit, I had called Neame at his home in Beverly Hills. He was nearly as guarded as MacQuitty and almost as old, telling me he was now put together with string. He remembered that Jill introduced him to Michael in the late 1940s. Ronnie had heard that Michael was a Communist and not a very nice man. On television, Michael came across as soapbox strident, a monomaniac:

> People used to come up to Jill and say, "What a shame you are married to that awful man." In fact, Michael is an absolute sweetheart. The only thing about him is that he is up in the clouds. He would like a world that is just not practical or possible.

Ronnie's arguments with Michael were always friendly and though he had not seen Michael in many years, he was obviously very fond of him.

10

Ronnie Neame echoed Michael's editor and publisher, Mike Bessie—another witness I interviewed before setting off for London in June 2000. Mike talked at his apartment off of Washington Square in New York City. Bessie, Michael's friend since the Second World War, regarded Michael as a brilliant writer, but also an imperceptive personality and a bungling politician. Almost the first thing Mike said was, "I wonder what kind of a source on Jill Michael is? He is so kindly a person."

But beneath that veneer was a controlling personality, Bessie went on. Michael often attempted to short circuit Jill, calling her "My dear child," a habit Barbara Castle regarded as a form of "gentle bullying." Mike Bessie interpreted the phrase as the effort of a man exerting his patience. Often the outspoken Jill did not give ground, but Mike never saw Michael lose his temper, no matter how outrageous her comment.

To Mike there was a mystery about Michael. For forty years he had asked his friend to write a book entitled "Why I am a Socialist" and for four decades Michael Foot had written books that avoided confronting that important issue, Mike thought.

"You know the central criticism of Jill?" Mike asked. She was ambitious for Michael and forced him into a political career, which ended sadly. "If it can be said that there was anybody not qualified to be the leader of the Labour Party at the time Michael became the leader of the Labour Party, it was Michael!" Mike said, his voice rising. "He has none of the aggression — when he speaks he is a demon," but that is not enough to make a leader, Mike implied.

Then Mike described a different Michael Foot:

To Jill has been attributed what many see as a wrong turn in Michael's career. If you didn't know them well, watching them in a room together, you would think that she was very dominant because what you wouldn't necessarily observe is that he would allow that to seem

so. It didn't deter him from doing what he felt he had
to do. He just didn't fight back in terms of argument or
discussion.

Mike wanted to know if I agreed. On two occasions I had
watched the dynamic he described while working on my
Rebecca West biography. I sensed it again when another
biographer sent me a recording of Jill arguing a point while
Michael played second chorus, so to speak.

Why did Michael permit such an impression to be
created—one that would continue even after Jill died, when
he would attract a kind of female confederacy around him? Or
did Mike feel otherwise, that Jill could orientate her husband
in directions he might not otherwise have taken?

I think the turn in the road was after Nye died. The party
came to Michael and said you must take Nye's constituency.
"You are Nye's heir and you must do that." I think Michael
had made up his mind about writing—God knows I wanted
him to write and we had begun talking about the books he
would do. But going back into politics that way—I think Jill
was one of the elements that persuaded him to do that. But
immersed in Labour Party politics through my friendship
with Dick Crossman, I certainly understood why Michael did
that.

If Jill did have a significant impact on Michael's political
decisions, it was, in part, because he really liked women, Mike
emphasised. Michael Foot saw a great future role for women
in politics.

When I entered Michael's life, he was rebuilding
his support system, superintended by Jill's close friend,
Jenny Stringer. He had an enlarging circle of new and old

companions shepherding him not only around London, but also accompanying him to Dubrovnik, Plymouth, Grassmere (to meetings of the Wordsworth Society) and even to Bermuda. The frail, pale figure I had met on the doorstep was beginning to burgeon, devoting more and more time to his beloved football team and serving on its board, even as he became, in his own words, even more rickety. As Mike Bessie observed:

> Michael is greatly changed. Even when he had his eczema [in the 1940s] and a certain shyness, he was not as vulnerable as he now looks—the eye [Michael had been blinded by an attack of shingles] and he just doesn't have the strength. His continued activity is a triumph of will. Each time I see him I wonder, "Where does he find it?"

Michael's energy did seem, in part, of a piece with his will to make a world in which he could think well of people. "Jill thought Michael lived in the nimbus of his qualities," Mike observed:

> He didn't really see how awful some people were. You had to do something pretty bad before Michael would criticise you. He might criticise your ideas, but of your character or behaviour he tended to be sympathetic or understanding. Jill would be much sharper about people. Michael could be a destructive speaker in the House and tear you down. But that was an argument about something, not about a person.

Especially in their last years together, "You had a feeling that Jill pretty much arranged Michael's life," Mike thought. Michael grew increasingly dependent on her—"perhaps we all do," said Mike, including all us husbands in his observation.

This reliance on women showed up early, in Mike's view. "Whatever affair or relationship he had with Connie [Ernst]" (who became Mike's first wife after she had ceased her World War II romance with Michael), "there was an element of dependence in it." When Connie told Michael he should move out of his crowded flat during the war, he seemed powerless to effect a change. How could he manage all his books? he wondered. Rather like Jill taking charge of Michael, Connie engineered his removal to more spacious surroundings, taking care to ship his precious library to his new accommodations.

"Did you seriously consider marrying Connie?" I asked Michael when I got to Pilgrim's Lane in June. "You bet," he replied. "Tell me about Connie," I prodded him. "I was very fond of Connie," he began:

> I had two Jewish friends that I fell for. The other was Lily Ernst, the Jewish exile I first met at Beaverbrook's and got to know during the war. She was Beaverbrook's mistress and I would have liked to take her off him. But I didn't have much success. She was a passionate Jew. Her mother had been taken to the camps from Yugoslavia. Beaverbrook had met her in somewhere like Cairo and said if you're ever in trouble, let me know. Now Connie I met sometime in 1942 through Mary Welsh.

This roundabout explanation was rather typical. Michael could recall significant events, such as being with Connie in

New York City on the night Roosevelt's death was announced, but he never clarified the nature of his emotional tie to her. I would remain in as much doubt about what Connie meant to Michael as Mike Bessie was. "For three or four years during the war we were going around lots of places together," Michael said of his relationship with Connie. I persisted:

[CR] Do you think that if she had not met and married Mike Bessie she would have married you?
[MF] Well, I'm not quite sure. I don't think she really wanted to live here. As it turned out, it was probably better for both of us.

I made another try:

[CR] As a personality, was Connie anything like Jill?
[MF] No. I don't think really. Just let me think ...

A minute went by:

[CR] Did she have Jill's feminist interests?
[MF] I don't know that she did exactly. She practiced it—that is to say, she was a strong liberal.

The word liberal triggered his mention of coming to New York in 1954 during the Army-McCarthy hearings. Michael and Jill stayed with Connie's father, Morris Ernst, famous for his defence of *Ulysses*.

Mike Bessie's discussion of Michael and women brought me to the issue of Michael's infidelity. I was keen to know what Mike Bessie, an old hand at publishing, would make of the "Lamia" story. I wondered how he thought I should handle it in the biography. "I have a suggestion to make," he began:

> You don't know how you will handle it until you do. If it comes out to your satisfaction and you are inclined to use it, I would give it—not send it—to Michael, saying, "Here's a part of my book that I believe to be true and that I would like to use, but it is not sufficiently important for me to use if it distresses you in any way."

Although at the time I agreed that this was good advice, I should have known that I would never take it. My vision of Jill's biography—any biography I chose to write--took precedence over anyone else's feelings. The truth came first, Dr. Johnson asserted, even at the cost of hurting others.[1] But how I would pursue that truth in the light of Michael's own trust in my judgment I had not decided upon.

At this point Mike's second wife, Cornelia, joined the conversation and I asked her for her impressions of Jill. Cornelia felt Jill was conflicted, playing the good wife to Michael, but being a feminist. "There were those moments when she and Michael disagreed," Cornelia said. "My dear child," Mike broke in, imitating Michael's habitual method of addressing Jill. "That must have been fun to watch," I said. "It was fun," Cornelia agreed, because "my dear child" would bring out the feminist in her. "All of a sudden she was on her hind legs snarling—sweetly snarling but snarling."

---

[1] See my argument in *A Higher Form of Cannibalism? Adventures in the Art and Politics of Biography* (Chicago: Ivan R. Dee, 2005).

11

In June 2000, I had settled into a cosy stay at Pilgrim's Lane. Only later would I begin to see that by providing me with so much access and comfort, Michael was buffering the biography. I don't mean that he made some sort of calculation that I would be indebted because of his generosity—although this is exactly what his nephew Paul Foot would later say: I was abusing Michael's hospitality by dealing with issues that for Michael's sake should be left out of Jill's biography. It was simply in Michael's nature, I believe, to extend his liberality, which easily segued into his thinking I would produce a biography in the same spirit of amity that characterised our jolly talks together.

I did not realise then that I could not count on Michael to be his own man. He had a minder, Jenny Stringer. I met her during the course of my June 2000 stay at Pilgrim's Lane. Although she promised me an interview, it would be quite some time before she would sit for one. "I better not stay." Jenny said after stopping by to look in on Michael and I think, monitor my progress. "Why not stay?" Michael asked. "I have things to do," she said." "Better not stay," Michael muttered, "doesn't sound very convincing to me." This was the sort of banter Michael enjoyed with the women — and it was mostly women — who catered to him.

Jenny was a friend of Victoria Reilly's, Michael's godchild and the daughter of Paul Reilly, whose father, Sir Charles Reilly, had introduced Michael to Jill at a London party in late 1944 just before Jill embarked on her most important film, *The Way We Live*. Jenny had not met Michael and Jill, however, until 1963, when they bought their home in Pilgrim's Lane, close to Jenny's home. Jenny became one of the younger women Jill encouraged, praising her as both homemaker and worker. They shared the same politics and Jenny was deeply involved in Labour Party affairs. When Jill realised she was dying, she began to worry about what would happen to Michael. Although Jenny never said so in so many words, I believe she made a promise to Jill to look after Michael. She was always cordial to me, but in her view, I was an interloper not to be trusted, especially since I always seemed to carry with me what she grimly called the "black box"—my cassette recorder.

12

The world seemed to turn on Michael's likes and dislikes—as I learned when I mentioned I was giving a talk about Dr. Johnson at Cambridge. Michael objected to him as though Johnson was just another Tory politician. Indeed, literature seemed another form of politics and one had to declare a position. "What's all this anti-Johnson stuff," Michael's brother John had asked him. "It won't stand up," John said. Michael explained his complaint to me:

It all derives from Johnson's attack on Swift. Several people I admire very much like Alan Taylor was also a tremendous admirer of *Lives of the Poets*. No one can deny what a wonderful book it is. But he describes Swift's madness without any kind of qualification. Once you look into it the story is absolutely false. He was not mad at all. Even Swift admirers like George Orwell swallowed the story of Swift's madness.

Michael took fire on the topic of comic geniuses, putting

Swift at the top with Shakespeare, followed by Rabelais, Charlie Chaplin, and Dickens. "I'm anti-Thackeray—I know that people will say that's a foolish thing to say—because of what he said about Swift. "They tried to destroy Swift. If they had their way, he'd be dismissed as an absolute maniac. Terrible, what Thackeray said about him. Partly it's because of his treatment of the women, but in my view he was in love with Stella and Vanessa." The "they" almost sounded like a political party.

Talk of Stella and Vanessa transitioned in Michael's mind to the question of fidelity and then to an old joke. A chap comes home and finds his wife in bed with another man. He upbraids her. She gets up and says, "That just proves you don't love me. You'd rather believe your own eyes than what I tell you."

13

After an afternoon at the British Film Institute, I returned to Pilgrim's Lane in quite a state of excitement, eager to read a letter to Michael that I had found in Jill's papers. She had written to Michael Balcon, a friend of hers and Michael's, asking him for the opportunity to direct a film. Although she had made her name during the war as a director of documentaries, her work had received mixed reviews and when postwar developments in British cinema closed off her efforts to continue her career, she turned to script writing for Ronnie Neame and his producer, John Bryan. Essentially Jill was making a pitch to Balcon for making films about contemporary women, a subject ignored or poorly handled in 1950s Britain, which she nonetheless had explored with considerable success in an *Evening Standard* series of articles.

Balcon sent her a polite but firm brush-off. I wondered if Michael knew about this letter and how he would react.

I read the letter to him in the living room while he played classical music. "An amazing letter," I said. [2] "Good, isn't it?" Michael replied. "How could anyone not hire this woman?" I asked. "Yes, I think so too," he said. "I daresay she was disappointed."

Michael asked again the date of Jill's letter. It was written in 1958. This was a shattering period for both Michael and Jill. He had recently lost his bid to recover his Plymouth seat (he had been out of Parliament since 1955). At around the same time Michael had had a row with Nye Bevan, his mentor, closest friend, and ally. Bevan's refusal to endorse unilateral disarmament came as a bitter disappointment to Michael, who continued to campaign for it, putting tremendous strain on the Bevanite faction of the Labour Party. The acrimony reached its climax when Bevan smashed one of Jill's antique chairs and called Michael a cunt in his own home.

In 1959, Michael reconciled with Bevan, then dying from cancer. Michael went on to write an acclaimed biography of his mentor. Michael reminded me that a year or so later he decided to make a bid for the Ebbw Vale seat Bevan had held until his death in 1959. Helping Michael, he acknowledged, became a full time job for Jill—"the election and the actual process of settling there [in Tredegar, part of Michael's constituency]." It was a distraction. I'm sorry to say it must have often happened. She was turning away from what she had been doing in the film industry." In fact, Jill's last substantial film work was a screenplay for *Windom's Way* (1957), a vehicle

---

[2] I include the entire letter in *To Be A Woman: The Life of Jill Craigie* (London: Aurum Press, 2005).

for Peter Finch. She did not produce another substantial work until *Who Are the Vandals?* (1967), a BBC television documentary about tower blocks and public housing. In that film she resumed her passion for architecture and town planning. She also caused an uproar in the Labour Party and among architects with two articles for the *Times* in which she accused both of reneging on their promise to provide housing on a human scale. Michael admired the ruckus Jill caused, but he seemed unable to understand why she did not continue with her causes. She would not make another film until the 1990s, when Michael's retirement from Parliament allowed him to put himself at her disposal. Initially he had balked at the idea of her doing a film about the Balkan Wars, but then he capitulated to a suddenly adamant Jill, determined to make the film no matter what.

Was he making amends? Or was he simply caught up in her own passion to tell the story about the breakup of Yugoslavia and the shelling of Dubrovnik, their beloved holiday retreat? If Michael was no Carlyle when it came to reassessing his marriage, was the film nevertheless an act of restitution?

I watched Michael mulling over Jill's letter to Balcon. Michael mentioned his friendship with the film producer but seemed unable to grasp that Jill had been rejected. "They should have pressed her more," he said vaguely. Who "they" were was in doubt. Jill apparently never told Michael about the letter, and to me that was as heartbreaking as the letter itself.

But then, Jill had another life that Michael acknowledged but did not share. A case in point was Tom Driberg , a part of the Bevanite faction. Driberg's personal affairs, as Michael described them, were a mess:

He had an unhappy life, Tom, because of his sexual ...
He was taking terrible risks before the whole change had
happened in the atmosphere of what could be done and
not done. Tom from his earliest days was a homosexual,
but he couldn't enjoy sex with members of his own class.
So he was constantly engaged in affairs ... you know ... in
a way that was not at all ... In his last few years he used to
come up here quite often and talk to Jill. He wouldn't say
all this to me. Jill was very good to him.

Michael then described a scene with a dejected Driberg
standing alone on the street with his belongings, not knowing
how to arrange a move into new lodgings. Jill understood this
kind of male helplessness—as did all those women around
Michael—and she soon had Driberg settled.

The 'Dribergs' — the hapless males of this world — often
turned up on Jill's doorstep, Michael recalled. The artist Stanley
Spencer would come calling, unwashed and dishevelled. He
would ask: "Why am I so attractive to women?" and he was,
Michael explained. At one point Spencer turned out a quick
sketch of Michael, which Jill thought awful. She destroyed it,
Michael recalled, adding that Clementine Churchill had done
the same with Graham Sutherland's portrait of her husband.

Just then Julie arrived. "How are you?" Michael asked.
"Okay," she replied. "Doesn't sound very enthusiastic,"
Michael said. Michael seemed to crave big entrances and
provocative pronouncements, and he liked to send visitors
away with some kind of provoking comment: "Drive
properly," he would say to Jenny. He knew that would get a
rise out of her and prolong, if only for a moment, their comic
crosstalk.

Julie got up to get us drinks, refusing my offer of help. When she returned, she handed me a whiskey (with Michael, I almost always drank whiskey, a cheap Scotch I would down while eying the superb collection of single malts—gifts from admiring visitors — displayed on the mantel).

I had brought a copy of my Rebecca West biography for Julie. "You should read it for your education," Michael said to her. "My ongoing education," Julie tittered. She would be the first to say she was not an intellectual. It had often been hard on her simply to be in the company of Michael, Jill, and leading lights in theatre, politics, and the arts who frequented the Foot /Craigie dinner parties. Julie loved private, domestic life and she had little patience for the sacrifices Jill made to Michael's status as a public man. She was fond of Michael but critical as well—as she was of her mother. Michael would eventually sour on me because I gave Julie so much of a voice in my biography of her mother. But Julie had also been a problem for Jill and Michael, running through three marriages (as her mother had done), borrowing money, and bitching up her life while wanting Jill and Michael to give her not only economic but moral support. To many of Michael's and Jill's friends, Julie's motives were mixed. To Julie, however, families were meant to help out, and she had certainly helped out at certain crucial points in Michael's and Jill's lives.

Just then, Julie was planning a two-week stay at the Villa Dubrovnik, where Michael and Jill had spent so many happy holidays. Jill's friends were assembling, as were many Croats, who honoured Jill and Michael for making a documentary about the shelling of their city. *Two Hours From London* marked Jill's astonishing return in her eighties to filmmaking. Of course, I had to be on hand to meet as many of her friends as I could. "Fun is to be had there," Julie said. "You're making it impossible for me to say no," I replied. "That's what we like to hear," Michael chimed in. Michael and his entourage planned the rendezvous for that September. I did not know then that he was paying the way for many of these people, including Julie.

14

After Julie left us at Pilgrim's Lane, I came back to the question of Michael and women, which he had alluded to when describing his period at Oxford. I pointed out to him that one of Jill's obituaries referred to him a "man about town" during the war, while another claimed he had been a "womaniser" in the period before he met Jill. "What I want to know," I said to him, "is how much of a ladies' man you were." "Well I wasn't at all, hardly," Michael replied. I laughed, "What a disappointment, Michael!" "I wish I could have made the boast," he added. "I sometimes had eczema so badly I wouldn't go out of the house. For quite a long time I didn't think any woman would look at me." The word womaniser bothered him. "It should be exterminated from history." Frank Owen, his colleague at the *Evening Standard*, seemed to attract women effortlessly, but Owen was no womaniser. In Michael's book, the term implied one-way gratification and in Owen's case the women received as good as they got. "I was in awe of such men and thought, 'How do you do that?'" Michael continued: "In the 1930s, I was tremendously inhibited about sex. I was very backward in such matters. I started reading H. G. Wells properly then. He liberated me." Michael adored novels like *Ann Veronica* and thought the world would have been a poorer place if H.G. had not had his affair with Rebecca, no matter how many hardships and griefs their liaison caused. Rebecca had attacked H.G.'s feeble characterisations of women such as Margerie in his novel *Marriage*. But in subsequent novels, Michael pointed out, Wells included much more complex portraits of women—some of them clearly based on Rebecca herself.

I was still trying to piece together what Michael was like when he first met Jill:

> **[CR]** She must have seemed an extraordinary woman. She was doing this film [*The Way We Live*]. She had been married twice before. She had a child. What was that like for you?
>
> **[MF]** Yes, oh well ... By the way, I was tremendously admiring of all the time she gave to Julie. Sometimes Julie poorly appreciated that.

I didn't think he was going to answer my question, but he continued:

> It didn't happen all at once, you know. After the [1945] election we started doing some things together. I was living at sixty two Park Street and she came up and saw there was no music, and she put a radiogram in the corner and played Mozart. Jill was the one who really made me understand what music was—all such things.
>
> **[CR]** Was it difficult for her to divorce Jeffrey Dell?
>
> **[MF]** I didn't know about that at all, really. I don't think it was difficult. We weren't pressing to marry, but my father was in favour of it.

Such dialogues were all too brief, with Michael often breaking off to discuss another book, another writer—this time it was V. S. Pritchett, who put him on to Disraeli's novels. "All the women are different," Pritchett pointed out, "not a stereotype among them."

Literature, especially Michael's favourite works, had a presence so palpable for him that it deflected discussion of his own emotional life. Personal experiences seemed displaced in literature, or rather, the crucial events in his life could only be approached in terms of literary analogies. For example, Michael's great friend, "Vicky," a newspaper cartoonist, a Hungarian Jew who had emigrated to England before the war, was quickly merged into a discussion of Heine, whom Michael revered for his melancholy Jewish sensibility. The witty yet often morose Vicky committed suicide—in large part, Michael believed—because of the sorry state of the world. The cheerful Michael was nonetheless drawn to apocalyptic visions and would recite—as he had for Rebecca West—the whole of Byron's holocaust poem, "Darkness."

Just then Jenny returned, having sorted out some business for Michael. But a good many items remained to be acted upon in what she called his "procrastination file." He was about to go out and she said:

> [JS] When you come back, I'm going to pounce on you and you're not going to have lunch until you said yes or no to every single one of them.
> [MF] Right.
> [JS] I'm going now.
> [MF] I'm coming with you to see you're not arrested.
> [JS] No, you better not. Arrested? For what?

[MF] Leaving your bloody car in the middle of the road.

15

Jenny mentioned as she was leaving that Michael might expect a call from Moni. "Who is Moni?" I asked after Jenny left. She had been James Cameron's wife, an Indian woman who figures in Cameron's wonderful book, *An Indian Summer*. Michael considered Cameron the best journalist of his generation. He was dead now and Moni had married Sir Denis Forman, former head of the British Film Institute and the producer of, among other noteworthy projects, *The Jewel in the Crown*. Forman, I was later to learn, had first met Jill during the war, when, as he put it, she was quite a nightclub hopper and girl about town.

Talk of Moni set Michael off on a trail of funny stories: the time, for example, when a Parisian friend with a weak grasp of English idiom wrote him on the eve of his first election campaign in Ebbw Vale, "I'm crossing my fingers for you." To which Cameron added: "I'm fingering my crosses." Michael did not have much to do with crosses or any sort of religion, he wanted me to know. When he spoke of Heine, for example, he described a man who rejected Judaism because of his "humanity." Heine seemed a greater figure than his friend Karl Marx, Michael added, because the former had a much better sense of humour.

Comedy, in fact, was a huge topic of conversation in the Foot household. Michael often quoted Jill's assertion that it was much more difficult to write a great comedy than a tragedy. The couple seemed to regard comedy as a capacious way of describing and understanding humanity, even a form of social justice. "If Karl Marx had only brought Heine over to London with him. It might have saved us all." Michael then paraphrased Heine: "I don't want a poet's crown. Say that I was a soldier in the fight for humanity."

This fight for humanity is the way Michael glorified the Labour landslide of 1945, which became his next topic of conversation. It was much more than a party victory and what drew him to Jill was her confidence—far greater than his—that not only would he win a seat in Devonport, Labour would triumph too. The turning point for her, Michael suggested, was watching Nye Bevan speak on Michael's behalf in Plymouth.

Michael never mentioned the passes Bevan made at Jill, but this subject did not bother him when others—including me—spoke of it. "You must make a list of the men who made passes at Jill," I told him. "An appendix," he suggested.

16

Michael's praise for Jill seemed extravagant to nearly everyone I spoke with about her. She was a filmmaker, a journalist, and finally a kind of historian, but she did not make history. But Michael wanted to make an epic out of her life:

> She was dedicated to the women's fight and in one form or another that's what she's doing for the rest of her life—in some ways I think better than anybody else. If you take it all together—at our commemoration for her I said that she called herself a William Morris socialist and I said that at the commemoration service they had for William Morris, Robert Blatchford said that William Morris was our best man. I said Jill was our best woman.

Michael spoke of how well Jill had taken his devastating defeats in Plymouth in 1955 and during the general election debacle in 1983. Turning to me, he said abruptly: "Now the way to recover from this defeat of hers is your book. It is very important to us. You understand, I'm sure. I'm tremendously pleased you're doing it. I'm sure she'd be pleased." I nodded, but I could not honestly say that my biography would be what Jill wanted. Michael wanted it very badly. He proposed a title: "Jill Craigie and the Fight For Women's Rights."

It seemed odd to me, however, that Jill's book, *Daughters of Dissent*, which I came to regard as her unfinished masterpiece, provoked so much uneasiness in Michael. "What happens about the actual stuff there [in the book] I'm not quite sure. I'll read it through again sometime, but I'm doubtful whether it should be published separately. If you think it should be, that's another matter ..." But he proved resistant to my proposal that it should be published with a foreword and afterword explaining Jill's intentions and how she planned to complete her work. She had left eighteen substantial chapters (well over 250,000 words), but Michael continued to balk at the idea of publishing because Jill never was able to write about the postwar years when women actually got the vote. When Michael Bessie said the book needed considerable editing and shortening to be published, that pretty much shelved the project in Michael's mind.

So far as I could tell, Michael never did re-read the book. I sat in Jill's study for days reading it all and marvelling at the way she created a great drama out of the Pankhurst and Fawcett family histories, including cameo appearances by John Stuart Mill, Disraeli, and many other 19th-century notables. Her book was pure story, it seemed to me, a wonderful narrative composed of multitudes of biographies. There was nothing dry about her approach or arcane about her use of sources. Her work in film and her love of music showed in the book's images and symphonic structure. Indeed, she had used this material to write a play with music about the suffragettes, eventually also a screenplay. Neither of these works were ever produced.

17

"So ... what's the time"—an expression Michael invariably used, especially around drink time. "10 to 6," I said. "I found a nice reference to Jill in Richard Crossman's diaries," I told Michael. "Yah ... Ah," he muttered. "I just happened to pick this up coming down the steps." It was hard to turn in any direction in the Hampstead house and not find a bookcase. This volume was in the hallway leading to the downstairs kitchen. Actually, the hallway was like an antechamber lined with shelves of Crossman's diaries and biographies of political figures. "I was looking in the index for an entry under Jill Craigie, but it was not there. It was under Jill Foot." "Good God, a scandal!" Michael said in mock outrage. "Page two hundred and thirty five," I continued. "He's talking about Celia Strachey, John Strachey's widow." I began reading: "She had been devoted to John all her life ... She has been a wonderful wife in the same way that Dora Gaitskill and Jill Foot are wonderful wives. All of them are possessive women who fight for their husbands like tigers and all of them, unlike Anne, are politicians themselves and not merely interested in politics."

I had been hoping to stir Michael to comment. I was already frustrated by his unwillingness or inability to analyse the role Jill had played in his political career. I would later learn from Leo Abse and Glennys Kinnock about this aspect of his marriage to Jill. Michael only asked me which of Crossman's diaries I was reading. "Volume one, Minister of Housing, 1964-66," I told him. "How do you think Jill would react to that?" I prodded. He paused, "Well ..." and I re-read the part about possessive wives fighting for their husbands. Michael cleared his throat and began talking about Crossman. "We became much more intimate in the last ten years of his life ... I'm just going to have a short sharp one [a nap] ..." and off he went to rest on the upstairs sofa.

Michael was more voluble later that evening, discussing the Callaghan government and its efforts on behalf of maternity rights. When Margaret Thatcher was elected Conservative leader, she showed no interest in women's issues, Michael observed with considerable dismay. After which he got on to one of his heroes, Lloyd George and Lloyd George's affair with his secretary, Frances Stevenson, a strong supporter of women's rights. Lloyd George said to her, "We can't have another Parnell case, you know." Michael mentioned that both he and Jill were interested in Frances Stevenson, whom Michael had met. He did not know that Jill had kept a diary with rather acerbic comments on the submissiveness of secretaries.

Talk of Lloyd George led to an aria about the poor record of Liberals on the subject of women's suffrage. Michael deplored Gladstone's opposition but saved most of his fire for Asquith, whose government force-fed the suffragettes. Jill, Michael noted, had given Roy Jenkins a hard time for not adequately dealing with Asquith's hostility to votes for women in his biography of the politician. Although Jenkins had made certain government documents concerning the Liberal government's treatment of the suffragettes available to Jill, she continued to hector him. "She would not let him off," Michael chuckled, "every time she saw him."

I seized my opportunity: "Do you think that's part of what Crossman meant when he said Jill was not just a politician's wife but she was a politician too?" "She wasn't a politician's wife at all," Michael replied. "She was very good to me, but she had her own ... " When Michael hesitated, I asked, "So a politician's wife would not speak up, right?" Well, a politician's wife might not put it the way Jill did, Michael conceded. "She was not doing anything to injure me," he quickly pointed out. "She did not meekly follow what the males were saying."

Hoping for further openings, I mentioned a passage in Barbara Castle's autobiography describing Jill's effort to corner Harold Wilson, then President of the Board of Trade, about more support for the British film industry. "Barbara said Jill became quite outspoken and she quotes you as saying, 'Jill, come off it,' perhaps because she was becoming a little aggressive." Michael lowered his voice, "I don't remember that." I continued: "My impression is that Jill was outspoken and not particularly concerned about being tactful." Michael seemed to agree that Jill was pursuing her cause "by the best available means." Jill could be tactless, but Michael asserted that she dealt better with people than Barbara did. Wilson was one of Barbara's heroes (he promoted and backed her), Michael reminded me, but Michael felt Jill was justly critical of Wilson's lukewarm support for British filmmakers. For a Labour Party member, Wilson evinced a shocking want of support for leftwing filmmakers and in fact seemed to Jill, all too cosy with rightwing rogues like Alexander Korda.[3]

"I don't think it would be much use, ever," Michael said, referring to any effort to silence Jill. I laughed. "But that did not mean that she lacked subtlety," Michael added. "I think she was both outspoken and charming," I offered. "Yes, she was," Michael agreed. "I also wonder if she had more latitude to be her own person. She wasn't a member of Parliament representing somebody. She was just representing a point of view," I suggested. "She wasn't representing my views. She knew much more than I did about film," he noted. According to Jill, the trouble started with Stafford Cripps, who seemed in the grip of reactionary filmmakers and then continued with Harold Wilson, Cripps's protégé. Michael Balcon would have supported Jill in this regard, Michael emphasised.

Michael remembered other instances when Jill had gone after Labour leaders—even Robin Cook for the Party's policy on the Balkans. This was before Tony Blair's first election victory when both Jill and Michael thought New Labour had not condemned Serb aggression in stronger terms. James Callaghan himself had come up to Jill to quietly suggest that perhaps she should "lay off." Callaghan and Michael had never been personal friends, Michael pointed out:

> But after we had the election [for party leader, with
> Michael losing by only a few votes to Callaghan] I was
> doing everything I could in the House of Commons

---

[3] Later, film historian Philip Kemp sent me a tape recording of an interview with Jill, who attacked Korda and remained unwilling to accept Michael's defence of the producer when Michael joined the conversation.

to keep that government in office. Also, I didn't want
Callaghan to resign. I thought there was still a chance
of winning the next election—much better than I would
have. I pleaded with him not to do it [resign]. He was
very nice to Jill. After the election [for party leader] he
invited us to Chequers and showed us around, saying,
"Five more votes, Jill and you would have been here."

When I asked him about it, Callaghan did not remember
saying this, but he saw no reason to doubt Michael's memory.

"How did you and Jill feel about coming so close—five
votes?" I asked.

Michael said he never thought he would win:

I didn't think I was going to come as close as that ... he
did that terrible thing about sacking Barbara and Barbara
will never forgive me [because she thought Michael
should have resigned from the Cabinet in protest over
her dismissal]. She thought from that moment onwards
the government made an awful hash of it. Not the truth.
My opinion is that Callaghan ran that government better
than Wilson.

"What happened to Wilson?" I asked. "Did he just get tired?"
Michael thought so: "Yes. Nobody knows for sure."

18

At the end of my London visit, I discussed with Michael
the possibility of joining him in Dubrovnik in September.
It was difficult for me to get away because of my teaching
and my two Scotties, which I refused to put in a kennel. My

wife could look after them, but more than a week of that became rather burdensome for her when alone. "I could never put Dizzy in a kennel," Michael said. I said I'd have to find someone in the neighbourhood to take care of the dogs if my wife came with me (a doubtful possibility). "That's what we did," Michael said. "Dizzy was quite adventurous with other people. He was very frisky. When we said he was a Tibetan, some people laughed. They're supposed to have a terrible reputation." Indeed, Julie had told him that the breed "yapped" all the time. "During the first two years he was a bit hard to control," Michael said, a massive understatement. "We got him just before the terrible election of 1983. On Sundays, I'd do seven or eight miles with him up to Kenwood [in Hampstead Heath] and all those other parts."

"How did Dizzy get his name?" I asked. "I was writing a piece about Disraeli at the time. Greatly undervalued as a writer. A better novelist than that bloody Trollope. Better on politics. . . He was genuinely interested in the women ... in women's rights." Thus Michael rewound the spool of his recollections. Sometimes it seemed like an endless loop.

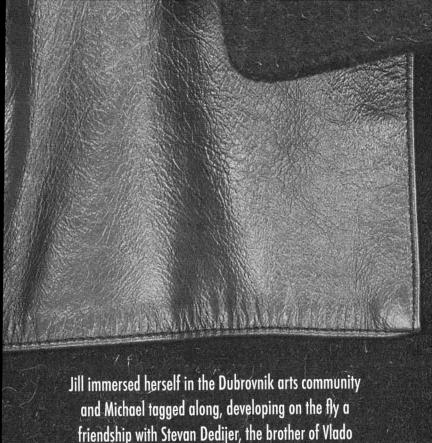

Jill immersed herself in the Dubrovnik arts community and Michael tagged along, developing on the fly a friendship with Stevan Dedijer, the brother of Vlado Dedijer, at one time one of Tito's staunchest supporters

September 2000

19

On my arrival, I found Michael and Julie sitting outdoors in the late afternoon at the Villa Dubrovnik—Michael's and Jill's favourite holiday spot in the last years of their life together. Michael wanted to give me the full history of his stays, so we adjourned to his balcony. It provided a wonderful view of Dubrovnik, a place so compact that Rebecca West, looking back on it as she departed, called it a "city on a coin." Michael said, "Now to come to this place and how we got here. Jill came to see this place better than anybody else and to understand what they were up to here." In 1980, after Michael was elected leader of the Labour Party, a Yugoslav diplomat asked him why the Communist Party in Belgrade had better relations with the Tories than with the Labour Party. "One reason," Michael replied, "is the treatment you've meted out over the years to our friend Milovan Djilas." Djilas had stayed with Michael in Hampstead, befriending Jill as well. In fact, after Michael reviewed several of Djilas's books, Jill proposed that her husband should do a book about him.

The persistent diplomat asked Michael to come to Belgrade on behalf of the Labour Party. Michael agreed, provided it was understood that Djilas would be the first matter he would raise with Tito's Central Committee. The diplomat did not object, except to say that he did not think

Michael would change any minds and that the whole Djilas matter now seemed passé.

Michael arrived in Belgrade just after Tito's death to address the Central Committee. He spoke to five or six of its members, apparently with no results. He was then invited to visit Dubrovnik. "They took me round the wall," Michael said. He was never one to describe what he saw: in this case, a marvellous walkway that encircled the old city. By the time I arrived, it had recovered from Serb shelling. There were no ruins, but new tile roofs were evidence of the effort that had been made to repair a world heritage site.

When Michael got home, he said to Jill, "I've discovered a new place for a holiday. We'll go there next year," and that is what happened. They came to stay at the Villa Dubrovnik. Between 1981 and 1991, they took their holidays in Dubrovnik, a world so self-enclosed that they never managed to visit such famous sites as Sarajevo.

Jill immersed herself in the Dubrovnik arts community and Michael tagged along, developing on the fly a friendship with Stevan Dedijer, the brother of Vlado Dedijer, at one time one of Tito's staunchest supporters, who braved considerable risk in coming to Djilas's defence during his trial. Michael extolled the delights of Dubrovnik. He would often call spots he loved to visit, "a good place to read." I decided to interrupt: "But what did you think of Yugoslavia then and what were your first reactions to the country's breakup? Yugoslavia as an entity ... " Michael broke in: "Well we didn't think it had any sentimental ... and we weren't favouring the breakup, nor were we saying that we thought everything was being run well." Informing much of Michael's thinking was Djilas's call for a more democratic society. Then came the autumn of 1991, the "first time I ever heard the words 'ethnic cleansing,'" Michael noted. "A Belgrade chap" (Michael seemed to recall he was a journalist) said, "They're going to claim every territory for the Serbs." Michael said, "There aren't many Serbs here, are there?" "Oh, they don't mean just where they have a majority," he was told, but any place where there are Serbs. In September 1991, the Serb attack on Croatia began in the North while Michael and Jill were still in Dubrovnik. "We didn't know about the scale of it. We discovered we had to take a new route home." Instead of flying home from Dubrovnik, they had to travel to Montenegro, take a plane from there to Belgrade and then change aircraft for the trip to London.

20

I gazed at the city in the distance and asked, "What were people thinking here? That separation was the right choice?" Yes, Michael and Jill went out and bought Croatian badges. By the end of September, at some public gathering having to do with the House of Lords, Michael spoke to Lord Carrington, suggesting how serious the attacks on Dubrovnik and Vukovar had become. The people in those cities had a right to self-determination. "Of course they have," replied Carrington. "We'll have a fresh look at it." A skeptical Michael told me, "He pretended then to be slightly shocked at what was happening. He bloody well should have been more shocked in my opinion. From that point on, he did not become exactly an apologist for the Serbs, but he and the foreign office were much too accepting of the Serb point of view about the breakup." The Serbs were bound to prevail, the foreign office thought, because they had such an edge in weaponry. Michael also thought that Fitzroy Maclean, a British agent who had played a significant role in Churchill's backing of Tito and his partisans during the Second World War, influenced British government policy. Michael knew Maclean well (they were both first elected to Parliament in the 1945 Labour landslide) and Michael surmised that Maclean had advised the government that whatever the rights and wrongs of the case, the Serbs, in control of the central government and its army, were bound to crush the Croats. But the British government underestimated Croatian and then the Bosnian, resistance. The Germans and the Americans understood the situation on the ground much better than the Major government, which made such a show of not intervening, Michael added.

Michael and Jill returned to Dubrovnik in December 1994, having followed a roundabout route by bus from Zagreb. Part of the twelve-hour trip took them near the Bosnian war zone, but these intrepid octogenarians were overjoyed to return to their beloved city. Dubrovnik, not yet fully recovered from the shelling, but bathed in sunshine two days before Christmas, seemed to Michael "never so beautiful." They wanted to make a film about the 1991-92 siege. "During that time we had been in touch with some of the people we had known before the war." They went to see their friend, the painter Duro Pulitika, whose studio had been used as a lookout post during the siege. A frustrated Michael had not even been able to persuade the British government to send in a food ship. It would be considered an act of war, he was told. "But the Italians are sending in a food ship," he replied in amazement.

Michael and Jill stayed nearly a month in the Villa Dubrovnik, then occupied by refugees. Jill and Michael interviewed the mayor and defenders of the city. Although Michael narrated the film, Jill's writing, editing, and direction were what counted, he told me again and again. He had a hard time adjusting to the role of narrator. Jill's grandson, Jason Lehel, a professional filmmaker who did the camera work, argued that Michael ought to be replaced. Instead, Jill coached Michael day after day, slowing eliminating the stentorian style that had become habitual after so many years on the hustings and in Parliament.

To obtain funding, "We went round to our friends with lots of bloody money," Michael recalled. One friend, Harold Lever, a multimillionaire, sympathised with Dubrovnik's plight, finding parallels with what had happened to Spain when the Western democracies failed to support the Republican government's resistance to Franco's attack. Yet he did not heed Michael's plea. Then a fund-raising meal with Sidney Bernstein, founder of Granada Television, and a Labour Party supporter, also proved a disappointment. "I had to pay for the bloody lunch in the end," Michael said, laughing. Michael resorted to using his own retirement money and Jason cajoled his friends in the film industry to work with no pay, except what they might receive should the film be sold to the BBC or ITV. Finally, a BBC showing of the film, with a panel discussion to balance the film's pro-Croatian bias, allowed everyone involved to just about recover their expenses.

21

"I had just finished my book on H. G. Wells," Michael noted, recollecting their September 1995 holiday in Dubrovnik. "Jill read it here. Couldn't do much about it then." I laughed, knowing that Michael was referring to her reservations. "I don't say she agreed with every word"—a vast understatement! "She thought I was too enthusiastic about Moura Budberg—

the magnificent Moura, as I called her." The mysterious Moura might have been a better appellation because of Budberg's murky history in the USSR. She has been accused of being a Soviet spy, exciting a good deal of controversy about her. Michael, an ardent champion—indeed an idoliser—of his heroes and heroines, had befriended Moura's daughter, Tanya. Michael was enchanted with what she told him about Wells and Rebecca West visiting Moura at her country home outside London on weekends during the war. "My mother could hold her own in any company, although with Rebecca she was inclined to be a little quieter," Tanya told an admiring Michael.

I could imagine the skeptical Jill listening to Michael's impassioned description of Moura's "wonderful, serene countenance—one of the most beautiful faces I've ever seen, in spite of all the turmoil she had. Jill didn't know Moura, but she said to me, 'I think you're a bit thick about Moura.'"

The talk of Moura reminded me of a joke I'd been told about Rebecca attending a funeral for one of H.G.'s mistresses: She turned to another mistress at the ceremony and said, "I guess we can all now move one up." Michael laughed. "Would you like to meet Tanya?" he asked. Moura and Tanya had nothing to do with my biography of Jill, but it was typical of Michael to corral Jill into the pen of his enthusiasms. He had extended a similar invitation for me to meet Stanley Kubrick's wife. Kubrick and Jill had had a casual friendship, meeting on a few occasions, and Jill was an extravagant admirer of his films, but Kubrick's wife had not known Jill—as Michael knew.

I shifted Michael's attention back to Jill's Dubrovnik film, wondering aloud whether any other subject could have galvanised her belated return to filmmaking. Michael still seemed to have Jill's letter to Balcon in mind when he said, "If you look at the whole bloody thing, I was stopping her from what she should have done. She should have been making films all the time."

Dubrovnik probably was the scene of Michael's finest marital moment. He put himself entirely in Jill's hands when it came to the kind of holidays they enjoyed there. He followed her directions for the making of *Two Hours From London* without so much as a quibble so far as I could tell. Kathy Wilks, an Oxford don who was made an honorary citizen of Dubrovnik for her heroic efforts to save lives during the siege, was aghast at how Jill ordered Michael around during the filming—until Kathy realised that this was how Michael wanted it. At first, Kathy, a deep admirer of Michael and his politics, had trouble getting along with Jill. I can see why: Kathy was like everyone else— especially women—who treated Michael as though he were a sort of saint, the man on the Left with the most integrity, a man who was also so gentle, obliging and incorrigibly cheerful. He was just as cheerful about doing Jill's bidding, believing that she was a master of the visual media, about which he knew little. As he had done with Aneurin Bevan, Michael adored submitting to those he deemed at the top of their form. In this one realm he wanted Jill to be a genius and perhaps that is why I could catch him in a vulnerable moment: admitting that he had not done enough to foster Jill's film career.

22

A lunchtime talk with Stevan Dedijer yielded surprisingly little about Jill. She had sent him a list of questions about the siege of Dubrovnik—none of which he could recall. He promised to send me her list, but I never got it. He was more Michael's friend than Jill's. I often had the feeling (as did Jill) that with

Michael around she simply did not count for much. As Julie said, "There were problems in the relationship. Michael was very much in demand." Julie recalled Pamela Berry luncheons in the 1950s. Berry, wife of the owner of the *Observer*, kept a sort of salon. She didn't like Jill, but this did not stop Michael going without her. Richard Crossman's diaries portrayed the "hardboiled, journalistic atmosphere" of Berry's "male-oriented" parties.

I later discovered a letter from Michael to Jill alluding to the Berry problem. He was writing shortly after their 1963 road accident and release from hospital. He was convalescing at Beaverbrook's estate in the south of France after Jill had returned to London for an operation on her gravely injured hand: "My dear child, I was relieved to get your telegram, although I am still shaken by our conversation. Whatever has arisen, it's sad that you should have fresh anxieties when you have enough to put up with. However, nothing can be done about this until we talk and I am confident then that all will be well." Berry had sent a letter or a book—Michael couldn't recall—and Jill thought that "there was a closer relationship with the woman than was the case," he said. "You weren't having an affair with Pamela Berry?" I pressed. "No, no affair," Michael insisted.

Julie thought the situation was especially hard for her mother because at that point Jill wasn't making her own money. In the early 1960s she had quit screenwriting, frustrated because directors made such a botch of her scripts. Then her life was thrown into turmoil when she crashed her car into a lorry. Michael was not expected to live (his chest was crushed and one of his lungs collapsed) and Jill, hurt nearly as badly, almost lost one of her hands. It was saved only at the cost of many painful operations and a physical discomfort she tried to alleviate with special bandages. It took her mother a long time to recover physically and mentally, Julie said.

The early 1960s was not a happy period for Jill, according to Julie:

> She sold a Renoir painting to help her mother and buy me a Leica camera [Julie was embarking on a successful, if short, career as a photographer]. Michael gave her housekeeping money, but it wasn't enough. He wasn't in touch with domestic life, to put it generously. I was hostile to him then because I thought he was treating my mother very casually.

This last comment triggered Julie's memory of a visit to Beaverbrook at his Cap d'Antibes estate. There Lady Beaverbrook, who was very fond of Jill (I found dozens of affectionate letters from her to Jill in Jill's study) observed that Jill did not have a very nice dress to wear and ordered one made:

> This humiliated my mother. She held it against Michael. I don't know how you can use stuff like that. She felt that he was oblivious when he humiliated her. He didn't know that £8 a week when my husband was giving me 20 and only earning a pittance wasn't enough. She never liked to ask for money. She had her pride. When she couldn't earn it, she'd sell something.

23

Julie told me that during the first week of Michael's Dubrovnik stay (I arrived at the beginning of their second week there) several of his London friends had flown over as part of his commemoration of Jill in the City she loved. The wife of Bob Edwards (an intimate of Michael's who edited *Tribune* after Michael left the job) told Julie that Michael was one of the most selfish men she had ever met. It seemed a shocking statement to me at the time; Michael was so affable and so obviously engaged with other people. He did not strike me as a monomaniac who would hold forth only about himself. But in effect, in Jill, he found a collaborator—as Carlyle had done with Jane—who might complain from time to time, but who never seriously challenged his own vision of himself or of the world he had a right to rule.

By making no demands (for example, "You must give up your career"), by seeming not to interfere in crucial decisions (should she abort the child she had conceived by him before they were married?) he effectively placed the burden of all decisions on her. She was the one who had to choose—over and over again. Michael could just be himself. This is the free ride men so often enjoy in their marriages.

Much later, when I interviewed Michael's parliamentary colleague Leo Abse, I discovered that Leo viewed Michael's solipsism in political terms; that is, because Michael could not see beyond the perimeters of the loving world constructed around him, he became (or perhaps always was) incapable of dealing with a world undreamt of in his philosophy. He was a partisan for his point of view, and it was very difficult for him to argue for any side other than his own. This is a common human failing, I suppose, but we seldom pursue our self-absorption with as much passion as Michael showed.

24

Jenny Stringer, as usual, was in charge of Michael's itinerary. She was concerned that he get enough exercise. It was difficult but essential for him to walk. When I first met him in the mid 1990s, he could still walk quite vigorously with a cane but since then, the muscles in his legs had atrophied. He should have had physical therapy regularly, with home visits, but he had stopped even his once a week visits to a Hampstead therapist.

Jenny announced that she would come for Michael at eleven:

[MF] I'm doubtful Jenny.

[JS] Oh for heaven's sake, it's ridiculous. You're not going to hang around here all day.

[MF] Hang around? I've got things to do.

[JS] I know. You can still come in [into town] for the walk. Can't you?

[MF] No. Tell you what I might do ... I don't want to disrupt your day.

[JS] You're not disrupting it.

[MF] What I might do with you is walk up those steps [the Villa Dubrovnik had a steep set of steps up to the street] and then walk the opposite way.

[JS] Would you like to do that now?

[MF] No.

[JS] Why not? Then you won't be doing any exercise all day. At the end of every day you say you need to get more exercise. The last three days have been very bad. You need to reform your ways. Let's do it.

[MF] If you'll just help me up the stairs. I'll walk that way [away from town], come back and have the lightest lunch in Christendom, possibly only bananas.

The conversation reminded me that in spite of how accommodating Michael could be, a resistant element in him defied even the most skilful cajoling. But Jenny and Michael were not through, now almost putting on a show. Jenny ventured:

[JS] Supposing I said Tony Blair had sent a Rolls Royce to be up there at half past eleven?
[MF] You know what a bloody liar you are. Very difficult to know when she's telling the truth, isn't it?
[JS] Now you're going to slump into one position and stay there.
[MF] No, I'm all against that too.
[JS] You heard what he said? He's all against it.

Michael finally got up from the table, reciting his favourite mantra: "One to be ready. Two to be steady ... " and with a succession of grunts he stood up.

25

There was no errand for Michael that Jenny would not undertake, no comfort for him that she would not arrange. Unlike many of the women surrounding Michael however, she was no adoring sycophant. She seemed sturdily independent and rather like Jill, kept him in line. Even so, *protecting* him was her mission, no matter how critical she might be.

I asked Jenny if she thought Michael appreciated Jill more during the last years of their marriage. Julie had said as much. "Well, he saw more of her," Jenny replied. Had I heard about any rifts between Jill and Michael? Jenny asked. Was she obliquely referring to 'Lamia'? I reported that Julie had told me Michael had alluded to rows with Jill. "Hm," Jenny considered.

After some inconsequential conversation, I decided to come out with it:

> **[CR]** Julie told me a very sensitive story, "I don't see how you can put this in the biography, but it's certainly part of the marriage and of who he is." She told me he had had an affair with a Pakistani woman.
>
> **[JS]** Yea.
>
> **[CR]** Paul Foot knew about it. I guess you know.
>
> **[JS]** I can elaborate on that. I can tell you how Jill felt **about it.**
>
> **[CR]** I talked to Michael Bessie about it.
>
> **[JS]** You'll have to talk to Michael about it.
>
> **[CR]** I would like to. I'm not writing a saint's life …
>
> **[JS]** Of course not. No.
>
> **[CR]** The marriage is strong enough to—if it's an important story—it makes him more of a human being and the marriage more interesting.
>
> **[JS]** Absolutely. You'll have to talk to him rather than to others about it.
>
> **[CR]** Absolutely.
>
> **[JS]** See what he feels about it. He's going to say, "Who told you that?"
>
> **[CR]** I'm sure he will.
>
> **[JS]** He adopts positions and it's very difficult to get him away from them. I'm always challenging him. His memory is quite selective now, too.

[CR] Oh sure.

[JS] This may be one of the ups and downs he needs to talk about. He trusts you. He's very fond of you.

[CR] I'm very fond of him.

[JS] Maybe in a discreet, subtle way you can get into it. He knows about other biographies and these things have to be revealed. I'm sure he'll come out with it when you're on your own sometime. I think it should [the rest of the sentence is unintelligible on tape because Jenny was speaking so softly]

[CR] That's my gut feeling.

[JS] Talk these things out. Otherwise, after he goes ... someone else will come up with something. Sheila and Una [one of Michael's secretaries] know, but I don't know that they will say anything until they know Michael wants to talk about it. Once you've got that established, I can talk to you about it. Her [Jill's] angle on that. It's very difficult, isn't it? interviewing very, very close and loyal friends ...

Jenny added: "I've been in politics so long ... "—the rest of the sentence is inaudible—but I can't help but believe she was alluding to how hard it was to be frank. Certainly her attitude here contradicted the way she later behaved, when politics and protecting Michael Foot the public figure became her sole *raison d'être*. Perhaps Jenny's attitude began to change once she realised how much of the 'Lamia' affair I already knew from Julie. In retrospect, I can see what was at stake: who had power and authority over this story? It alarmed Jenny, I'm sure, that Julie had made herself such an important source. Julie was the wild card Jenny could not control, except by trying to mitigate what Julie said. I understood as much, but only now do I see how worried Jenny was that the indiscreet Julie would challenge the control Jenny wished to exercise. "What is her theory on why it happened?" Jenny asked me. "He just fell in love? It happens to every bloody MP"—again the rest of her sentence is inaudible. Here I made a strategic error, telling Jenny what Julie said. I told Jenny I had asked Julie how Jill had come to suspect Michael. "Well," Julie had said, "when a man like Michael begins taking perfumed baths, [I laughed] "and starts paying attention to his personal hygiene in a way he hasn't before ... " Jenny was not laughing and I should have understood what a mistake I had made. Julie would not have minded my repeating her words, but Jenny, I think, was appalled that Julie's account amused me. Jenny said less and less and then switched the subject back to Dubrovnik and how important that story was to the biography. Thinking I had made enormous progress, I had no idea that in another sense, I had dealt myself a significant setback.

26

In Dubrovnik, Michael established a celebratory mood, cloaking his days with Jill in the city in such lavish ardour that I did not have the heart to discuss anything that might cast a shadow on his memories. I would have to change the terms of our conversation. To scale Michael's "politics of paradise" (the title he gave to his Byron book) would take some manoeuvring on a different terrain.

"It's very interesting, Julie, where we're headed on this," I said. "Eventually I'm going to have to ask him about this Pakistani woman." A startled Julie said, "Oh, are you?" I had to, I told her. "How do you know it happened?" she challenged. I laughed: "You told me." "I know, I know," she said, "but I don't want you. . ." I laughed again: "I won't say that. I talked to Jenny last night about it. But she would say almost nothing. 'Once you've talked to Michael, I'll talk to you,'" she promised. I wasn't sure the affair belonged in the book, I said to Julie, but I wanted to write a real biography. "The relationship survived it," Julie observed, even though at one point a distraught Jill ran away to Venice to sort out what she should do about the affair.

Julie now elaborated on her mother's discovery of the affair and how Michael took it:

Just after my son was born (1970), I went to see my mother and she was sort of drooping around the kitchen in a very peculiar state. I said, "What's the matter? There's something wrong." She said "I'm not going to talk to you. I'm not going to talk to you." I said, "Yes you are, there's something wrong." So she broke down and told me. Then she kept me informed all the time and things came to a head very quickly and Michael couldn't make up his mind. My then husband, Mike Randall, went round there and sat Michael down and said, "Shit, or get off the pot." Mike was then editor of the *Daily Mail*. Michael had great respect and admiration for him. So Michael had to. One of the strong influences was not just his love for Jill but ... he was not going to move out of that house. No way he could move all those books. Into a flat with a Pakistani? Jill wasn't about to give up the house, which happened to be in her name, because of the libel case with Kemsley [a newspaper publisher]. Everything was transferred to her name so that they couldn't be bankrupted. She had him, really. He'll never admit that. How he'll react ...

[CR] Well, so far he's had a free ride with me. I've just listened because I think that's important. I don't want to cut him short. There's a truth in all he says, but there's another side you're talking about.

[JH] His thinking will be this is a book about Jill, not about his flaws.

[CR] But I will say to him, "This had an impact on Jill. I already know that." Then either you will be seeing me again, or I'll be off working on another book.

[JH] Have you met Paul yet?

[CR] No.

[JH] I would not approach Michael until you've seen Paul. Paul knows. So Michael won't know where it's come from.

Perhaps it was good advice, but I had no rapport with Paul yet and I was keen to test just how strongly Michael trusted me to tell the whole story.

Julie continued:

"Jill was very distracted. There were late night sittings in the House. She was at them. She never used to go. He was a completely free agent. She clung to him ... went right to the other extreme. Then there was the odd business of learning how much money he had spent on her [Michael's mistress]. They went to the accountant together. He'll never tell that."

Julie said my biography would be no good if it became just a book of praise. "It'll be boring." I agreed: "No one will read it. This is the Carl Rollyson who usually gets in trouble doing his biographies and suddenly he writes a saint's life?"[1] Which prompted Julie to say:

"My mother had an enormous amount of anger at Michael. I don't think he was aware of it. She occasionally had rows with him, but her anger was always turned on me. The tiniest thing would trigger off a lethal rage at me, which I never understood."

There were also long periods when mother and daughter did not speak to one another. It took considerable effort on Michael's part to reconcile Jill and Julie. He was good at that and wanted peace between them, believing that Jill had done the best she could with her daughter.

To Julie, Jill had become Michael's devotee. "She would give an opinion tentatively as her own and if I wasn't obviously very impressed, she said, 'Well Michael doesn't think ... ' She was deeply insecure about herself, which was strange seeing as though she was so accomplished in so many ways."

---

[1] My controversial biography of Martha Gellhorn could not be published in the UK until after her death. UK publishers also feared publishing the Sontag biography I wrote with my wife, Lisa Paddock, because they thought Sontag might sue for libel in British courts. In the U. S., Lillian Hellman's estate and Norman Mailer's agent opposed my biographies of Hellman and Mailer. But I have never actually been the target of a lawsuit and much of this attack on my work has been an attempt to use the copyright and libel laws to silence an unauthorised biographer. Michael Foot deplored these efforts to censor my work.

27

I joined Julie and Jenny for drinks on the balcony of Jenny's room. "I don't know what you think, Jenny, but I think Carl is going to have a very difficult time writing this book," Julie ventured. Jenny muttered, "God, yes." "Well, all I can say is that it won't be the first time," I replied.

The conversation with Jenny and Julie lasted a good two or three hours, late at night over drinks. Julie repeated a good deal of what she had already told me, dismayed Jenny (frequently dismayed) attempted to contradict or dilute Julie's acerbic asides. The next day, Jenny spent an hour cautioning me about Julie, who had tended to rely on her mother or on a man to support her. This habit, Jenny implied, coloured much of what Julie had to say about Michael and Jill. But what about Jenny's bias? She was the caretaker, the damage control operative—more sensible in some respects than Julie but also a politico palliating vexing situations. Julie was direct, Jenny oblique. Julie exaggerated, Jenny temporised. Jenny spoke of "scenarios," implying that Julie had a tendency to fictionalise. Everything had to go "according to her plot." Jenny spoke so low I wondered if my recorder could pick up her voice (it did just barely). She spoke, it seemed to me, as though she were trying to fly under the radar.

28

"What was your father like?" The question came during dinner with filmmaker Fiona Cunningham-Reid, one of Michael's recent finds whom he had invited to Dubrovnik. Michael responded in typical fashion: "A wonderful chap. He was the happiest chap I ever knew—all his life. Wordsworth's happy warrior. I don't say he did not have his trials. He lost more elections than he won." We learned that Isaac and Jill got on very well, but we did not learn much else. I always found it astonishing how little Michael had to say about his family. Granted, our focus was supposed to be on Jill, it still seemed extraordinary to me how unwilling Michael was to reminisce about his upbringing.

"Your mother?" Fiona asked. "A very strong Methodist, anti-drink," Michael said. Jenny brought up Lady Astor. "My father fought against her when she was first elected." That was 1919, when Michael was only six, but he remembered going around Plymouth in a coach, electioneering with his father. "The Labour candidate got about twice the vote my father got. But my father got very friendly with Lady Astor. She was a very great spokesman for Plymouth. She had a lot to be said for her." Lord Astor, too, earned Michael's admiration for supporting the ambitious plan to rebuild Plymouth after the war. Michael loved to quote a line from *The Way We Live* concerning Lord Astor's effort to interest the House of Lords in the rebuilding plan: "Such was the power of the House of Lords that nothing was done."

Fiona was full of questions about Parliament because she was researching the life of her grandfather, an MP who had had some dealings with Michael. She asked him if Parliamentary speeches had been recorded. "Only in shorthand," Michael explained and then the MP was allowed to check over the transcript for errors. "That was how I met Mrs. Thatcher," Michael said. It must have been 1976, just before she was elected leader of the Conservative Party. Michael had just given a speech: "I went up to look at it, and there she was. She said to me something like, 'They won't let me say what I want to say.' I said, 'They will, sometime.' She said, 'Maybe.'" This recollection reminded him of another event in 1978, which marked the fiftieth year since women had been able to vote on the same terms as men. Callaghan was prime minister, with Michael as his second-in-command in charge of the House of Commons. "We decided to have a celebration in Westminster Hall." Michael called it a "nonparty affair," with invitations going out to all sorts of people. Jill had a big part in the planning of this event, including suggestions about who should participate. "We sent an invitation to Thatcher," Michael recalled:

But she wouldn't come. There was no kind of reason why she shouldn't have come. She didn't like to think that she owed anything to the women's vote. Stupid woman! It didn't endear her to Jill. But to do Jill credit ... she gives her a fair share because Thatcher came out with you've got to resist [the Serbs]. Jill said if she had still been there [in power] perhaps the war could have been stopped. Jill showed her in the film saying that.

Later Thatcher wanted to use Westminster Hall to stage a reception for a sitting U. S. president, Ronald Reagan. Since it would be a state event, she had to obtain the consent of the Labour Party leader, who then happened to be Michael Foot. He refused. Westminster Hall had received such figures as Charles DeGaulle. Thatcher said to Michael, "That's very small-minded of you. Why are you opposing it?" Michael said, "Don't you understand? He's going to stand for election again." It would be like electioneering for Reagan, Michael argued. "Our people don't want him re-elected. It's nothing like a nonparty event." So Reagan had to deliver his speech in a room off of the House of Lords.

Michael was astonished to see Reagan reading his speech

off of the teleprompter. "I'd never seen it before. Everybody does it now. But it's an outrageous thing. It absolutely destroys the idea that the chap is making a real speech. Of course Reagan's delivery was amazing. He could give a very good speech."

After quite a long discussion, Julie stood up (bored, I suspect) and said, "Right, I'm going." "What?" Michael asked. "I shall have a read, contemplate the weather and either go to the beach or into town." For two days the weather had been blustery and we were dying for a swim. Into the noisome wind, Michael said, "It's quietening down, isn't it?" "No," Julie said. He had been predicting milder weather almost hourly—that was Michael.

29

After my week in Dubrovnik, I returned with Michael to Hampstead. Jenny arrived and began to talk about how things had changed since Jill's death. The house, especially the downstairs kitchen and dining area, were untidy. Michael just dropped books and papers everywhere—a habit Jill refused to indulge. "He can do what he likes now," Emma, the housekeeper, chipped in.

"There's no point in talking about anything current," Jenny said. "He's out of touch now. He can get away with that in the Aneurin Bevan Society. They like history and that sort of thing. It's all about ideology anyway." Jenny was preparing to drive Michael to a talk. Then later in the day there was an event for *Tribune*. It was remarkable how many events Michael might pack into a day, although he certainly had learned to pace himself with his afternoon naps.

Jill's death had exhausted him, but he was making a

remarkable recovery. The last year or so of Jill's life had been hard on him. When she was really ill, he would sleep on a sofa next to her. She was so weak it was hard for her to make it to the loo, which was just off the sitting room where she slept. She could no longer go upstairs or down stairs. Michael never talked about how he had waited on Jill during her last illness. What he did, and how he did it, would become a contentious subject later on in my interviews with his friends. Julie seemed a sore point with some. She helped out, but they thought her help was spotty.

Jenny thought Julie might try to seduce me, the biographer-in-waiting. I certainly saw Jenny's point. But I felt like a double agent, since Julie was a precious source, but whatever her limitations and a surprising number of her stories checked out. I've read a novel or two in which the biographer beds a source, but such situations seemed ill advised and Julie never did pursue me.

None of this might be worth reporting, except that Jenny went on to say that Michael was well aware of Julie's designs on me. Now *that* interested me because I did not think he had an eye for such shenanigans. "Carl's arrived," Jenny recalled telling Michael, when I first appeared at the Villa Dubrovnik. "Julie's taken him off." Now Jenny added, "He sort of sniggered under his breath and said something incredibly rude: 'I expect they're hard at it in the bedroom now.'" Emma laughed, "He didn't!" I exclaimed. Then, on second thought, I added: "So maybe when I start to press him on other subjects, he'll say, 'Well, I know a thing about you.'" Jenny piled on, suggesting I use this approach with Michael: "I've told you about me, now you tell me about you."

30

Even though I was staying with Michael whenever I came to London, I found it hard to have him entirely to myself. At home there was always a housekeeper, many calls, and visitors. So I was delighted when Emma said she was going out shopping. "Have you got everything you need?" she asked me. "I do," I said, "I have my man." Michael, who often missed parts of conversation, asked, "What's he got?" I repeated Emma's question and my answer. "Ah," Michael said. I don't think he understood that I was leading up to something.

I started out in as disarming a fashion as possible: "I'm going to tell you what I think of Jill's book [*Daughters of Dissent*]." I told him how impressed I was with the writing. Although the book was not complete, Jill had done a good deal of revising as she went along. I then began to discuss autobiographical aspects of the book, passages that dealt with wives of politicians and women with homes and careers. I read Michael a passage where Jill expressed her regret that biographers had so little to say about their subjects' private lives: "Consequently, we are left with the impression that the Fawcetts were rare specimens who knew nothing of personal tests and fluctuating emotions. Clearly, much more was happening beneath this artificial surface.""Jill is raising the issue of what biography is," I said to Michael. "Yes," he answered. Listening to the tape recording of his response now, I seem to detect the faintest note of resignation in his voice. "You bet she is," Michael said. I commented on the reticence of Victorian biography, in particular the trouble Froude encountered when he attempted to be candid.[2] Michael broke in with "Yah, yah. Yes. He made Jane Welsh, in effect, right, I suppose."

I took a breath and said, "I have enormous admiration for Jill and I think this long-standing marriage you had is a wonderful story. Absolutely wonderful. But people are ... not going to want to read a saint's life. Everybody has faults.

> **[MF]** Yes [the word was drawn out rather meditatively].
> **[CR]** What got me thinking about this was this passage [the one I had read to him]. Then I came across a little book in Jill's study.
> **[MF]** Huh.
> **[CR]** The book is called "Odd Reflections." I don't know if you know that Jill kept this book.
> **[MF]** No.
> **[CR]** It's a kind of diary.
> I read one of her statements: "We are creatures of habit. That is why it is fatal to permit a husband to prolong an affair."
> **[MF]** Yea.
> **[CR]** "Nothing will convince me that life has anything better to offer than a marriage in which both partners rate each other's welfare and happiness of supreme importance—give or take a few adulterous moments."

I read another of Jill's statements:

> "Marriage is like democracy. It may not work, but no one

---

[2] I deal with Froude in *A Higher Form of Cannibalism? Adventures in the Art and Politics of Biography* (Chicago: Ivan R. Dee, 2005) and in *Biography: A User's Guide* (Chicago: Ivan R. Dee, 2008).

has thought of a better system."

[MF] Yea.

[CR] "Nothing destroys a relationship so much as disloyalty. Infidelity is not necessarily incompatible with loyalty." That's an interesting one, Michael.

[MF] Huh.

[CR] This is something Jennie Lee is supposed to have said, "Love may be deaf, dumb, and blind, but it can count."

[MF] Yes, that's pretty amazing. She was obviously ...

I foolishly cut Michael off before he could finish the sentence, eager to tell him that I had read in Jill's correspondence that Michael had discovered some poetry Bevan had written to a woman he loved before he knew Jennie. Jill wondered how Jennie would react to the poems when she learned about them. "How did Jennie react?" I asked Michael. He responded:

> I showed it [proofs of his book including the story of Nye's love affair and poetry] to Jennie. She didn't want it in ... She said, "If you put that in, it will be sensationalised ... and she was quite right about that. If I had included it, the press would have been round to the woman, who was alive. I went to see her and she wanted it in, because it was the truth ... I daresay Jennie also wanted it out because she didn't want any rival ... It's not of great importance from your point of view.

But it was. Michael had done exactly what I could not: put his book in the hands of another to censor.

Michael now knew where I was headed: "I'm not saying, of course, that you should ... sometime ... about my [he chuckled] relations with Jill. Some of those remarks she made ... " I have not excised any of his words. He was stumbling onto the new ground I had broken, and I was just as hesitant to plough ahead. But as Michael went on about how Jennie had become the love of Nye's life, I saw my opportunity slipping away. Michael was, in effect, justifying his decision to abide by Jennie's desires.

But then Michael broached the subject of adultery, although he didn't use the word: "One of the necessities for people maintaining decent relations is that they shouldn't know about such things if they happen." "Yes," I said, cutting him off with another statement from "Odd Reflections": "Nye Bevan said that affairs should be clandestine. But that didn't stop him making a pass at me in a car in a traffic jam in the middle of Hyde Park corner." Michael laughed, "Well, that's it, you see. That's true. Nye didn't want Jennie to know he did have affairs. One was with Sonia Orwell after Orwell's death." Then Michael was off, expatiating on the subject of how badly biographers had treated Sonia, who had become Jill's friend as well as his.

Finally, Michael came to a full stop. He tried to begin again: We, ah ...

[CR] In writing Nye's biography you were right to include ...

[MF] Well...

[CR] The story about the woman. I understand Jennie Lee's point about sensationalising. The press does that. It's unavoidable.

[MF] The *Daily Mail*—the way they deal with these

things. It's even worse now. They're less restrained than they would have been then. The newspapers had old scores to settle against him. He called them the most prostituted press in the world ... He was bitterly opposed to the way they intruded into these matters.

[CR] Did you consider changing the woman's name?

[MF] Well, no. In the original proof I had her name.

I was just beginning to grasp that Michael's first loyalty was not to biography, but to friends and to anyone else whom a given biography might hurt. He and Jill had vowed never again to rile Jennie after Michael's row with Nye over unilateral disarmament. That pledge overrode everything else—even Michael's own convictions about what ought to appear in a biography.

Nye's passes did not alter Jill's opinion of him, Michael said. I found that evaluation to be true. She was one of Bevan's most ardent admirers and I told Michael I liked the fact that she never hid his sexual side when speaking or writing about him. But Michael ignored the point about Jill's candour and turned to describing Nye and Jennie. They married, to begin with, as a matter of political convenience, Michael suggested, although they grew to love one another. "Our marriage—mine to Jill—had nothing to do with political convenience, although the political convenience came in because we had to be careful about not offending the nonconformists in my constituency." Michael recalled his first years as an MP for Devonport (1945-1949), during which Jill was still married to Jeffrey Dell even while having an affair with Michael. Marriage as an institution meant little to Michael but a great deal to the voters and in that sense the decision to marry Jill was a political one. If, for example, his trip to Nice with Jill in 1946 had come out in the newspapers, he pointed out, "It might have been damaging for me." In fact, the press had learned of this trip, but Michael was able to quash the story by threatening to write articles about the love affairs of newspaper proprietors. Marriage could act as a safeguard.

Then, to my surprise, Michael said:

Let's come back to my relations with Jill. Of course, we had some tensions too, some upsets too and it wasn't all plain sailing throughout, or anything like it. I did some things that she didn't approve of ... some of those remarks there [in "Odd Reflections"] ...

[CR] Well, I have to ask you about that. This is the hard part. I have to ask you about what happened, what she didn't like.

[MF] Yuh. You have to [he lowered his voice].

[CR] Jill made a comment once in a newspaper interview—somehow the question of marriage and fidelity and adultery came up and all Jill said was, "Michael is very secretive and whatever he's done, I'd rather not know about it."

[MF] That's right.

[CR] But the problem is I feel I have to know [I laughed].

[MF] Ahuh, ahuh.

[CR] It's difficult because this is going to be an enormously sympathetic book ...

[MF] Yes.

[CR] But because it is so sympathetic ...

[MF] No, you ...

[CR] You see where I'm headed. I don't want people to

simply say, "Well, he really didn't do the whole life. He just presented the good aspects."

[MF] No, of course you must ask me. I'll think of the answer.

[CR] Then I have no problem when I write the book. I want you to see it. I want it to be accurate. I know you told me it's my book ...

[MF] Yes.

[CR] At the same time, it *is* your life. There may be things in the way I write ...

[MF] Yes, I know. I made a mistake because I said to Mervyn, "It's your book ... we'll come to this, Carl. I'll tell you some of the rows we had. Whether I can do it just at this moment I'm not quite sure. Of course you can't do something that is misleading ... No point in writing a book at all in that case.

I was encouraged to go on, since he seemed to concede my point. In retrospect, though, I can see that he wanted tighter control over me than he had over Mervyn. But at that moment I felt I had to nudge him just a bit further:

[CR] Also, I deal with the fact that I'm interviewing other people and they tell me things. I don't want to be in a position of hearing all these things and then not being able to ask you.

[MF] Yea. A-huh ... A-huh

[CR] Certainly from talking to various people who knew you and Jill, and also I can tell from reading this little book ["Odd Reflections"], huh [I now hear the stress in that sound] there had to have been some adultery.

The silence, as they say, was deafening. The orchestra of sound that usually emanated from Michael cut out.

[CR] ... which I know is really hard to talk about.

[MF] Uh, well ...

We were sitting on the second floor, with Michael reclining on a couch. I was in an upright chair, my tape recorder perched on a foldout desk to my right. Michael gazed upward, apparently lost in thought. I looked down — anywhere but at his face. And we sat there. I decided that rather than press him again with words I would just simply wait to see how he would respond. For nearly four minutes he did not say a word. After about ninety seconds, his customary mumbling returned and nearing the four-minute mark (I felt like a swimmer under water wanting to come up for air), he seemed to pull himself together, drawing in his breath. He paused another few seconds, then said:

Two or three of the women are alive. One or two are not. Let me just think about this.

[CR] I know.

[MF] I know I must talk to you about it.

[CR] I want to do this as sensitively ... I'm not even sure how much of this gets into the book.

[MF] I understand.

[CR] The idea of the whole story. To me, it is a magnificent story. I don't want it to get less magnificent.

[MF] I know you don't. But I must just think about it.

[CR] Yes.

[MF] Do it properly.

After two more minutes of silence, Michael said, "So, I'll think about it. I don't want to do it now. I don't think so. But I must sometime, of course. It's a ... " I did not know how to end this session, so I continued:

> Michael, I know you don't want to talk about this now,
> but Jill has a whole page here [in "Odd Reflections"]
> about secretaries: "The most sinister of all relationships
> is that between a husband and his secretary. A secretary
> has more power over a man than his wife. The
> subservience of secretaries is disgusting.
> [MF] Subservience, she said?
> [CR] Was one of the women you were involved with a
> secretary?
> [MF] Not Una.

I had heard much talk of Una, but never met her. She had been Michael's last full-time secretary. She died before I could meet her. Like many of the women who worked for Michael, she had formed a very strong attachment to him, although in this case not a sexual one.

> [CR] But one was.
> [MF] One was, yes. That was Elizabeth [Thomas].[3] She's
> still alive. . . A man may be in love with two women
> ... at the same time ... and that's what I was. One of
> the reasons I was interested in Swift was because he
> was in love with both Vanessa and Stella. I was quite
> sure. Otherwise the poems are absolutely terrible ...

---

[3] No hint of Michael's true relationship with Thomas is given in Kenneth Morgan's sanitised and authorised biography.

That's where I got the Vanessa name from. When Julie gave us a dog, we called her Vanessa. I don't say that Jill approved of all that, but she understood what I was saying. Swift was more advanced about women than most people thought. It is a beautiful story, in my opinion. Now he was secretive. If he hadn't been, the whole thing would have been bust up much earlier. So when Jill talks about secretive, well I used the word about Swift too, you see.

[CR] This is what will make the book come alive. Your books have this intellectual ... but they also have this emotional ... that's what a biography is. That's wonderful.

I was coming to the point of diminishing returns as Michael launched his lecture on Swift, happily remembering his father's suggestion that Michael write a book about Swift's arrival in London, "and I did," Michael said triumphantly (*The Pen and the Sword*, one of Michael's finest books). Writing this book had been therapeutic, since Michael was recovering from his devastating election defeat in Devonport in 1955. "I was out of Parliament for some time" [until his win in Ebbw Vale in 1960]. He had tried to regain his Devonport seat but was defeated again, even more badly. Swift became a passion during the years Michael was out of Parliament. But I wanted to hear about Elizabeth: "How long was she your secretary?" She had been with him from 1950 to 1955, as he recalled, but he had also worked with her from 1955 to 1960 in the *Tribune* office.

[MF] We knew each other from then until now. We've always gone on well together. You should go and see her sometime, maybe.[4] She's a fine woman. But that's not the only thing that happened. There was something else that happened that I will tell you about a bit later.

[CR] This book is about how marriages stay together, even when there are these strains and tensions.

[MF] That's right.

Emma had returned, bringing in a picture of Michael and Callaghan (why, I can't remember). "You look quite lively there," I told him, "ready for action." He took a look. He turned from it in disgust, "It's terrible. Good God," he whispered.

"This looks really good," I said, perusing a copy of *The Pen and the Sword* he had just handed to me. "I did that with Elizabeth too, you see," he said.

[CR] Mervyn told me that he thought Elizabeth adored you.

[MF] Well ... Jill knew her quite well and they never had a row. Elizabeth was tactful, you know. However, there are other matters that I've got to talk to you about, which ... [he was starting to read through a newspaper Emma had brought in for him].

Any intimate talk with Emma in the house was impossible. I wished I had asked him then, "Was your love for Elizabeth different from your love for Jill?" I suspect he would have said yes, although I doubt he would have accepted my interpretation: Elizabeth was one of those women who put

---

[4] When I later called Thomas, she refused to talk, claiming not to have anything to say about Jill. She gave me no opportunity to bring up her affair with Michael.

herself at his service, an alternative wife who never voiced, as Jill did, any criticism of his behaviour.

31

"I remember we used to have interesting conversations about Michael and her whole demeanour in that house," Ursula Owen said. We were sitting in her Index on Censorship office, discussing how Ursula met Jill and got to know Michael in the late 1970s. I had previously interviewed Ursula for my biography of Rebecca West. Ursula had been one of the founders of Virago Press, which reissued a number of West's works. Jill had come to Virago, with feminist scholar Jane Marcus in tow in order to connect with the second wave of the women's movement. Ursula described how she had worked with Jane and Jill persuading Rebecca that Virago should republish her.

Ursula then began to tell me about her visits to the Foots' Hampstead home.

I'd have supper with Jill until Michael came back from the House of Commons ... But what I thought at the time and actually feel in a way myself is that she decided that love is important and she loved him. I think he didn't understand that. I don't think he ever did. I love him dearly, but he doesn't have a clue. I think she saw that he was never going to understand it. She looked after him. I understand that better now than I did then. She thought that was important and actually I thought that was. I think it's what he needed. I have also since then worked in the House of Commons for two years. I can see the way those marriages and those lives intermesh. You really do have to do a lot of looking after those guys and that's the life they [Michael and Jill] had. ... At Jill's memorial service, he stood up and said, "All the women are going to speak first. What's I've discovered is that women do the job so much better than men, and they're going to come first." *That's* his understanding of feminism, which is not really my understanding.

We laughed. "It's sort of touching, sort of being on her side but not really knowing what the issue was," she concluded.

Ursula was fascinated with the Koestler rape story. She wished she had asked Jill why she hadn't told Michael about it when it occurred. I told Ursula that I had asked Michael the million dollar question: what would he have done if Jill had told him about the rape right after it occurred? I told Ursula that Michael said he would have written Koestler a letter breaking off their friendship. "But Michael wouldn't have knocked him down," Ursula said. "Exactly," I replied:

[CR] When I talked to Julie about it, she said: "That was one of the things my mother was afraid of ... "
[UO] That he [Michael] would knock him down.
[CR] No, she was afraid that he wouldn't knock him down.
[UO] She couldn't bear that. Understandable.

Ursula was sixty-three and described herself, in the 1970s, as at the "top end" (in terms of age) of the generation of women in the second wave of feminism. "The men in my generation had to think about women, whether they wanted to or not," she observed. For Jill, it was a different story. Jill did not feel it was possible to confront Michael with what it felt like to be a woman, Ursula explained:

> She wouldn't put up with any nonsense from Michael about that [women's issues], but the way of life ...
> **[CR]** That's right, everyday ...

It was one of those moments when biographer and interviewee don't even have to complete a shared thought. During the best interviews a moment comes when a rapport is established that stimulates the interviewee to say more than she perhaps intended: "Then there were two very extraordinary, very funny occasions, one of which I remember Jill vividly at, and this is a tricky one because I'm not sure Michael will like it." By the end of the sentence, Ursula had dropped her voice to a mutter so that I could barely hear her:

> **[UO]** The first ...
> **[CR]** I'll tell you what he said to me. It doesn't mean that he couldn't be hurt by something or be mad at something somebody said: "Write what you want. It's your book." Which is what he also told his biographer Mervyn Jones.
> **[UO]** I'm sure. Well, it was Michael's birthday. She invited me and Bill [Ursula's companion] and she also invited Jill Tweedie [a *Guardian* journalist], Alan Brien [another journalist and, like Tweedie, old friends of the Foots], Ian Aitkin [another journalist and one of Michael's confidants], Neil and Glennys Kinnock and a whole lot of other people. Later in the evening everyone sat in a huge circle—there were probably twenty five people there ... It was the time Tony Benn and Denis Healey were

competing for the deputy leadership of the Labour Party. I was pretty leftwing, so was Jill Tweedie and there was this huge feeling that Tony Benn was the villain. Suddenly Michael got to his feet and made this extraordinary speech. Well, you think he's going to have a heart attack. It's so impassioned ... a pretty savage attack on Benn. Jill Tweedie defended Benn. At some point an angry Brien said something against Kinnock and Michael's part in Ireland. Glennys turned to Jill Tweedie and said, "How dare your husband talk about my husband like that." Suddenly Jill Craigie shouted across the room, "I want to hear what Ursula has to say," in this ringing tone that only Jill could make. Sounding like Joan of Arc I gave an impassioned speech, "Nobody gives a damn what these internal fights are about. What they want is socialism." It was rather sort of yucky.

But at the time her talk somehow calmed the atmosphere:

[UO] I remember we all walked off in a daze. It was very aggressive.

[CR] It must take people really by surprise when Michael turns that sort of thing on. He's so charming ...

[UO] It was terrifying ...

[CR] People think this man couldn't have been a politician, but when you see the other side ...

[UO] He seemed quite out of control, actually. I don't think he was actually ... But what I liked about it ... was that these people let such an event happen in their house. I'm sure it happened more—that such a big row could happen and implicate them and didn't freak them out and think that everyone's got to be well behaved. Good for them.

The image of Jill enmeshed in Michael's politics brought up the subject of the husbands and wives dinners [regular gatherings of the left-wingers in Wilson's 1974-76 cabinet]. "Jill did talk to me about that," Ursula said. "She must have complained about Barbara," I suggested. "I think she did," Ursula agreed. Ursula thought that Barbara was "rather in love with Michael." At Jill's memorial service, her behaviour toward Michael was conspicuously flirtatious.

Ursula wanted to know about how Michael was coping with Jill's death. Ursula knew that he had a regiment of women looking after him. I told him about Emma, the housekeeper-cook who had been married to two writers. She seemed to suit him perfectly. "Emma told me that he had stopped walking on the Heath [it had been a daily ritual]. But with me he's been walking. He walks ahead of us teasing that we can't keep up with him and Emma keeps poking me in the ribs and saying, 'This is a performance. He hasn't done this in months.'"

32

I dashed from Ursula's office over to Julie's flat in Stoke Newington, where I met her daughter Esther. Julie brought out a cache of Jill's letters to her that would prove a godsend for my biography. Julie read one her mother wrote during Michael's tenure in Harold Wilson's cabinet. Jill described how much Michael enjoyed his job. He was upset over nuclear testing and had written a "stiff note to Harold." Michael considered resigning, but he felt his work with the unions was important. Jill was proud that her husband had not forsaken his unilateralist principles and he might still resign if the testing continued. On this issue, however, no one in the Cabinet shared Michael's convictions.

"Michael thinks Tony Benn cracked. He really is slightly mad," Jill confided to Julie. Yet Tony could be quite amusing and good company. Jill worried about the upcoming election in 1979:

Michael is so much happier in office. He's born for it and it's tremendously good for our marriage. In many ways, things have never been better between us, or at any rate not for some time. He takes me out quite a bit. . . If we lose, I shall start worrying again.

If he returned to the back-benches he would have too much time to "play around." Jill reported Michael's easy dealing with Healey in cabinet. They got on well and Healey seemed concerned to befriend Michael. Jill called his wife Edna 'a Foot fan'. It was time for Wilson to go, Jill reported, but no-one liked the prospect of dealing with Callaghan, a much hated figure. He was "two people, different in private life than in public. In public, he's a good humoured, amenable uncle; in private, he is surly, stubborn, reactionary, and hellish." Neil Kinnock thought Michael could get the leadership in the unlikely event of a showdown over Wilson, but others feared that Callaghan would triumph.

The letter was vintage Jill and provides a view of politics on the level of personality that Michael could never have shown me. He shared Jill's misgivings about Callaghan, but to his surprise he and Callaghan later made a wonderful team. Jill's description of the private Callaghan simply did not register in Michael's reminiscences of their years of staving off their minority government's defeat. It is hard for people to remember that before Michael became leader, before the 'donkey jacket' incident, it did not seem quite so unlikely that he could become PM. If he had won the leadership battle in 1976, after Wilson resigned, he would have had a fighting chance.

Esther had been quiet during this long recitation of Jill's very long, chatty letter, so I asked her about her first memories of Michael. She felt distant from him. He was not a cold man, but he seemed so far removed from the world of children. He was a "busy man. He was Jill's priority." Jill did not want Michael to be perceived as a grandfather, Julie suggested and so little attempt was made to involve him in the children's world. "I do remember going on these ridiculously long walks with Michael," Esther suddenly spoke up, "with Dizzy, on the Heath." Esther was then only seven and didn't like walking the dog in the cold. "He didn't tell you stories that you remember?" I asked her. "No, I'm sure he told us all about the Labour Party." We all laughed. As Esther grew older and developed an interest in politics, her bond with Michael strengthened.

Esther had seen Jill shortly before she died and I wanted to get her reactions to the hospital scene. Julie had been quite critical. She concluded that the consequences of Michael's purblind socialism had cost Jill her life:

It's a mega scandal, which Michael tucks up because he is so loyal to the National Health Service. He is 'Mr. Nice Guy'. If a nurse comes in and plumps up her pillow and gives her a pill, he thanks her profusely as if the nurse is doing her a favour. Even if a nurse was surly, he would say, "She's a very nice woman, really." Jill was dying and a doctor stood in front of her saying, "You're doing very well." They bungled it completely.

Michael swore by the Royal Free [in Hampstead]," Mervyn Jones had told me, "though I had my doubts." Mervyn's wife had been advised to go another hospital because of her doctor's concern about the Royal Free's standard of care.

Julie's son Jason thought the Royal Free handled Jill's nutrition badly during her final illness. When he suggested to Michael that he seek the advice of a nutritionist, Michael erupted. To him, it was an attack on the National Health Service and his beloved Aneurin Bevan. "What are you trying to say? That I've done everything wrong?" he asked Jason. That was not Jason's view, but Michael responded as though he were under political attack.

When Jill lay dying, a frightened Michael kept telling her she was doing well, but Julie and her son Jason believed Jill wanted to be released from her responsibility for Michael. Jill took Julie's hand and said, "Please let me go." Michael said, "No, no, no." Julie then snapped at Michael, saying, "Let her go. You'll be all right, Michael. Let her go." He would not say to her, "My child, it's all right. You can go."

Then Esther recalled Jill's final illness, when she had to be returned to the Royal Free, struggling with the consequences of her weakened heart. Esther remembered seeing Jill the day before she died. "How are you?" Esther asked. "I'm dying. I just want to die. I've had enough. I only get better so I can get worse again!" Michael interrupted: "No, no, my dear child, you're getting better today." Esther saw the heart monitor. "Jill's kidneys had failed by then," Julie added. There was still plenty of fight in Jill, but "she was really completely angry with Michael who would not allow her to let go." "She felt very lonely," Julie said. "He also couldn't hear everything she said."

"Did you see Michael right after Jill died? What was he like?" I asked Esther. "He was in shock. He sat there, holding her hand and stroking her forehead, saying: "Oh, my dear child, you're going to tell me off any minute now." He remained in shock for quite a while.

"So how much change have you seen in Michael since Jill's death?" I asked. "Do you see him going through phases?"

"Yes," Esther answered:

In the beginning, all he would talk about was Jill. At the same time he didn't want to know what happened to her ashes [Julie had told me the same thing]. On Christmas Eve [just a few weeks after Jill had died] I asked him, "Don't you wonder if Jill is still with us? That she will send a sign?" "No, no, no," he replied. But then he told me a story about going to a football match and Peter Jones [who drove him to matches] had a new stereo he was showing Michael and when it was turned on, lo and behold, the piece of music was the same piece of Mozart Jill had played for him when they first met."

"This was the piece he was playing over and over again," Julie said. "There was some kind of dialogue going on in his head," Esther continued, because he told the Peter Jones story to others. "He's become a lot more loving and more able to show himself to me." "Oh definitely," Julie agreed. "Very passionate—a grandfather."

Michael had, for example, become very concerned when Esther shared with him her desire to have a baby. She and her husband had doubts she would be able to conceive. "We had long conversations about it. He shared with me that he and Jill could not have children." Esther asked him if he would use the current technology—is it not playing with nature? "We would have done it," Michael assured her. "We had lots and lots of tests." Indeed so. He had shown me one of the doctor's reports. "I'm afraid it was more my faults than hers," he said, although the report I saw said it was possible, but perhaps not likely, that Michael could impregnate Jill. "She never thought that," Julie broke in. "She felt guilty that she could not give Michael a baby."

Esther thought Dubrovnik had become an essential part of Michael's recovery. "Dubrovnik cures all," she had heard him say. "I wonder if he feels at peace with everything in Dubrovnik?" she said. "It helped him to heal and advance his grieving." Now, she thought, "Michael is living very much for the moment." "Yes, I suggested, "on the one hand, he's very strong. He's still got that strong voice. He's still *there*. But he goes through these periods—when we were in Dubrovnik, it's all sort of a monologue and he keeps repeating things." He had been doing that for about a year, Julie said. Jill used to say, "For God's sake, Michael!" He was quite aware of his digressions and his recapitulations, but he seemed powerless to stop them.

My biography of Jill, the trips to Dubrovnik, were all part of Michael's effort to recoup his loss and turn it into a kind of celebration. "He was totally consumed with the memorial service," Julie remarked. Now, Esther said:

He's at peace, even though everything Jill created [in the house] is all around him. He's still going to the Labour Party conference. But he's not going to change his checks, which have Michael Foot and Jill Craigie on them. Simple things like that. He's also more involved with his family, his nieces and nephews and his sister-in-law. He's spending more time with them now. He is moving on.

Michael had lost his brothers and had only one remaining sister, now in a nursing home. There had been seven siblings. For all his fragility, Michael was incredibly resilient. "He just doesn't need to have a fall. That's the fear we all live with," Julie said. "It's amazing how he gets through the day. Every time he stands up, I'm just perched to catch him," Esther said. "He takes the bus by himself. He gets off and goes to the Gay Hussar [his favourite restaurant]," Julie noted.

"I don't want to alarm you, but he had a bit of a slip last night," I reported. I wasn't even going to mention it, but he was so insistent that I tell you. They came back late from the Labour Party conference. He was so eager to get into the house. He opened the car door and bolted out and fell in the street. It was around midnight. I was already asleep. I heard Jenny's voice, "Carl, I need your help." I thought I was dreaming.

Where were you? [Esther asked]

[CR] Sleeping in Michael's library. I put on some clothes and ran downstairs. He was sitting in the street.

[JH] Not on the steps?

[CR] No, right off of the curb. Jenny said, "Take one side and I'll take one side." So we picked him up. Under his own steam he got into the house. We sat around, had a little drink and talked about it. He claimed he was perfectly fine. I said, "We won't know until the morning. You could have a bad bruise."

I told Julie that I thought Michael was still feeling a little shaky, but he had had a nap and we then had a long talk. "Did you ask him the leading question?" Julie wanted to know.

[CR] I did.
[JH] Did you get a response?
[CR] Yes, yes. He was silent for ...
[JH] Esther knows about this. "Lamia", the Pakistani girl. His wandering [Esther said] we called it.
[CR] Actually, he wants to take it in chronological order.
[JH] Oh yes?
[CR] I don't want to say too much because we just broke ground today, but he is going to talk about it.
[JH] Is he?

Julie kept wanting to know more, but I was at such an early stage of my discussions with Michael that I felt it would be risky to reveal more. I could tell she was surprised, but then what she said next seemed to confirm how much Michael wanted Jill's biography to be written—at whatever cost to himself:

When you first made contact, Michael phoned me up immediately and said, "Come over, I've got some really exciting news! Because Sally Vincent was going to do it while Jill was alive ... well was thinking about it. But as I told you, she couldn't interest a publisher and she felt pressured into it anyway. So Michael told me who you were. He was *so excited*. For him this is his shrine to her. This makes her life an important event in history.

[CR] The reason I asked you if he has gone through certain phases, this is my third trip to talk to him about the book and the first two trips were about how wonderful Jill was. I felt all that had to come out. My agent said, "Deal with that [the adultery] later." But I thought, "This is just about the right time."

Although I realised Michael admired my work, I thought now he was investing more confidence in me as a human being. "There's a greater degree of trust," I said.

"So Carl, I'm coming to an obvious conclusion," Julie said:

As you're seeing a side of Michael the outside world obviously doesn't see, you're going to be the obvious choice to do his biography.

[CR] Yes, that's occurred to me, too. Which I'd be quite happy to do.

[JH] Well you better work fast because there will be quite a few people [biographers]. Would it be published before Michael dies?

[CR] Well, that's the question. I would guess ...

[JH] We don't know how long Michael has. It may be one year; it may be fifteen.

Writing Michael's biography had not occurred to me when I first contacted him. I was not prepared for this conversation and dropped it.

Julie warned me that I did not have quite as free a hand with Michael as I thought. When I repeated his oft expressed vow that he would not tamper with my book, she said, "Yea, but … " In my enthusiasm about how the book was shaping up, I cut her off. It was still heady days, when Michael would wake up in the morning, come down to breakfast and say, "In the middle of the night I woke up with three things I have to tell you," and he just rattled them off.

33

Julie reminded me of a conversation we had had in June with Jason (her oldest child) about his perceptions of Jill and Michael. I had asked Jason about his impressions of Jill and Michael together:

> They had a quality I wish I had. They had an
> understanding. They were doing a similar job, as it were.
> It was nice to see the support. He was able to criticise
> her work in a very nice way and she would take it very
> well. Or, if she didn't, she would be very strong in her
> defence. They loved each other. He pissed her off, but
> I never saw him pissed off with her. He didn't show off
> that kind of emotion. But she would—if he was scruffy
> or watching too much football. I've got a great video
> of him at home watching the FA Cup final. You can't
> see Jill. She's out of the shot. There's the television and
> him in a chair. He gets very excited. He goes, "Whey!
> Whey!" and his chair is moving around. You can hear
> Jill's comments, "Michael, please get back, get back!"
> Constant conflicts about football. He used to enjoy that
> bait, putting it out there. It made her wind up and made
> him feel sure she still loved him. It was a fun game they
> had together. It was nice to watch.

At a dinner Julie prepared, I asked her about any domestic upsets between Michael and Jill. "He was always breaking things and hiding them," Julie said: "I was cooking a meal. There were ten people coming to dinner. Jill would lay the table and sort out everything. She would say, 'Michael, can't you do the drinks? Can't you take the glasses upstairs?" No, Michael couldn't. Jill would declare, "He's hopeless. He's hopeless." Then Julie would interject, "Don't worry. I'll do it." While Julie was busy cooking, Jill laid out a tray with coffee cups. She turned around to ask Michael to take the tray upstairs only to find that he had already done so. She went upstairs and found on the stairs a bit of one of the coffee cups. She noticed that two cups were missing from the tray. On her way down, she glanced at the bookshelves at the bottom of the stairs and saw Michael had placed the broken cups where (Julie surmised) he thought they were hidden from Jill's gaze. "He wasn't going to tell her and then he was moving some books one day and taking a long time doing it. Jill went up to see if he was all right and found a mirror on the floor smashed. She said, "Michael, darling, why didn't you tell me you smashed the mirror?" He said, "Oh, I didn't." Jill did not think the mirror had fallen off the wall by itself. Michael steadfastly denied any fault. She never got really angry, just irritated and then she would say something sharp, Julie recalled. When I interviewed Jason on my second trip in June, he listened to his mother imitate Jill's manner of speaking. Jason thought Julie had caught Jill's tone spot-on. He remembered another occasion when Michael served coffee with salt instead of sugar.

Julie said Jill wanted quite another life after Michael retired from Parliament in 1992. Jill wanted to sell the

Hampstead house, have a nice big ground floor flat and some money in the bank. Michael resisted not only moving but also any changes in the house itself. "You know the shower room upstairs?" Julie continued:

> She'd been trying to get that made about eighteen months before she got ill. It [the space for the proposed shower] had a large bookshelf and Michael would not move these books. So Damon said he would move them. We said, "We'll all move them!" He'd lose his temper at the table and Jill said, "I must have a shower room. When I have guests to stay, they have to use my bathroom on which there's no door. "No, I'm not moving my books." I said to her, "Why don't we just move them?" "Oh," she said, "I wouldn't dare. He can get quite nasty." So when she was in hospital, she was told by the doctors, you can never have a bath again [she had broken her hip and apparently could no longer get up out of a bath], you have to shower. I said to Michael, "Do you realise what the doctors have said?" "Rubbish," he said. I said, "No, no, she can only shower." "Well," he said, "it's not possible." I said, "What you're saying is that you care more about your books than you care about my mother." He was so shocked at that, he said "Okay, go ahead."

After Michael retired from Parliament, Jill made him take an office because she found it difficult to write when he was at home. "She wouldn't have him in the house, but he kept coming back for lunch," Julie said. She advised her mother, "Go off." But Jill demurred: "I need all my things." "Then send Michael to Jamaica." "Oh, he couldn't manage without me."

34

"I've *never* in my life seen two people that age so tactile, so devoted," said Esther. Julie interrupted Esther, "But she was so irritated by him most of the time." Then Julie stopped herself, "Oh, you mean before she was ill." Esther said yes: "The dialogue between them—it illustrated an incredible love." That had been my impression, I said, when I met Jill during work on my Rebecca West biography. "It wasn't always like that," Julie persisted. "Of course," Esther agreed. "There were long periods when it wasn't like that," but she could not be contained: "They always admired each other and sung each other's praises." Esther repeated, "Quite tactile." Julie agreed: "He will hold your hand, my hand, *your* hand [meaning mine]." It was true. He had already done so. "They slept in the same small bed," Esther said, prompting an outburst from Julie: "I think they became extremely close once his dick ceased to work."

Esther wanted to talk about how wise a grandmother Jill had been, about how involved she was with everything, including politics. I mentioned how Barbara Castle had scorned Jill's political opinions. "She was quite a driving force behind Michael," Esther insisted. It was a partnership, Julie and Esther agreed. "She claimed she never influenced his career," Julie said. "But that's not quite true. At some point he was on the verge of being offered Ireland [this must have been during Callaghan's term in office], and she stepped in there. She said, 'Everybody goes down in the bog of Ireland.'" She denied it later, "But I was there," Julie said.

35

Michael spent the next morning preparing me for visitors, Peter and Celine, who had become Michael's devoted friends. Celine had been Ronnie Neame's lover. They had had a falling out and Jill took Celine's side when Ronnie reneged on a promise to give her the house they had lived in. Jill helped Celine win her court case and the house.

Peter and Celine had devoted themselves to Jill during her last days, taking food to her in hospital and then looking after Michael just as faithfully. "Nothing is too much trouble for them. They are warm hearted friends," he averred. They had taken Michael to Jamaica for a holiday and made certain that he was feted and treated like a major star. Amusing newspaper articles recounted Michael's jovial visit. My first meeting with Peter and Celine did not amount to much— it was always difficult to get anyone to speak candidly while Michael was present—but later on I was able to count on their independent view of Michael, his household and family.

I followed Michael upstairs to the living room, where Emma had prepared drinks. "I know we have some other matters [Michael's lovers] to talk to you about at some stage," he said, almost chuckling. Then Celine and Peter arrived. Michael reclined on a sofa, leaning against a soft pillow, prompting Peter to remark that Michael must be recovering from his fortune-telling at Brighton (the site of the Labour Party conference). "You didn't see your picture in the *Times*, did you?" Peter asked Michael, knowing that Michael would not have a Rupert Murdoch newspaper in his house. "He did. We showed it to him," I told Peter.

"Filthy newspaper," Michael said, adding "I had a rather unfortunate return from my bloody conference. I came back absolutely sober, I may tell you." After he had made this point three times, Peter interjected, "He doth protest too much."

"I got out of the car and stumbled and fell over like a bloody fool. Right on the pavement here. He [he indicated me] had to come and pick me up out of the bloody gutter." Michael said his leg was a bit twisted, which is why he had it sort of straddled across the sofa, making him look a bit sybaritic. "I saw the doctor this morning, and he says it is okay."

Talk turned to current affairs. When the Bush-Gore election came up, Michael noted, "We discovered that to the credit of Gore he said his favourite book was *Le Rouge et Le Noir*." Stendhal was one of Michael's all-time favourites. "That settled things for Michael," I said. "Yes," he quickly agreed.

"How's Plymouth Argyle doing Michael?" Peter asked. "It's dreadful. We've had the worst beginning of a season for years," Michael replied, dropping his voice in disgust. "So we don't need to press *that* subject." We all laughed.

Michael started to rise with his usual stagger. "Are you all right, Michael?" Emma asked.

"Just let people help you," Celine suggested. "I know," Michael said. "You must do it," Celine insisted. "You've always been independent, but it's not in your best interests." Celine was the only one of Michael's friends who was quite this direct with him. While in Bermuda, Celine and Peter had provided a wheelchair for Michael, so that he could get around more quickly.

Celine pressed her case in a jolly way, nearly always punctuating her remarks with laughter. A former centrefold, she was short and zaftig. She recommended that Michael find a nice girl with long hair to give him a massage. "It might work," Michael agreed. He kept saying his legs had been getting better in Dubrovnik. I saw no sign of that, but I did marvel at how he negotiated the three sets of stairs from the kitchen to the living room (at street level) and then up another flight to where Jill's study and his library are and then yet another all the way up to his bedroom. It was a very long haul that he laboriously climbed up every evening and then down again in the morning.

When Jill could no longer manage the stairs, Peter had recommended that a chair lift be installed. It was ordered, but then Jill died and Michael cancelled the order. Every morning he performed his act of courage. I would be in the kitchen and starting about seven thirty or eight, I could hear him on the stairs shouting "I'm coming. I'm coming." Although he would groan and wheeze, he always sounded so cheerful, so ready for the day, that I could see why he would regard a wheelchair as a sign of defeat.

36

"We used to read Hazlitt in all those different places, especially in Venice."

I had trouble imagining Jill actually reading Hazlitt. Upon further questioning, Michael explained he used to read his favourite passages to her. He brought out one of Hazlitt's books and on the inside cover were the dates and places they had read Hazlitt together. Sometimes Michael added a note about what they read. Jill indulged him in his intellectual passions, I think it is fair to say, but I did not see any evidence in her study or her papers that she really took an interest in Michael's revered authors.

Hazlitt, Swift, and Stendhal filled Michael with all sorts of conceits about the nature of love that grew to have for him a consecration of its own, perhaps best exemplified in Hazlitt's *Liber Amoris*, Michael's Bible of love and his justification for his affair with "Lamia". Hazlitt had been besotted with a servant girl who eventually spurned him for another. What was the servant girl's point of view? Now *that* question would have interested Jill, but Hazlitt, like Michael, confected instead a romantic cocoon that excluded the voice of his beloved. "Lamia", like the servant girl, was never given a voice in Michael's brief and halting comments on his affair.

Michael and Jill stayed at various hotels and pensions in Venice from the 1950s to the 1970s, twenty years of fortnights, before Dubrovnik became their favourite holiday spot. "We stayed at the Danieli," Michael said:

Where Hazlitt stayed. When we first went there, I didn't know about Byron's connection with the place. Byron knew more about it than anyone, pretty well. When we first wanted to stay at the Danieli, I went and looked at the price. I wasn't sure whether it was for the week or the day, but I discovered to my horror it was for the day. So we moved around a bit then. When I was in the government, we had our holidays arranged by civil servants with all these nice appurtenances.

Michael had a whole library of books about Venice. He singled out John Ruskin, Gore Vidal, Mary McCarthy and Jan Morris, the latter a friend. "It's difficult to write badly about Venice, you know," he told me. "We knew every inch of it. A lovely place for walking." Walking was his exercise and I daresay he put more miles on his feet than any of his contemporary politicos. "Hazlitt wrote about Titians," Michael said. "We went to see the Titians."

I heard a light tread in the hallway. "Who's that lurking?" I asked as Jenny entered the room. "We were just talking of Venice and love," I said. "He's been pulling books out of the shelves and reading Michelet to me." "How are you?" Michael asked Jenny. "I have a few things for you to sign," she said but she went downstairs and let us talk on.

"We read Byron's letters there [in Venice] together. Then we were going up in the world, having the bloody government pay for our holidays. . . Venice revived him [Byron]. It restored him," Michael insisted. "Venice is the happiest place on the planet, in my opinion. That's why I can't stand the Thomas Mann business." I laughed. "A damn travesty," Michael asserted. "Venice is not like that at all. Stendhal's got all that in—how and why it was the best place in that time ... He was staying with his wonderful woman—whatever she is called—at the time that Napoleon escaped from Elba. He had just established his relations with the woman,and nothing was going to break that. Not even Napoleon. He [Stendhal] stayed there throughout the whole of the one hundred days."

Michael often spoke of his father and their book discussions. Isaac Foot would visit London nearly every fortnight, Michael recalled, and they would see each other. Michael rarely spoke of anyone else in his family. Even more than Michael, Isaac was immersed in the world of books, accumulating a huge library. Sooner or later Michael seemed always to take up the books his father had prized. Montaigne and Conrad became part of the Foot canon during his convalescence after the car accident.

On one of his trips with Jill they visited Montaigne's tower, "twenty miles outside Bordeaux," said Michael, who liked to pinpoint the author's biographical geography.

> We also went about to several of the other places where he had been and so I read every Montaigne essay in a year or two either at the place he'd written about or in the vicinity. I have it marked. It changed my life. Mostly I was reading it with Jill. It's got the whole humanist case of how you should look at the world. Jill and I were absolutely captivated by it. I started collecting Montaigne's other translations. I've got a Florio ... which Shakespeare read. Not my particular copy, you know, but the same edition ... Hazlitt himself wrote about Montaigne. His own essays ... were obviously inspired by ... Swift also translated Montaigne.

The only genealogy that meant anything to Michael was a literary one and that is why his father was the only family member admitted to this pantheon. For all his effort to include Jill in his bibliophilia, I wondered how she stood for so much hero worship. "Both of us, Jill and I, were absolutely caught by Montaigne," Michael went on.

I decided to test my doubts:

[CR] Did Jill have a favourite Montaigne essay?
[MF] Favourite one?
[CR] One that she liked to re-read?

The flow of Michael's reminiscence suddenly stopped. "Yes," he muttered. It was as if he was coming out of a reverie. "Um

... There's a famous one on the classical ... I daresay that is one we read more than the others ... " Plainly, he had nothing more to say about Jill in this regard. We were interrupted by Julie's arrival. Time for dinner, which Jenny and I went to retrieve from Michael's favourite Thai restaurant.

When we returned, Julie began chafing Michael about the mess of newspapers piled up on a long table and about the downstairs kitchen/dining area:

[Julie] Jill use to do a big sweep-up and out it'd go!

[MF] No. Will you have a drink, Jenny?

[Julie] You change the subject quickly.

[Jenny] She kept you trained.

[Julie] There was never a book in this room, or a newspaper.

[Jenny] In those days, Julie, for God's sake, Michael could get up to his study much more easily.

[Julie] Even so, even so, when Jill was here this was a different setup. Jill was very strict.

[MF] Not the proper word at all.

[CR] What's the right word, Michael?

[MF] She was discriminating.

I laughed. Julie scoffed.

[MF] Now she had a very good complaint about the library.

[Julie] You bet!

[MF] My father used to say to her, "Let the boy be known for his library." That's why we took this house. But I have to admit that—I don't know—four or five years ago ... [Julie grumbled]. A bit later than that maybe.

[Julie] Fifteen years ago.
[MF] No."
[Jenny] It wasn't *Julie.*
[MF] There was a slight decline in the way the things were organised.

Michael said this last bit with the jauntiest lilt to the word "slight." I couldn't stop laughing. "She had a perfectly good case about it," Michael said. "I acknowledged that. The library that you [indicating me] sleep in now is not as it should be. It has too many books all over the bloody place. But it is being cleared up, although you may not have noticed it." I roared. Michael continued, "Before and after Jill's departure, I've been engaged in it. I think the next time, when you come back at the beginning of the year, you'll see a library without any books out of place." "I'll put money on that," Julie interrupted him. She would have won the bet; I never saw any discernible improvement.

Michael said he had agreed with Jill about the overcrowding and that he planned to sell off his Defoe collection to make space for the books that were threatening to buckle the floor. "So there is a slight element of truth in what Julie says," he concluded. Julie tittered. "That gets us back to some sense of reason," was his capper. These sorts of comic scraps were quite droll and brought out Michael's playful nature.

Michael then turned his attention to Jill's library and to her book, saying, "I think it's best of all if her book is published at the same time as Carl's." He later withdrew that notion—a terrible blunder in my opinion, for it would have made Jill a much bigger figure to reckon with when my book came out. Julie was all for publishing and so was Jenny, but it was typical of their rivalry that even this issue got turned into a sort of power struggle. In a low, barely audible voice, Julie said:

She'd turn in her grave ...
[JS] No, she wouldn't. She'd be delighted. If she was alive and Carl appeared ...
[MF] What?
[CR] Julie said she'd turn in her grave.
[JH] She has said to me *so* many times ...
[MF] What?
[JH] "If I don't finish it, you ought to scrap it."
[MF] Hm.
[JS] She never said that to me. She was always ...
[JH] You're not her daughter, Jenny.
[JS] I *know* I'm not her daughter.
[JH] Well, she said it to me many times. There was no argument about it.
[JS] I'm not *denying* she said it to you Julie, but she never said it to me.
[JH] Well, why should she say it to you?
[JS] No, because what she said to me was she would really like a good editor.
[JH] That's another matter. She said if it's not finished, she did not want it published. I didn't agree with her. It was her wish.
[CR] Hm.
[JH] That's all I'm saying. It can't be contradicted.
[JS] I didn't contradict! She indicated she would quite like some help in finishing.
[JH] If she was still alive, yes.

At this point, I said: "Well, I can understand that." Jenny could understand that, too, she said. "Yuh," Michael muttered. "I think it's right to go against her wishes," Julie said. Finally, Michael said, "What we have is a real independent view of it from Carl. He's the only person whose fully read it through and that's his view. It should be published that way [incomplete but with a preface outlining Jill's plans for finishing the book]." So we all, temporarily, came to a consensus. It strikes me, though, that only Julie remained faithful to her mother's attitudes. Jill had a unique vision; the book was her baby. The idea of anyone carrying on with it was preposterous. Only Julie had the candour to say she was overruling her mother.

"*So*, what's the time?" Michael asked a second time. "The same as it was two minutes ago," Julie replied. "Ah, time for me to be staggering up to bed," he said. "You're allowed to," Jenny said. "What happens if I do?" Michael asked. "If I'm not doing the washing up, how are you going to get on?" I said we'd feel very sad and go to bed. "Did you get a lot done today?" Jenny asked. "Yes, we went through twenty years of holidays," I replied.

"I'm off," Michael said. "I'll see you—some of you—in the morning."

Whatever lingering bruises (mental or physical) he had suffered from his fall seemed invisible as he made his jaunty, wheezing way up the three flights of stairs to his bedroom, keen to turn on the radio and listen to the latest developments regarding Milosevic, whose power had begun to wane as the opposition to him mounted. Jenny and Julie attributed Michael's early retirement (it was barely nine) to his fall, a shock to the system that only showed up two days later. The doctor had said to watch Michael carefully for forty-eight hours after the incident.

37

The next day, Michael introduced a new subject: "One of the reasons I've never been in favour of writing autobiography is because you can't tell the truth." I agreed. "All the great autobiographers have been charlatans," Michael said, warming to his topic. He named Casanova but then was interrupted when Emma brought in tea. This discussion, I soon learned, was not merely academic:

When you write these things [autobiographies] you have to be careful with people who have a different interest in life and whose lives may have developed in quite a different way —and that applies to the two or three people I'm going to mention to you now. Each of them, you see, is a person happily married and if we had an affair—connections, whatever you like to call it ... The first one, Elizabeth Thomas, was already married when she became my secretary way back in the '50s and we had a kind of sensation—affair—two or three years after that. But she never contemplated leaving her husband and she lived happily thereafter with him. . . In the 1970s, she came back as my so-called political advisor [employed by the government] for another three or four years. Along with Brigid Brophy she was the main person from my department's point of view who put into operation the whole of the Public Lending Right which we carried through right at the end of 1979. So that's one. What she told her husband about it, I don't know. We had an understanding about that all through [the affair] and that remains the case today and I would of course hate anything that appeared that was embarrassing to her. There's no reason why that should happen.

I had lots of questions, but I dared not risk interrupting Michael. He had obviously braced himself for this confession and had in mind a certain way of presenting details. The next affair had also been with a secretary, now happily married. He provided a few more details but in a sense these details were irrelevant, since I wanted to concentrate on "Lamia," the only lover who had disturbed Michael's marriage in any fundamental way.

Now Michael came to the crux:

There was a much different case — also a woman who is still alive so far as I know. A woman called "Lamia" [I've changed her name] who was at the BBC. She was a beautiful black woman. She was as black as you can be. She was very good and we had a kind of affair about 1970. To some extent, it was like what I was reading in Hazlitt about the chap who has an affair and he gets an obsession about her and he doesn't know it until he's got out of the obsession why he's had it. . .. Of course I had read the Hazlitt thing before. It did not last that long. But I must say I was absolutely taken by it. What's happened to her I'm not quite sure now. After two years I had a separation with her because I said, "We can't do anything about this. It would be too damaging to Jill and to everybody else." She didn't mind it all that much.

But I had seen a letter from "Lamia' to Jill that showed just the contrary. "Lamia" had been quite bitter, whereas Michael said they "had a good sexual time together, but I broke it off and I told Jill about that. She didn't like it and she was obviously hurt. I don't think she was altogether surprised and she took it quite well." Had Michael's memories of this affair faded? His account was nothing like Jill's letters about it. Jill had gone off to Venice to decide what to do, writing letters to Julie about her consternation. The affair, in fact, came close to shattering Michael's and Jill's marriage. "After 1981, there were no more disturbances in these matters" [such was Michael's way of referring to his sexual affairs]. In fact, our friendship and love became stronger all the time."

"So it was just the three women?" I asked. "Yuh. There's another woman, Dr. Roberts, who I met when I went to Ireland. It had nothing to do with sex." Still Michael counted her as one of his loves. Julie liked to call her the "vampire lady" because the woman had an obsession with vampires, which Michael later confirmed. He was quite secretive about this woman, Julie said, putting away a picture of her after it piqued Julie's interest. "I've known her [Dr. Roberts] the last three or four years—perhaps a bit more," Michael told me. Julie later reported the woman was going around saying, "Michael has been in love with me for years."

It seemed time to ask more questions:

[CR] Are you *sure* Jill didn't know about either of the secretaries?

[MF] I don't know about that.

[CR] Because she wrote those statements about secretaries. She was angry. She suspected, but she didn't know.

[MF] Well, I'm not sure which it would be. Unless some people said that to her. We went to places where I used to meet them [that is, engage in sexual activities with secretaries], you see, at the party conferences. Jill didn't usually come—not always—sometimes she would come. At that time [the 1950s] she didn't want to come.

Thomas continued to work with Michael on and off for more than twenty years, but their affair was over by the end of the 1950s.

> [CR] Did you consider yourself in love with these women?
>
> [MF] Yes, I did.
>
> [CR] Especially with Elizabeth?
>
> [MF] Yes. As I told you, I think people can be in love with two women at the same time. That's my 'Swiftian' excuse. If you say it's not true about Swift, then you have to say he is a charlatan and I'm sure he was not that. The women didn't like the treatment they were getting from him, no doubt; each of them did not like the rival being there.

Whether it was Byron, Wells, Hazlitt, Swift, or himself, Michael saw mating with women through a romantic screen that ennobled him and his heroes, no matter what grief they caused others. He also wanted to believe that Jill had become reconciled to his vision:

> From my point of view and from hers, I hope, we had a pretty good relationship in many ways. Some people would say that if she hadn't married me she would have done more and better films and the rest of it and more time to do it—well, she would have had more time. There's no ... On the other hand, what she wanted to do was to see political ideas put into practice. You can see from this last affair about Dubrovnik and all that how strong her political passions were.

I tried to bring Michael back to the subject at hand:

> [CR] Now when Jill departed for Venice, were you worried that she might actually leave you?
>
> [MF] Well, I was very shaken. Maybe that's the reason she did it. I couldn't bear the thought of her being there in Venice without having a nice time there. . .
>
> [CR] Did you ever seriously consider leaving Jill?
>
> [MF] No, not me. I hope she didn't. She was very good about my escapades.
>
> [CR] I wanted to ask you about that. It's a very personal question. Rebecca West said that after men get married they lose interest in their wives sexually after about five years.
>
> [MF] No, nothing of the sort. I don't think—certainly not five years.
>
> [CR] What about Barbara Castle. You never had a sexual relationship with her?
>
> [MF] No. Never. I wanted to, maybe, but in 1938 we went across the channel together, waiting to start on our new jobs. I had asthma terribly then. I had it that night. She did not know what it was. She thought the boat was sinking or something.

Michael explained that in 1938 Castle already had a lover, William Mellor, who edited *Tribune* before the war. Michael regarded Mellor as a mentor and Barbara as a colleague. They often attended public meetings together and discussed their reading of Beatrice Webb and other socialists.

[CR] Do you think Barbara ever fancied you?

[MF] No, no. She doesn't like people to [he did not complete the sentence, but I know he meant she disliked speculation that she and Michael had once been lovers]. Some things she did I didn't agree with. She had a great row with the trade unionists, you know. But she was a good minister, the best socialist minister. I knew she wouldn't like what I wrote about her diaries. It's still the truth in my opinion; it had to be said and now when I go to her parties ...

[CR] How did she react when you asked her to speak at Jill's memorial service?

[MF] Very pleased.

[CR] Was she surprised?

[MF] A bit. Well, I don't know. I was slightly surprised how much she went into the disagreements [between her and Jill]. I couldn't help respecting her for it.

[CR] Very honest.

[MF] Some people say she stole the show.

[CR] Well, I'm going to be careful when I talk to Barbara Castle. I'll just ask questions and let her talk.

[MF] It's quite right you should see her. I was a bit nervous about what she would do [at the memorial celebration]. I thought she would be less explicit.

"What's the time, by the way?" Michael asked. This was a tic of his that made me think of the rabbit in *Alice in* Wonderland. I think Michael was tiring, but I pressed on:

[CR] Was Jill flirtatious with you?

[MF] Flirtatious? Yea.

[CR] Did she tease you?

[MF] She could do what she wanted [he said it quite coyly and made me laugh].

[CR] Playful? I'm searching for words.

[MF] Yes.

[CR] Aggressive?

[MF] Oh, not aggressive, playful certainly. She thought sex was a matter for some ridicule.

[CR] Did she have fun with sex? Was she playful that way?

[MF] Yes. She didn't take it too seriously. It was all part of her belief that comedy was the greatest of all operations. She'd rather go see something that was laughing at it [sex].

[CR] So the last thing we would say about her is that she was squeamish or inhibited.

[MF] No, no, not in the slightest. But she thought there ought to be mockery as well as the serious aspect. I'm sure she appreciated Byron on that account. He is mocking it as well as treating it as a serious subject. When I went through *Don Juan* the first time [in hospital], every time I got to a part I wanted to read it to Jill as soon as I get back here.

[CR] I forgot to ask you Michael—it just occurred to me—why did you feel you had to tell Jill about "Lamia" when you didn't tell her about the others?

[MF] Well ... it came up. How did it come up?

[CR] Did she find out about it? Did she suspect?

I knew the answer, already supplied by Julie. It made no sense to me that Michael would confess an affair to Jill. He did not suffer from guilt. He had made plain that H.G. Wells and Bertie Russell had liberated him from such compunctions. What was the point of telling Jill, especially if he never seriously considered leaving her? What he had said so far, while revealing, did not entirely compute. As he fumbled about, I asked him:

> How were you seeing "Lamia"? You weren't seeing her at party conferences.
> **[MF]** No. She had her place where I used to visit her. I think I told her [Jill] because I was breaking it off then.
> **[CR]** Do you think telling Jill was part of breaking the obsession? Making it impossible to continue?
> **[MF]** Well, I had broken the obsession before then, I hope. But there you are.

But where was I? Either Michael was concealing something from me or from himself. "Who knows, exactly?" But I knew from speaking to Julie and from Jill's letters to Julie that Jill had taken a much more active part in ridding Michael of "Lamia".

Michael seemed vaguely aware that Jill had tried to break through his literary obsessions. Why hadn't Hazlitt backed the case for women's rights as he should have done? She wanted to know. Michael conceded this weak point in his hero's armature, but her criticism hardly changed Michael's behaviour. Her good-humoured frustration often comes across in TV documentaries, where Michael gets the last word, but her incisive criticisms at least abate the tide of his enthusiasms.

[MF] What's the time?
[CR] One o'clock. That's a lot for one morning. Maybe we should stop.
[MF] Okay.

At such moments, I felt I had strained Michael's patience to the limit. He was never short tempered with me. He simply evaded questions, took refuge in silence or deafness and asked the time, a question that had become, I suspected, a reflexive way of moving beyond the moment.

38

At lunch, Michael began:

We had a chap, Solomon Stevens, the local baker and we heard he was going to be knighted at Buckingham Palace. He said, "I'll tell you what happened there. She [the queen] said, 'Down on your knees, Donut! Arise, Sir Fancy Cake!'" That was my introduction to the House of Lords, you see.

Michael always found the Lords a subject to ridicule and steadfastly refused any titles for himself. Emma interrupted this hilarity to report "Una sounded good this morning." Una was terminally ill but still concerned about Michael. "Is he being a good boy?" she wanted to know. It seemed every woman in Michael's life wanted to mother him. Emma had declared that she never wanted to leave Michael and was arranging to have all her holidays coincide with his so that she would never be away when he was home. Just how dependent Michael could be on women became clear later when Molly replaced the unfortunate Emma. The first hint that all was not right with Emma came the morning when she told us about her troubles with her son, who had lost two cell phones in pubs in a week and had just now had his car towed for a parking infraction.

"So, I'm off. I'm just going to have a sleep upstairs," Michael said. Before he went up, Michael said he was "nervous" about my taking away a photograph of him and Jill sitting on a sofa in their Beaverbrook cottage. It is a charming picture that sums up their love for each other. I returned the photograph to its treasured spot on a cabinet downstairs, making a note to contact the photographer to get my own copy. I didn't blame Michael a bit. Certain photographs and objects had an almost totemic value and it made him uneasy to think of parting with them, even temporarily.

39

I was having dinner with Paul Foot, journalist Sally Vincent (Julie's friend) and Julie at Julie's flat in Stoke Newington. Sally mentioned that she had heard Michael downplay Jill's achievement, saying she was more of a visual person than a writer. Paul roared with laughter: "Absolute rubbish!" "I *believed* him," Sally said plaintively. Both Sally and Paul were shocked to learn that Jill had written eighteen solid chapters of her book, with only two remaining unfinished. They had supposed the book had been all talk.

Then we got round to Michael's health. "He's reached a rather difficult stage," Julie said and began to talk about Michael's digressions, his seeming inability to get to the point or stay on it. It was so. But I added: "If you call him up and you say, 'I want to ask you about this, this, and this and give him the night to think about it, he'll come in the morning and for an hour or two he will do perfectly well." Michael recognised the problem, I said. He called it "wandering." "Well, that was his problem when he was leader of the Labour Party," said Paul amid our laughter.

"You do know about the case, don't you?" Sally asked me. Michael had been party to an accident in which a passing vehicle had hit the open door of Julie's car, resulting in a lawsuit that had to be settled in small claims court. Michael had to appear as a witness and an attorney asked him about his eyesight, implying that he had opened the car door without seeing the approaching car. "Would you say your eyesight is exceptional?" she asked. Michael whisked his glasses off and he pointed to his blind eye and said, "This eye *completely* blind. This eye [pointing to the other] sees all the mischief in the world."

After Paul departed, Julie said, "He wishes that nobody knew about "Lamia". "I told Julie I had gathered that. "You'll find him very, very reticent," Julie added. "That why I said I had talked to Michael," I told her, adding, "He [Paul] thinks the personal life should remain the personal life and not part of a biography." Julie thought otherwise and related memories of her youth when Michael used to tease her about her boyfriends. Michael used to embarrass her. He used to sing, "Ma, he's making eyes at me" in a loud voice. "He'd sing the whole bloody thing."

January 2001

40

At breakfast, Michael announced some startling news:

> The woman who is coming in—I haven't met her yet—
> to do Emma's job ... I'm very sorry about what happened
> ... She was led astray by her son. She was doing things
> that could have caused lots of trouble. When we were
> away in Ireland, Jenny here had a phone call from
> Emma saying that the police were coming and they
> were threatening to prosecute her for participating in
> perverting the course of justice, along with her son. That
> is what he is being charged with. She had that day to go
> off to court for a preliminary hearing. Very sad, because
> she was a delightful woman, you know. The chap was
> very stupid and he behaved very rudely to Jenny here.
> He got into the bloody house ...

41

At dinner, Michael talked about Salman Rushdie, who had a
column that day on the recent U. S. election. Michael had not
seen him since before Jill's memorial celebration. He still had
fond feelings for Rushdie and defended the expense that the
British government had incurred protecting the writer from
the fatwa against him. Indeed, Michael had played a role in

getting the Thatcher government to provide Rushdie with a security detail and safe houses. "The whole thing was done partly on my representations to the Home Office," Michael said. "To do them credit, they did what they should have done. Several people who should have known better were attacking him [Rushdie] ... Prince Charles made some stupid remark ... dreadful." Later, I searched Michael's shelves for Rushdie books and found in one of them a letter from Rushdie thanking Michael for coming to his aid in his hour of need.

Michael and Jill revelled in Rushdie's visits—security detail and all: "He talks almost as brilliantly as he writes. He would let loose, a wonderful story teller," Michael said. "The first time he came here with the American woman [his second wife, Marianne Wiggins], and later she wrote harshly about him. We didn't like her. But then when he took up with Elizabeth [West] we were very friendly with her, a lovely woman. When this breach between them happened after Jill's death, she [Elizabeth] said, 'What would Jill say I should do now?'"

Michael recalled that even before the couple's split, Rushdie had been agitating for a move to New York City. Jill and Michael took Elizabeth's side, saying, "Elizabeth's more sensible than you about it. She wants to bring the child up here." Michael loved Salman's (he always called Rushdie by his first name) satirical sensibility, calling Mrs. Thatcher 'Mrs. Torture' in *The Satanic Verses*. But Michael acknowledged that this satire did not go down well with certain British readers. Rushdie was fiercely funny about the racism of Londoners.

Rushdie was rather rough on Indira Gandhi and the Nehru family—all heroes in Michael's book. "He was also quite critical of the standards of the vernacular Indian press,"

Michael noted. "A rather sweeping remark ... attacking more than he should have been. So he does say things like that which get him into trouble on his own account. When you take him all in all ... up to this affair [with Elizabeth] ... so sad." Over a ten-year period (during the fatwa), Rushdie visited the Hampstead household perhaps twenty times, Michael estimated. "More than that, maybe. He gave us nice presents and we gave him some presents, you know. He gave us the most expensive wine we had drunk in our lives up till then."

42

Our discussions in the late afternoon or at dinner always were accompanied by Scotch, Michael's in a silver tankard with water and after I arrived and asked for ice, he would put that into his Scotch as well.

I asked him if he knew that Jill had kept a diary during his first year as Labour Party leader. This came as a surprise to him, but all the same his lack of curiosity about what she wrote mystified me:

> [CR] Tony Benn seems to have been an incredible headache.
> [MF] Yes, he was.
> [CR] She asks this question: "Should Michael be tougher on Benn and the other trouble makers?" But she fears that if you do, there will be a party split. Do you know what she said about your speeches? When you dealt with other people's writing, they didn't allow at all for your own speaking style. She felt you were constrained by that.

[**MF**] Well, that's true, no doubt. And to read a
speech—I should never have done it. So ...

[**CR**] She sees you on TV: "Michael lacks the cosy,
avuncular, reassuring style of Callaghan and Healey."

[**MF**] True. She was absolutely right.

[**CR**] "Too inclined to shout, which gives the impression
that he is haranguing the audience."

[**MF**] All that criticism is right and that is what made it
worse for her.

In person no one could be more avuncular and reassuring
than Michael. His shouts within his own circle were merely
hearty greetings, an "eccentricity of energy," Sally Vincent
had called them.

[**CR**] Jill says, "Cocktail parties are a barbaric ritual. We
have *never never* given one, nor will we."

[**MF**] Quite true. What we did do is give decent meals
down here. The friendships we had through her were
wonderful.

I read another passage from Jill's diary: "Michael's not
depressed. He can laugh. Live in the present." He gave a
half-laugh and said, "Yes. It's what we need to do. It was a
terrible defeat. The bloody Social Democrats. If they had
done slightly better and we had done slightly worse, the party
might never have recovered and some of our friends who
went down—like Albert Booth—wouldn't have been defeated
if it had not been for his association with me and the party."

Jill had a nice passage on Neil Kinnock: "He has wit, a
good sense of fun, and he is clever—indeed a true radical in

facing realities. A far more rare quality in a politician than might be supposed." Michael assented: "All that is right. She saw that from the beginning." Michael and Neil used to go walking in the Welsh mountains together and come back to the cottage in Tredegar that Jill had fixed up so charmingly. "I think it'd be a good idea if we went out to Wales sometime," Michael said. I thought that a wonderful idea. Jill had bought a run-down miner's cottage for two hundred and fifty pounds and spent about two thousand pounds on it. Michael had written much of his Aneurin Bevan biography there.

Back to Jill's diary and her comments on Michael's sartorial difficulties: "Jennie Lee used to say, 'Don't let the Tories dress Michael.'" He got a big kick out of that. She also mentions meeting Denis Thatcher and finding him "deadly and quite cheerless." "He was, too," Michael agreed. Jill used to imitate him, Michael told me:

> We went to Downing Street twice when she [Thatcher] was there. In *Private Eye* they have him [Denis] calling for a "tincture" when he called for his drink. When he came up [for a drink], I said, "Just a tincture, please."

Jill mentions Michael going to a reception with Prince Charles and Diana: "All the women were in semi-formal dress, so I was surprised to see Diana resplendent in a low-cut off the shoulder evening dress of taffeta. She has lovely shoulders and arms and looked quite beautiful and talked to everyone with animation, charm, and enjoyment. It was easy to see why people do go mad about her." Michael had no gift for calling up or appreciating such observations. His only comment: "Well, there you are."

"December 8, 1981," I real aloud to Michael. "For the first time Michael has an approving press." Only a few more days were recorded in the diary. "That was it," I said to Michael. He made no comment on the diary itself. I regretted that Jill had stopped keeping a diary because she was an unpretentious and candid writer. She understood Michael's strengths and weaknesses.

This period (1981-83), when Michael was Labour Party leader, had been devastating:

> Some things helped me—the Byron Society—Byron
> helped me to recover from that. He never gave in. Just
> after the election, I was becoming quite active in it [the
> Society]. I read, by the way, *Don Juan*, in hospital after
> I had been elected leader of the Labour Party. I had
> slipped coming down the stairs and broken my ankle
> [and surgery was necessary to put it right]. The only way
> to read *Don Juan* is right through and that's what I did.
> I spent the whole of Christmas doing so — leader of
> the Labour Party I was supposed to be [he laughed] ... it
> [*Don Juan*] put me in a good temper.

The Labour Party faithful loved Michael Foot, finding in him the soul of unassuming integrity. He had never expected to be leader, had never really wanted the job, but in the end had acceded to his importunate advisors (including Jill and Neil Kinnock) who suggested he had a responsibility to his party that could not be shirked, especially so because of the possibility that Denis Healey would be elected leader if Michael did not declare his candidacy, and Healey (to the party's leftwing) seemed too much like a Social Democrat in

Labour clothing. Although a man of the left, Michael was seen as having the stature of a party stalwart, an honest broker, who could keep the party's warring factions from destroying each other. In the event, of course, he never developed the mechanisms to rid the party of its extremist elements and he left Neil Kinnock with the unpleasant task of expelling hardcore, neo-Trotskyist elements that had formed a virtual party within the Labour Party.

43

Julie and I were on the road to Northumberland to see her friend, Gilly. Julie had known Gilly since the war, when they were young girls in Hampstead and Jill was not yet married to Michael. Jill had met Gilly's father when they were both involved in the ARP. Gilly would prove a crucial witness, not only corroborating—even as she criticised—Julie, but also providing a sense of the world that both Jill and Michael only dimly apprehended.

While Julie drove, I filled her in on my recent talks with Michael. Whereas Michael always presented Jill as a committed and campaigning political wife, Julie witnessed instances where her mother had been rather recalcitrant. I could believe it, having reading Jill's *Evening Standard* columns, where she made no secret of her distaste for life as a constant canvassing of the electorate. In 1955, when Michael lost his Plymouth seat, she had become involved in his campaign only in its closing days, when she seemed to sense that Michael's female opponent had outclassed him in making contact with the voters.

"When people come up to Michael, he doesn't keep walking. He stops and says, 'How nice to see you' and all that," Julie said. "He behaves as though they are somebody he should know." That was true, I said, I had seen it myself when we made the rounds in Hampstead: "Somebody came up to him in Dubrovnik and he greeted them and he did actually say, 'Well, off you go.'" Jenny was surprised because usually he did nothing to hurry people along. He did not have the calloused cordiality so many cold-eyed politicians cultivate.

We moved on to other subjects. When I told Julie about Elizabeth Thomas, Julie was quite surprised. "She was in and out of the house in the '50s. She was always around. I never had any inkling of it." I relayed Michael's views about being in love with two women at once. "That's a cop-out," Julie said:

You've got a wife. You've got a good life. A good home. You don't want to hurt her. So you say you're still in love with her. So that allows you to say, "It's all right to be in love with two people." In the meantime, the wife can go on the back burner, keep her safe.

Julie remembered that by the late 1950s, in their Abbey Road house, Jill and Michael were sleeping in separate beds and that her mother told her that she seldom had sex with her husband. "He would be in her bed occasionally, but more often than not he was in the other room," Julie said. "That would have been Elizabeth Thomas' time too." "But they slept together in Hampstead?" I asked. "Well, after "Lamia", he tried to make love to my mother a lot but he couldn't really get it up. He kept trying."

I then laid out my problem with the "Lamia" story: "He said he told Jill about "Lamia"." "Bullshit," Julie said. I went on: "Well, I never got a convincing answer from him. He told me he told her because he had decided to break it off." Why would he tell her then? I wondered. "He's not telling you the truth," Julie declared. Julie then reiterated how Jill began to suspect her husband of adultery. He was taking more care of the way he dressed—and so many late night sittings in Parliament, Julie recalled:

Jill was very troubled, preoccupied, distant. I was around then. One day she found a letter, which absolutely laid it out. She confronted Michael with it, lying on the sofa in the library in an obviously distressed state. He said, "What's the matter, my child?" She tried to get him to confess and when he didn't, she produced the letter.

Not only had he not broken his obsession, according to Julie, but Michael wanted to "string them both." Then "Lamia" called at the house. "There was a very ugly scene at the front door." So there was—as Jill's housekeeper told me later. Nearly everything Julie told me, I could corroborate either in Jill's letters or with others who knew the story. Michael's version simply could not be true. As Julie put it, "He was found out." This was hardly the heroic Hazlittian way, publishing one's love to the world.

[JH] Paul knows. He's reluctant to talk [she meant to me].
[CR] I'm sorry to hear that.
[JH] He talked to me. He obviously knew of others because when I said, "It seems there were four"—I had lunch with Paul after you had told me—he said, "Oh, is that all?"
[CR] Well, I'll talk to Paul.

More than anyone else I was to interview, Julie would contradict Michael without compunction. I mentioned, for example, Michael's fondness for recalling what he and Jill read together:

> She *hated* it when he read to her. When she was ill,
> he was reading all those letters from Rebecca West.
> I'd arrive and wait until he had finished that page or
> whatever. She would then be able to say, "You can stop
> now, darling. I'd like an orange juice."

That would get Michael out of the room. "She'd look at me and roll her eyes. I could never tell him this, but he is the world's worst out loud reader. It's all a monotone, and there's no ... " "Inflection," I added. "She said she never ever told him that," Julie continued. "He did indeed read to her quite often, but she tried to find as many ways as possible to stop him from doing it without in any way hurting him."

How deeply Jill respected Michael's separateness as a person and how little he really knew about her own feelings. Anything that might shake his confidence—it was clear from her diary—she would keep to herself. She remained a prop to his ego and that attitude took an enormous toll on her—as I learned when I began to hear more accounts of her dying days from Jason, Julie, Esther, and Celine.

44

Gilly was fond of Jill and Michael and yet had no compunctions about criticising them or explaining that she came from a Conservative home. "Did you know that Michael gave us the run of his flat in Park Street? [The girls were then about twelve or thirteen. Anything to keep us sweet," Gilly said, prompting the following give-and-take between her and Julie:

[G] He did, yes, but he doesn't even remember I was ever there.

[J] God, I remember the smell of that place [the musty odour of books]. I'd never been in a bachelor's ...

[J] It was all wood and books.

[G] A squeaky, sloping wood floor ...

[J] ... And the bed in the sitting room had a very prickly Moroccan type rug on it you had to sit on. Being little girls with shorts on this was extremely unbearable to sit on.

[G] But the draining board in the kitchen was alive—it was wooden, and it had years of filth. You know how it sort of grows green and ...

[J] I don't remember ... how extraordinary!

[G] We had no supervision. I don't remember Michael being there.

[J] He never paid any attention to us.

45

When Julie excused herself for the evening, I had an opportunity to speak with Gilly alone. I explained that Michael could only see Jill as good mother, one constantly concerned about her daughter's welfare. "But to me in a very negative way," Gilly spoke up. "He won't allow himself to see that," I told her. "The method or style of the mother's concern is not even an issue with him." Gilly thought about it. "I don't suppose he did [see how critical Jill was of Julie]. I think he was too involved with his books." I agreed and said, "All he heard was Jill saying something like, 'What am I going to do with Julie?'" It never changed, Gilly said.

I tested my impressions out on Gilly: "I think Jenny

identifies with Jill and sees Julie through Jill's lenses. Removed from seeing the interactions you saw as a child and as an adult, to Jenny—as to Michael—Jill only wanted to help Julie, give her money, whatever Julie needed." Whenever Gilly called Jill, the word about Julie was always the same: "Julie was making too many demands." Gilly felt like saying to Jill, "It was ever thus." Gilly remembered Michael's role: "Jill would say [to Michael], 'I'm just telling Gilly [about Julie].' He would say, 'Oh, she doesn't want to hear about that. She doesn't want to talk about that. Come on, pour a glass of wine and let's talk about something else.'" Gilly said what I had been thinking: "Goodness knows why we're still friends." Given Michael's incomprehension of Julie's point of view and Jill's constant extolling of Gilly's talents, I could only presume, I told Gilly, that she had remained friends with Julie because there was nothing Jill could say or do that changed Gilly's loyalty to Julie. Even at sixty, Julie would call up Gilly and ask, "You are still my best, friend, aren't you?"

I steered Gilly back to Michael:

[CR] Do you remember your father ever discussing Michael Foot's politics?
[G] I would go home and say, "So and so came to dinner and they talked politics." Daddy would say, "Oh, that would be *Labour Party* politics. Because I was such a wimp about any controversy ... I would do anything not to have that. There was a rule when Aneurin Bevan and Jennie Lee were around ... that if I was there, politics were not to be talked about because they upset me. I became deeply embarrassed. I did not know how to cope with all this political fervour. I was the odd one

out. Everybody else thought that the Labour Party was wonderful and there was a lot of banging and rushing that never happened in our household ... It got to the stage one night during a conversation and Jill said, "You mustn't talk politics in front of visitors. It's embarrassing" and Julie said, "She's not a visitor. She's a regular customer." Politics would not be talked until the girlies went to bed. So Aneurin Bevan would sit there and say, "Isn't it bedtime for the girlies? Aren't you going to bed girlies?" ... Everything they were saying was against what my father was saying. I was too young to answer back.

[CR] Did you like Bevan?

[G] I *did*. He was jolly, nice to us. He was different, loud. When you saw him on television, he was very similar to what he was in the kitchen.

"As I was growing up," Gilly said, "my friends and relations [many of whom met Julie when Gilly took her to family events] would say, 'Are you still friendly with that Michael Foot's daughter. He's a dreadful man. He says terrible things. He would lead this country into ruin.'" Gilly would insist, "He's a lovely man."

Gilly added, "If I had suggested to my father that we have Jill and Michael to tea, my father would have thought it was a bit like inviting the devil." Well, if not for the war, I said to Gilly, she and Julie would not have become such friends. Jill often made that point herself, but neither she nor Michael ever acknowledged or pondered the chasm that existed between their views and those of Gilly's family. Jill admired Gilly's father, calling him a natural leader, but she never considered why he would be a Conservative. She and Michael were too sure of the rightness of their own convictions. In their world, there were a few honourable exceptions to their way of thinking—Disraeli, Mrs. Pankhurst, Lady Astor, Randolph Churchill, Tories who won Jill and Michael's hearts because of idiosyncrasies that absolved them of conventional Conservatism.

46

Back in Hampstead, I watched Julie's son Damon come downstairs (he occupied a flat in the top story of the Hampstead house). Julie promptly told him he needed a haircut. "To hell with that!" Michael said. "Jill cut my hair for thirty years." "It got odder and odder," Julie said. "Did she put a bowl on your head?" I asked. "No," Julie quickly intervened, "but that's how it looked." "No, no not all," Michael objected. "I was itching to do it," Julie admitted. "Balls," Michael answered.

But after Jill got ill, she said to me: "You better get it cut." She said that to me once or twice. I wasn't too pleased because I'd much rather—anyway, she said, "You must do it." So I went up here [to a shop in Hampstead] and went in and said, "Can you give me a haircut now?" They said, "Yes, we can." I said, "How much is it?" They said thirty pounds . "Ridiculous," I said, "but I've got to have it." Jill thought it all right. A couple of months later, again the thing seemed to be growing and she said, "You really have got to get another haircut." I said, "I don't approve of haircuts, but if you say I've got to, I must." So, I left. I was meeting Una, my secretary and I said to Margaret, her daughter, "You wouldn't like to cut my hair, would you?" She said, "I've never done anything like that before, but if you want, I don't see why I shouldn't." She took very great care, and she did it. So when I got back here, Jill said, "Your hair does not look bad at all." I said to her, "I took your instructions. If you can guess how much it costs, I'll give you the money. So she started guessing from ten quid to twenty five quid—something like that and then I told her. I'm very fond of Una but I also go for the haircut.

It was a funny story all right—Julie and I laughed throughout his telling of it—but it was another example of how women have groomed Michael Foot from cradle to grave.

I mentioned a television documentary Julie and I had watched at Gilly's house and that Jill remarked on how his Park Street flat was filled with women's cosmetics and perfume bottles in the bathroom. "What?" Michael exclaimed. Sometimes I thought the word was not a sign of deafness but of stalling. Jill had suggested Michael had quite a full love life before she met him. "Did she?" Michael asked mildly. "So what I want to know," I said raising my voice, "did you get around or did you go out and get that stuff to impress her." Julie tittered. "I don't know where it came from," he said in that sort of comic-evasive tone he was good at slipping into. Julie brought up Gilly's comment on the draining board in Michael's flat. "What's that?" he asked. Julie suggested he had selective hearing and could even hear what others said quietly when he wanted to. "What's that? Say it again," he said, with a straight face.

47

Jenny arrived and I took her and Michael out to dinner, over which he reminisced about the years with Jill at Abbey Road, a modern flat they occupied for five or six years in the late 1950s. This period coincided with Michael's years out of the House of Commons when he appeared regularly on programs like the "Brains Trust" and earned his reputation as a fierce disputant. He was very fond of his Tory opponent, Bob Boothby, who by the end of the program almost sounded like a Labourite, Michael thought. Although the arguments could get "hot and strong"—to borrow one of Michael's favourite phrases—he said the debaters dined together and actually had quite a jolly time of it.

Dinner ended with my mentioning Julie's story that Michael had nearly drowned in Cyprus:

> **[CR]** Julie said you were shouting for help and she started to call for assistance and she said Jill was quite calm.
>
> **[MF]** "Let him sink," she said.

Michael said this quite cheerfully.

April 2001

48

Michael had a new housekeeper, Molly, by far the best one I had encountered. She was discreet but engaging. We had many long talks together. She had an affectionate yet shrewd understanding of Michael's strengths and weaknesses. Molly became an important witness to his life, although I never formally interviewed her. Unlike Emma, she did not join in conversations unless she was invited to do so.

Just then I felt I must confront the question of whether I was to do Michael's biography as well as Jill's. From our first meeting, Julie had been urging me to do so, to make sure I got my place in line ahead of everyone else. I took to the idea, since I had always wanted to write a biography of a political figure and I had such unprecedented access to Michael. But Julie, in her typical eagerness, had been pressing Michael:

> **[CR]** Julie said that when you were in Jamaica she asked you about my doing your biography. She's talked to me about it several times.
>
> **[MF]** I see.
>
> **[CR]** Ah, I'd be delighted. After Jill, it would be natural to do that. You may have somebody else in mind. Or there may be something else you want to do, Michael.
>
> **[MF]** No.

[CR] I was a little taken aback. I didn't realise she was going to do that.

[MF] Well, it's up to you. I'm not going to write anything further myself, excepting book reviews.

[CR] I've got plenty to do and I'd be delighted to do it, but I don't want you to feel as if this is premature.

[MF] No, if you want to do it, it's got some point from your point of view. So ...

His voice trailed off. It seemed to me Michael had given me leeway, if not exactly his blessing.

We spent the morning discussing Michael's role at *Tribune*, guiding the journal's policy toward endorsing the creation of NATO and establishing an anti-Communist stance earlier than most other leftwing publications. George Orwell had become a welcome figure to the staff at *Tribune*, even though readers protested: "Why do you take after the Russians all the time? We're still allies with them." Part of Michael's friendship with Ernest Bevin was founded on their staunchly anti-Communist views, strengthened by their dismay at what happened to Poland, Czechoslovakia and other Central European countries that became Soviet satellites shortly after the Yalta agreement.

I brought up Michael's passionate support of Indira Gandhi. "I read *The Asian Age* every morning, you know," Michael said by way of stressing his deep concern with Indian politics. Much to the outrage of Michael's fellow Labour Party members and supporters, Michael went to India during the emergency Indira Gandhi had enforced. "It was because of what was happening to George Fernandez that I went there," said Michael, separating himself from the allegation that he had gone to India in support of Mrs. Gandhi. Fernandez, a member of the Indian Socialist party, had become a cause celebre for the Labour Party. Fernandez was imprisoned because he had been conducting strike action. Michael had decided to protest Fernandez's incarceration: "We should not let this slide without making some representations," I said to Callaghan. "I would like to go to India and raise these things [the anti-democratic nature of the emergency] with Mrs. Gandhi because I know her quite well and see what she's got to say. I think it's much better that I should do that than to just have a row with her." I don't think the Foreign Office liked it very much. They gave me some kind of briefing ... Crosland was the foreign secretary at the time. I don't think he was especially interested in how this was developing, but I was. I didn't want to see an estrangement between us and India. When we [Jill accompanied him] got to the airport at two in the morning, the High Commissioner met me, terribly alarmed, saying "I don't really know what you've come here for, but you won't be able to do much with Mrs. Gandhi. We don't want a breach." I said, "I don't want a breach, either. I've come to raise a number of issues with her and see what she's got to say." Then I started mentioning the issues [Michael laughed]. He said, "You can't do that. If you say that to her, she'll just kick you out or something." He had a completely false idea of what I could say to her.

Michael was told: "You better go back home." "I can't do that," he said. He was to meet Gandhi that morning. The situation was tense. One British journalist, Mark Tully, had been thrown out of the country. Every subject Michael was told not to raise, he raised—"especially the Fernandez one." But Mrs. Gandhi was circumspect. She could not interfere with the Fernandez case while it was in the courts. Of course Michael understood, but he wanted to convey to her the strong feeling about Fernandez in Britain. Fernandez was a member of the Socialist International, and "we would be doing the same for anybody else in the Socialist International anywhere in the world in such circumstances." To Michael, Gandhi seemed "calmer than almost any political leader I've ever met. She defended her position. She said she had to be careful: "I don't want to have happen to me what happened to Allende in Chile."

For Michael, Mrs. Gandhi redeemed herself by allowing the election to go ahead. "When she didn't win, what she did, in my opinion, was absolutely crucial to the whole salvation of India because she took the defeat ... Then she made her comeback. An amazing thing. I don't think there's any such case in history of how a democratic leader has come back."

49

At lunch, Michael began to reminisce about his first election in Wales, when he was selected to occupy Nye Bevan's seat. A brief kerfuffle had resulted when his name did not appear on the short list of Labour Party candidates for the seat. Evidently some locals preferred not to take on Michael in spite of his association with Nye. Jennie Lee, along with others, intervened and Michael not only made the list but also was selected and won his seat in the general election. He had a wonderful photograph of himself and Jill, with their dog Vanessa between them. The happy looking dog in the centre looked as if she had won the election, I told Michael. "It did, too," he said.[1]

---

[1] Michael had grown up with several dogs in Plymouth and Cornwall, including a St. Bernard that looked just like the Tory leader the Marquis of Salisbury. "My father called him Salisbury."

Talk of Vanessa reminded Michael of the terrible 1963 accident. Vanessa and Jason (in the backseat) had escaped harm. "We were saved by the Health Service," Michael believed. Taken to the Hereford hospital, Michael regained consciousness and gave the staff there the name of their doctor and friend, Jerry Slattery, "a great supporter of the Health Service." Slattery knew how to work the system and called on specialist consultants.

When Michael awoke the first morning after the accident, he heard the words of his favourite childhood hymn, "Look away across the sea where mountains are prepared for me." For a moment Michael thought he had arrived in the hereafter, but it was the Salvation Army playing the hymn outside the hospital.

50

After dinner, Michael vouchsafed to me that he had had an encounter with Barbara Castle at a recent *Tribune* event:

> **[MF]** You told me about what she had done ... in your case. [Castle had asked for a fee as the price of an interview and I had refused.]
>
> **[CR]** I was really surprised.
>
> **[MF]** She spoke to me about that the other day. I don't want to cause any trouble. I don't want her to think that I've got any grievance against her because it won't serve any purpose. You know, we're longstanding friends and I'm now on very good terms with her ... She'd been in on the foundation of *Tribune* ... We've had our quarrels ... It was quite shocking—Barbara's reply to you. She shouldn't have done anything like that, but ... she's losing

her eyesight. I may wake up any day to see that she is dead. I had quite a talk with her ... She was feeling very guilty about what she said to you, and she came out with it in some way or other, and I said, "No, no Barbara. You don't have to worry about this." I wouldn't ask to see her again.

Very handsome? chivalric of my biographical subject, but not so helpful to me, I thought.

I asked Michael if he thought she could have become the Labour Party leader: "I don't think so, really," Michael answered decisively. "What stopped her?" I asked. "The business of understanding other people's positions and working together—I don't think she [Barbara] had much ... " Michael did not complete his sentence but switched instead to saying Callaghan had a much better sense of the whole party. I observed to Michael that Castle's diaries revealed that she often found Michael's behaviour in cabinet difficult to understand. "You were responding to other people's positions ... and therefore you would seem less focused than she was." Quite right, Michael said.

"She sees you in her diaries as this fiery backbencher, and then you get in the cabinet and you're behaving (to her) differently; that is, you seemed to be more of a compromiser. She found this almost shocking. I don't find it surprising at all: "If you're going to be in the cabinet for God's sakes ... " I began. Michael finished my sentence: "You have to compromise." Michael added: "I sometimes said to Jill if I'd had the experience of being in the cabinet before I wrote it [the Bevan biography] I would have written somewhat differently. He was making compromises to get through the main things he wanted. He had to keep on his side people like Dalton and Ernest Bevin. Herbert Morrison was the one who was opposed to the way he [Bevan] was doing the Health Service and he had to be prepared to compromise."

I asked Michael why Castle had gone into the House of Lords. She needed the money, the perks, that went along with the position, Michael suspected. He believed she had anxiety attacks about her finances. I asked him, "What if you had said to Jill, 'I've changed my mind. I want to go into the House of Lords'"? Michael laughed. "I don't know. She wouldn't have believed it." Celine La Frieniere, on the other hand, claimed that Jill would have enjoyed the honour and was put out with Michael for not pursuing the matter.

When their brother Mac went into the Lords, Michael remembered Dingle saying, "It's enough to make your blood run blue." The very notion of a House of Lords seemed risible to Michael. He used to tell me that it was the only club where they pay you for your drinks.

51

Peter Thornburn, Jill's gardener, arrived. He was still caring for her precious garden, which Michael felt quite proud of while at the same time happily confessing he knew nothing about it. "It's been a cold winter," Peter informed Michael, "quite a few things died." The wind had been a problem. "Why can't you stop the bloody wind?" Michael asked. He had an easygoing relationship with Peter and trusted him to do the right thing for the garden. This was Michael's way with everyone who merited his confidence.

I walked out in the garden to speak with Peter alone, curious to learn what he had noticed about Jill and Michael.

At the start, he was reserved, as I'd expect of an employee who had just met me. "A lovely couple," he said. I'd tried to draw him out about distinctions. Jill was concise; Michael tended to digress. "She didn't miss much," was Peter's contribution, but then he warmed to the topic:

> She'd get quite exasperated with him. Sometimes I think he would feel ... sometimes she would say, "Michael has disappeared. He's trying to avoid laying the table." I felt she was the boss and he was quite happy with that.

I suggested that Michael never felt comfortable doing any sort of domestic chore. "I sometimes thought he felt quite useless," Peter observed. One time for example, Jill had asked Michael to pick up some potatoes and he had come home with kiwi fruit.

Peter was fond of Michael, calling him a "teasingly affectionate man." He immediately added, though, that Michael was no saint and could be "quite grumpy. To be honest, since Jill died, I've seen much more of him. He was more grumpy when Jill was alive. It's almost like, in a sense—I hesitate to say it—he feels more at home. Jill was quite a dominating presence." Safe with his books, Michael was fine, but anything to do with the home, Peter concluded, Michael had to be "on his mettle."

52

By way of preparing me for a visit to Paul Foot, Michael told me a story about the time Paul, then 14 and a public school boy, visited Jill and Michael at the Abbey Road home. He was shocked that Jill and Michael had no interest whatsoever in going to Princess Elizabeth's coronation. Paul was to accompany Isaac Foot to the great event. Michael said, "We're going back to bed." Later they mocked Paul about his reaction. Michael wanted me to ask him if he had recovered from witnessing Michael and Jill's disgraceful behaviour. Of course, Michael well knew that Paul would now scoff at his once reverential attitude toward the royals.

"We were invited to some of these royal functions," Michael said. Jill wanted to see what they were like. They had gone to Prince Charles's wedding to Diana. "There was a lot of nonsense about it. We had to be there two or three hours early. I took a book with me, as I always do on such occasions and I read Hazlitt's 'Spirit of the Monarchy.'"

Second only to the royals in Michael's gallery of good-for-nothings were, of course, the Tories. John Major occupied a special page in Michael's book of bad ones. The trouble began when Suraj Paul, a staunch Labour Party backer and friend to Michael, invited him to the festivities celebrating his twenty-five years of doing business in Britain. Lord Paul had built a factory in Michael's constituency and another one in John Major's. A fortnight before the grand event, Lord Paul rang up Michael to say he had encountered a "terrible difficulty. I hate what I'm doing, but I've got to. I have to say to you that Major [then Prime Minister] had said that if you're coming to the ceremony, he won't come." Michael was flabbergasted: "I hadn't any great antagonism with Major or anything of the sort." Of course, Michael relieved Lord Paul of his problem by not attending the event. "I've never told anyone. Nobody's put it into print. But I see no reason why it shouldn't go into the book. The pettiest thing I've ever heard of. Naturally I don't think much of him on that account."

The Thatcher/Major years, as far as Michael was concerned, had wrecked the world that the 1945 Labour landslide had inaugurated. Shortly after the incident with Major, Michael traveled to Manchester from his constituency in Wales. The trip required a change of trains in Abergavenny:

> I used to go down there when I first got to that part of
> the world—1930s in the Monmouth constituency was
> the first place I fought a campaign. Abergavenny was
> a nice little busy railway town—the best supporters
> of the Labour Party—a thriving little market town.
> When I turned up [at the railway station] two days after
> I heard Mr. Major in London announce we were to
> have a classless society—the whole place was absolutely
> deserted. The ticket office was closed. Everything was
> closed except the lavatory. The only thing that was
> working was the bloody condom machine with some
> posh title called Empire—Elite! That's it! The only thing
> working in the Major station was the Elite Condoms. I
> didn't need one at the time, I may say, but there you are.
> That was my introduction to Major's classless society.

The discussion then returned to Paul Foot, who had not only outgrown his school boy reverence for the monarchy but had metamorphosed into a Socialist Workers' Party member. Like his colleague, John Pilger, Paul, so Michael said, took a "Trotskyite, anti-American view. He says the Americans are responsible for agreeing to the dissolution of the former Yugoslavia. It's absolute balls when you look at the detail of it."

Michael did not seem to me anti-American in the slightest.

Unlike many of his English contemporaries, he felt no resentment towards the world's only super power. Of course, he could be quite critical of American policies, but his voice never had the edge that crept into Jenny Stringer's whenever America and Americans became the subject of conversation. Michael took people as they came. Then, too, Michael was bound to admire any country that was a republic. Thomas Jefferson was one of his heroes.

"What time is it?" Michael asked. It was 6:30 and time for a drink, then dinner.

53

Over dinner I joshed Michael about Jill's garden:

> **[CR]** Did you ever help Jill plant her plants?
> **[MF]** No.
> **[CR]** Never?
> **[MF]** No. [Molly laughed]
> **[CR]** She knew it wasn't a good idea.
> **[MF]** That's right. She had better people to help her like Jillian.

I would be interviewing Jillian shortly. She lived just down the block in the house that Julie and her first husband, Victor, (now married to Jillian), once occupied.

Michael remembered that Jill came home with croissants after her early morning plant-buying excursions to Columbia Road. "So that's how we're going to do it this time." He would have the croissants ready for us when we returned from our re-enactment of Jill's gardening jaunts.

54

One of Michael's favourite pastimes was hauling books down from his shelves and reading to me, or pointing out comments he had made on the flyleaves. The astringent Brigid Brophy never failed to amuse him. Her invective, he claimed, "would put anybody in a good temper. It's my favourite cure for any kind of depression." Michael read out a newspaper clipping reporting an apology concerning something Brophy had written that the press council deemed pornographic. A reader had complained about her article on Lucretius, the newspaper report noted: "Referring to the Latin language Ms. Brophy wrote, 'yet, though non-colloquial Latin is rhetorical and declamatory because its sounds ooze forth, though its meaning has to be teased out, tension and internal contradiction are inherent in the language. I can't believe it didn't create in its users a psychological predisposition to tension like masturbating with one hand while playing chess with the other." We roared. "It's hard to beat. It makes me laugh like anything," Michael said. He spoke of Brigid Brophy constantly. "It's wonderful," he chortled.

55

Michael was keen to visit the new Tate Modern and arranged for an outing with Peter and Celine, who always seemed happy to indulge him. They drove us from Hampstead to the museum and then obtained a wheelchair for Michael, a necessity if he was to be able to move with any facility through the galleries.

On our return to Hampstead Michael said, "I didn't see a single woman in that place [the Tate] today that wasn't wearing pants." The comment startled me. It wasn't like him to make such observations. What else did he see that he did not comment on? "I wasn't watching," Peter said. "I was," Michael insisted. "Not a single one with a skirt. Some very neat, I must say," Michael observed.

56

After Celine and Peter dropped us off at Michael's home, I asked him about his attitude toward wheelchairs:

> **[CR]** Here's how it goes: Some people want to help you by making sure you'll never get into a wheelchair.
> **[MF]** Yes.
> **[CR]** Some people think they are helping you by putting you in the wheelchair.
> **[MF]** Yea.
> **[CR]** Which do you prefer?
> **[MF]** I like a bit of both.
> **[CR]** I think that's right.
> **[MF]** If you go to the Tate museum, a chair is a perfectly sensible way to go.
> **[CR]** They're [Peter and Celine] very put out because the chair [they had bought him one] was not used around this house. I understand they want to be very helpful, but it is probably better for you—unless you are in pain or just can't walk—not to use the chair.
> **[MF]** That's right. They understand that too now, I think.

The chair had been a great success on the Bermuda trip Peter and Celine had arranged for Michael. On their return to Hampstead Celine and Peter proposed to start wheeling

Michael out on the Heath. Michael politely declined, saying he thought he should try to continue walking there on his own. They understood his feelings, Michael said. I persisted anyway: "I'm not criticising them, but I do think the more they have you in the chair, the more, in a sense, control they have." Michael muttered, "Yes." The idea, however, that they might have mixed motivations did not appeal to Michael. Still, I pursued him: "You have all these people who want to help you, but the question is how much should they help you? And how much should they allow you to be yourself." I didn't realise then how important this issue was. Only when Paul Foot and others began to speak for Michael, to say what they thought was good for Michael, did I realise how they wanted to cocoon him. What Michael remembered, and rightly so, was how during Jill's last nine months, when she was in and out of hospital, Celine and Peter were indefatigable in visiting her and striving to make life as comfortable as possible for Jill and Michael.

Michael was not unaware of Peter's quirks. "He always caps the thing," Jill used to say about Peter, Michael told me. "If you tell him something extraordinary, he will have something even more extraordinary to top it." I saw Michael's point. "If I tell him something about New York, he will tell me something about it that I don't know." "That's it," Michael agreed. "Jill would laugh about it. It's not a terrible crime, in my opinion."

57

"I wanted to ask you about Elizabeth Thomas," I ventured. "What was she like as a person?" "As a person?" Michael asked. "Yea, what kind of personality ... what you found attractive about her?" He thought about it: "She was a good looking woman, as my father would say. Very good looking. Not as good looking as Jill, but she was very good." Michael provided some details about Elizabeth's family, but the kernel of their affair—what really sparked it—remained Michael's secret.

Elizabeth had typed the manuscript of *The Pen and the Sword* and I was curious to know if Michael had formed a sort of intellectual partnership with her during such projects. He seemed somehow nonplussed when I asked him about it. I never got any sense of how Elizabeth —or Jill, for that matter —really figured into his working days. Were they just sounding boards? I expect so. While Michael and I sometimes had give-and-take discussions about his reading and writing, more often than not, dialogue turned into monologue.

I tried once more: "Was Elizabeth's personality anything like Jill's?" Michael mused, "I must think carefully about that." After several digressions, I asked the question again. No response. "Sense of humour?" I asked:

[MF] She had that, too.

[CR] Was she flirtatious like Jill?

[MF] Yes, I should think so. Quite a lot.

[CR] So what did you do—make a pass at Elizabeth?

[MF] Indeed, a few.

[CR] Did it take more than one pass, or was she very receptive?

[MF] Oh, she was pretty receptive. It was about the time I was defeated in Devonport [1955] and the Aldermaston marches and the row with Nye—1957, 1958, 1959. Elizabeth was very much involved in all those [events].

She was as strong on those subjects as Jill was. So anyhow…

His voice constantly trailed off and I would try to nudge him along. "I'll show you a picture of her, but not at this moment."

[CR] Did you feel you could confide in Elizabeth the same way you could in Jill?
[MF] Confide? I see … uh huh … Well … Not quite, I suppose. However! … I'm just going to go and have a little sleep. We can talk about these matters later.

I never detected any irritation on Michael's part with my constant questioning. Either he really had not considered such questions, or his perpetual dodging was his way of coping with uncomfortable biographical inquiry. Rather than refuse me outright, he retreated.

58

[CR] I was reading another of your books in your library last night—Herbert Morrison's autobiography. He's got one paragraph on you. It's the nastiest piece of business, calling you a TV personality. He doesn't know if you have any influence on anyone and he refers to your election defeat in Plymouth. He loads it on. Do you remember that?
[MF] Ernest Bevin is supposed to have said of Morrison when someone else said, "He's his own worst enemy," "not while I'm alive."

Michael had no other comment on Morrison. He rarely spent time on those he disliked.

Just then he was preparing to visit the ailing Peter Shore, a Labour Party colleague he esteemed for an ability to articulate important ideas:

> He was the very best of them almost ... Some people said he should be the leader of the party next after Callaghan went. I think he would have been very good if he had. That's when I stood and some people said Peter resented it. But I don't think he resented it very much. I don't think he thought he would have won and I don't think he would have won. Of course, you can never be sure of what a chap thinks about such things. I still think Neil was the best chap to do it ... I thought he would become Prime Minister if we ever came back [into power]... We all thought it was going to happen in 1992.
>
> **[CR]** Do you think John Smith would have done as well as Blair?
> **[MF]** Yes—better in some ways. He had better links with the Labour Party. There are some things he [Blair] seems to be careless about.

When I later interviewed Neil Kinnock, he rejected Michael's view that Shore had not resented Michael's entrance into the leadership contest. Kinnock was emphatic about Shore's big sulks and Denis Healey's autobiography portrays Shore as quite troubled by Michael's decision. Was Michael really not aware of this estrangement? As with Mervyn Jones, Michael could be obtuse about what his friends really thought of him and Jill.

Another departed favourite was Donald Dewar, who lodged for nearly two decades in Michael's upstairs flat. Michael seemed amused at the way Dewar always took the blackest point of view:

"We would be defeated. We would never recover." But he was a highly intelligent chap. When he died the other day ... it shows what a bloody fickle lot they are ... the bloody newspapers were absolutely disgusting, every kind of way saying he was unfit for the job [Education Secretary] when was he coming out to say something. He was in hospital then. I was amazed at the fury of it ... Then he died suddenly. Overnight these same bloody newspapers said what a great man he was, Scotland's greatest hero, quite unqualified. But the venom before was terrible.

Michael admired Dewar's skill in debate in the House of Commons, as well as his humour. "We had lots of fun with him. Every time we thought the news was bad, we said, 'You wait to see what Donald says about it. You won't cheer up then.'" There was no lodger as good as Donald, Jill often remarked. He hardly left behind so much as a dirty towel.

I asked Michael about Tony Benn, wondering if he would dilate on the figure who had given him so much trouble in his brief tenure as party leader. Benn's wife, Caroline, had died just a few months before. She had got on with Jill. The two women shared an interest in women's rights, and Caroline had authored a biography of Keir Hardie, one of the male heroes in the fight for women's suffrage. Michael attended Caroline's memorial service, an act Tony appreciated. "We've had a kind of reconciliation," Michael said, "In this week's *Tribune*, however, he's written ... the same old stuff about Yugoslavia, which is all wrong and cock-eyed. So I'm going to write to him. He took the easy ways. He wouldn't face the difficulties. But he's got many virtues as well."

A few minutes later Michael provided this addendum:

Tony sometimes talks as if he is the only just man. ... He's a very persuasive speaker. You think he believes every word of it and I think he does, actually. That's why he comes across. There's no fake in it. But my impression is that his family—two or three of them—don't agree with him. They don't say it because they don't want to hurt him. In the first cabinet where I was—who you sit next to is quite important—you see how the other chap operates. Of course, Tony had been in many cabinets ... Tony was on one side and Tony Crosland on the other. I got more fun out of it that way, I must say. Tony [Benn] was keeping his diary ... Crosland was an interesting chap. Quite a lot of arguments with Tony Crosland ... I had an argument with him on one occasion about Hazlitt because despite the fact I was in the bloody cabinet, I saw that it was Hazlitt's two hundredth anniversary. They [the *Times*] asked me to do an article and I did it—this was before Murdoch had taken over. The next week [during a cabinet meeting] Tony Crosland says, "Fancy a chap who has time to write articles when he's in the cabinet. We're not like that. We have to get on with the bloody work." I said, "Well, it so happens I've been waiting a long time to write that article. That's my excuse." But I got back on him because he produced a book called *Socialism Now*. Three or four weeks later [in cabinet] I said, "*Socialism Now*— that's a wonderful title. We are trying to work on a decent incomes policy and here I read a book by you called

Socialism Now. I've looked through it ten times. There's no chapter on incomes policy."

This conversation took place over a simple dinner (a salad and an omelette) I had made for Michael—the only meal I prepared during my many stays at his home. It had been a wonderful evening, uninterrupted by a housekeeper or a ringing phone. I should have arranged more of these occasions, when Michael seemed altogether more relaxed and performing for no one but me.

"So, what's the time?" he asked. It was just after nine. "I think I will stagger up to bed," he said. "I'll just put the plates in the sink," I said. "I'll see you off," he said, referring to the fact that the next morning I had an appointment with Jillian to visit the Columbia Road garden market she and Jill used to frequent early on Saturday mornings. I told him not to worry about getting up. "I'll put the croissants in the oven, that makes them better," he emphasised. He got up muttering, "All this doddering now."

59

Michael did indeed have the croissants on hand when Jillian and I arrived home from Columbia Road. Immediately a jolly argument erupted between Michael and Jillian:

[MF] I never protested about flowers coming into this house. I wasn't such a fool as that.

[J] You were amazed at the amount.

[MF] What?

[J] At what a huge amount: "Not more! Not more!"

[MF] Never said that.

The discussion later turned to Jamaica, which Michael had visited in January. Noel Coward had spent a good deal of time there, Michael noted. Michael met Coward once in a hotel: "He took me upstairs. He didn't seduce me. I didn't know about such things then," he claimed. "An innocent abroad," I commented. "Yes, I was."

Michael's nephew Oliver had cosseted him during the Jamaica trip and although Michael enjoyed the beauty of his surroundings and sumptuous meals at the private home of the owner of Jamaican Airlines, he chiefly remembered, as usual, his reading. That time it had been a book on India. "I'm terribly slow, reading, but I was able to read it all there." He had to bring the book to within inches of his good eye and scan the text like a jeweller appraising a diamond.

60

Julie and I met the journalist Ian Aitkin for a drink. He had known Michael since 1953, when Aitkin had come to work for *Tribune*, relaunched, as Aitkin put it, as the "voice of Bevanism." I told Ian that virtually anything he said would be relevant since I would be doing Michael's biography after I completed my work on Jill.

"Perhaps I should describe the *Tribune* office then," he began:

> It was at 217 The Strand, which was also rather grandly known as the "Outer Temple." There was a corridor that ran down from The Strand into the Middle Temple— you know the legal ...
> **[CR]** Oh, yes.
> **[IA]** It was terribly run-down. It had the most

extraordinary lift, which was operated by a man who smelled of horses. A very large and elderly gentleman who had been a drayman for one of the breweries. It worked by hydraulics. He pulled the ropes generating enough heat up to a dark and gloomy windowless hallway with a row of glass doors with such light as there was coming through. It was like a railway carriage with the doors connecting to each other. The windows opened on to a frightful dank and gloomy area ... dreadfully dusty and absolutely chaotic. Circulation and advertising were in one room and there was me and anyone else who happened to be doing a turn for *Tribune* in another room, and Michael and his secretary Elizabeth in the next one and Bob Edwards [another editor] in the gloomiest room of all. The problem was whoever came in to see Michael would encounter constant traffic going through the rooms unless it was something frightfully private—in which case they would go out into the hall.

[CR] Was Michael's office tidy?

[IA] No, but newspapers offices aren't. He used to write columns for the *Daily Herald* in longhand. Have you seen his writing? It looks like Greek—very jagged.

[CR] He marks his books that way too—with daggers.

[IA] Elizabeth then typed it up. When he was writing his columns, you were expected to fall silent [Ian laughed].

[CR] Would he get upset by noise?

[IA] He rarely got upset about anything, except the state of the Labour Party.

[CR] Is the Michael of today the Michael you knew then?

[IA] He's not as intense now. You could tell then how upset he was by the [Ian made the sound of a vaporiser, which Michael used during asthma attacks]. If you heard it frequently, you knew things were pretty damn bad. He was completely fearless about what he wrote.

The period Ian described had to do with the Gaitskill leadership, when Bevan and his followers faced expulsion from the party for advocating a strenuous socialism that Gaitskill aimed to mitigate. Jennie Lee would often arrive [she was on *Tribune*'s editorial board], urging an attack on one person or another who had menaced the Bevanites. Ian startled Julie when he concluded, "On the whole, *Tribune* did Nye more harm than good." "Would Michael agree with that?" Julie asked. They answered the question simultaneously: "No." Laughing, Ian added: "Not that I cared. I thoroughly enjoyed myself."

I was curious to know if Ian detected political differences between Michael and Jill. Not many, he observed, although she became more outspoken, he thought, as she grew older. Ian did remember that "Michael had the most amazing put-down of her, 'My dear child, you don't know what you're talking about.'" Nothing ever deterred Michael, Ian asserted. "There were quite a few things he was ignorant about, but that did not stop him from holding forth." Did Jill have any influence on Michael's political views? I asked. "Absolutely zero," Ian thought.

Did Ian witness any big blow-ups between Michael and Jill? I asked. Jill got quite testy, he remembered, when Michael retired from Parliament in 1992. "She used to say to me, 'It's God awful. I've got to get him out of the house!

I can't stand it any longer" and Michael would trundle off to the *Tribune* office.

"Can you tell me a little bit about Elizabeth Thomas"? I asked. "An *amazing* woman," Ian shot back. Why didn't Michael express that kind of enthusiasm? I wondered to myself. He never spoke of their relationship using that kind of register. He seemed unable to rekindle in memory his passion for her. "Very good looking," Ian continued:

> In a non-sexy sort of way, rather elegant ...
> **[CR]** A small woman?
> **[IA]** No, tall and slim. Her husband George went to football matches with Michael. An innocent woman. She once told me that when she and her husband got married, neither of them had the faintest idea what to do.
> **[CR]** But they sorted it out.
> **[IA]** Yes. George was not a spectacular philanderer ... He liked flirting. Elizabeth adored Michael. The way she gazed at him. She made no attempt to conceal it. Michael appeared to be totally unaware of it. Would have been a bit tricky for Jill, I suppose.
> **[CR]** Did you suspect they were having an affair?
> **[IA]** Who?
> **[CR]** Michael and Elizabeth?
> **[IA]** They were?
> **[CR]** Yes.
> **[IA]** That comes as a thunderbolt! Wow! There he was going off with George and bedding his wife at the same time?
> **[CR]** As Michael would say, it is possible to be in love

with two women.

[IA] Yes, but ... [Ian laughed, perhaps a bit uncomfortably].

Ian turned to Julie and asked her if she was aware of this affair. No, she was very surprised, Julie said: "I was good friends with Elizabeth. I never saw her in a sexual light." Ian agreed, "No."

Ian wanted to know how I got Michael to talk about such matters and I explained what I had discovered in Jill's diary and what she herself had said about the need for candour in biography. I also mentioned that four-minute silence in which Michael seemed to be calculating what to say. "I know those silences," Ian said, laughing again. "It's going to be a good book," Ian told me. "I've learned more from you than you have from me," he added. "I try to give good value," I replied. "So Elizabeth was not the innocent thing I thought she was," he marvelled. I suggested perhaps nothing would have happened if Michael had not taken the initiative. "He did?" Ian asked. "How do you know?" "Because I asked him," I told Ian. "Michael is not the man we always believe him to be," Julie said. "There are other sides to Michael Foot, " I announced, "which is what one should learn in a biography." Ian wondered aloud about what the *Daily Mail* would do with such a story. Both Ian and Julie cautioned me to have nothing to do with the tabloids; publishing there would set Michael off. "Michael Foot: A Sexual Life," Ian said, and laughed. "Michael Foot in Love," Julie countered. "There is a passion there, yes," I agreed. " I always thought his interest was academic," Ian noted. "No, it ain't," Julie said.

Julie reminded Ian that they had once been lovers and

that Michael had discovered them in his bed. Michael later said to Julie, "I don't mind what you do, but not in my bed. By the way, how was it?" Ian laughed, remembering, "The awful sound of his footsteps coming up the stairs!"

After Ian left us, Julie said to me, "You really shocked him." I agreed: "I wanted to learn more about Elizabeth Thomas, a physical description, and Michael is not good on such things. I said to him just yesterday, 'What did you do make a pass at her?' He said, 'Yes, I did.'" But I could not get much more out of him. "He made a pass at me," Julie said. "Did he?" I tried to say levelly:

> **[JH]** It took me totally by surprise.
> **[CR]** I should think it would. How old were you?
> **[JH]** Oh, somewhere around 28. I was living in the country with my second husband Mike, and he [Michael] came into the kitchen and gave me a French kiss. I repelled him.

Julie remembered earlier instances when he had touched her in a more than friendly way. "I've never told anyone this," she said. "I don't think you should remember that." I said, "I presume you never told Jill. That would be so disturbing to her." Julie had not. We agreed Michael had a yen for young women. I mentioned how he had commented on the women at the Tate. "He's very interested in the sexual right now," Julie reported. "There was a time when my daughter Laura was quite beautiful. Michael used to home in on her and my mother used to be exceedingly bitchy about it.

61

Returning to Michael's Hampstead home, I found him keen to tell me about his latest dream—though not before providing me with a windup. Right up to the time of that catastrophic car accident in 1963, Michael had suffered severe asthma attacks. In hospital, he had been advised to remain as quiet and calm as possible, since another attack, given his chest injuries, might prove fatal. He remembered having quite a few attacks during the period he and Jill occupied Beaverbrook's cottage—an annoyance, Michael noted, since he thought the country air would be salubrious.

He had tried everything, even smoking what he called "asthma cigarettes." He did not think they helped much. Smoking was not a factor, he thought, because he had had asthma before taking up smoking. Until the accident he had been smoking over 60 Woodbines a day. But an operation on his throat convinced him that whatever else he might do, giving up smoking was a priority. Good as his word, he never smoked again.

For two or three years after the accident, he still had the urge to smoke, especially when writing. "I took hours doing reviews. After the first paragraph, I'd get stuck, wanting to smoke." Once he got over that brief period, the urge to smoke left him forever. Michael's anxieties about being able to complete his writing seemed tied to fears that his asthma would return:

> **[MF]** I've had twice a dream, thinking the asthma had come back. I was dreaming that I had had an attack of asthma and when I woke up, it wasn't [an attack]. Of course I was relieved. But the dream was absolutely as

if it was happening. There were other dreams often wandering on some bloody trail, wondering where I was going. I had that one constantly. Mostly I would tell Jill about the dreams.

[CR] What did Jill make of your dreams?

[MF] I had to be careful.

[CR] Did Jill ever tell you about her dreams?

[MF] No, I don't think she ever did.

[CR] Well, that wasn't fair.

Michael got something stuck in his throat and our conversation ended. "Want me to get you some water, Michael?" I asked. He paced back and forth until the choking sensation subsided.

62

Later in the evening, Michael spoke highly of Denis Healey's efforts to maintain party unity during Michael's brief tenure as leader. Denis had as much love for the party as he did, Michael emphasised and Healey even went out of his way after the 1983 defeat to say that Michael should not be saddled with all the blame.Healey and Michael certainly had their differences, but they worked well together, agreeing to approach Brezhnev and broker a deal that would ease tensions concerning the Cruise missiles in Britain and in other parts of Europe. Michael and Denis were concerned about an escalating Russian response. How to stop this super power competition? "We were protesting about it," Michael said. "We talked to Brezhnev. We said, 'What about a zero option? To have no new Cruise missiles on either side of Europe?'"

The Tory government claimed the Russians rebuffed Foot and Healey and that "we'd made fools of ourselves," Michael said. Douglas Hurd in the Foreign Office ridiculed the zero option proposal. "Two weeks later, Reagan came out and used the exact phrase, 'Why not a zero option?' The Foreign Office then changed its tune. We had a quite sensible foreign policy," Michael added, "and we were treated as innocents who did not know what was happening in the bloody world."

63

This day, for some reason, was a particularly important one to Michael. We ranged over all sorts of subjects, some of which forged a bond between us. Suddenly Michael said, "So, Carl, one of the best moments of my life was when you rang me and said, 'What about doing the biography?' And it's all going to come off.'" Actually, he had rung me, but in effect he was right, since I had written to him first. In retrospect, his trust in me remains gratifying, but it also sounded a cautionary note. How could anything I wrote ever have lived up to his ideal of the book, especially when it became a projection of his own dreams? He said the book would be "very good for the health of the world. I'd just like to be there when publication takes place." He almost never mentioned his mortality. I responded, "I'm glad you're happy about it." He was exultant: "I'm thrilled about it." I confessed that "when I proposed it, I thought it was a good idea, but I thought maybe it was premature." He said, "No, just right." "If you didn't do it now, the thing would fade. I'm sure you'll get the whole thing, the spirit of Jill into the book."

We had a lengthy discussion of the difficulties I had had working on other biographies and the efforts made by Martha Gellhorn, Susan Sontag and others to prevent publication. Gellhorn's representative, Bill Buford, sent a threatening letter to my publisher. Michael, a journalist first, called Buford a "dirty dog." I never dreamed, then, that he, too, would, in the end, assume a rather high-handed attitude towards my manuscript, ordering me to make changes and deferring to the feelings of others. On this day, I said: "I don't respond well to those threats. I don't allow them to intimidate me." "We don't believe in authorised biographies," Michael concluded. "All authorised biographies are hereby condemned." I would remember these words later when Michael the Apostate appeared.

64

Later that afternoon Michael and I paid a visit to Paul Foot. Watching them was always a treat. Michael got on to the subject of Jill's horrible childhood and her terrible mother, who at one point put Jill in a Belgian convent. "That's why Jill hated Belgians," Michael pointed out. "I don't mean to say she was racist or anything like that…" Paul interrupted, "No, she just hated Belgians." We laughed. Michael just went on, seemingly oblivious to Paul's foolery.

While his young daughter and a friend traipsed through the kitchen, taking the pizza that Paul had put in the oven for them, he served lunch—a feat for a man still recovering from a stroke. "Quite amazing what you get here," Michael said to me, as Paul delivered our cold cuts to the table.

Michael's devoted secretary, Una, had just died and Michael and Paul spoke tenderly about her. Who was helping Michael now? Oh, he had Sheila Noble on hand, he said. She was, I knew, as devoted as Una. "Sheila's lovely, a marvellous person," Paul said. "Don't know how you get all these left-wingers to come and work for you." Michael replied: "Another of your supporters." "She isn't one of our supporters, but she will be," Paul said. "What do you mean?" Michael said. "Well, she's not in the SWP [Socialist Workers Party]." "Are you still in it?" Michael asked. "I've been in the SWP for 40 years," Paul replied.

"Are you ready to answer some questions?" I asked Paul. He was quite willing to oblige. I asked him when he first met Michael. Paul's earliest memory of Michael places him at the Foot family home in Pencrebar, just about the time of the 1945 general election:

[PF] The only thing [of importance] to us was how many members of the family were going to get elected. The information we had was no chance for Michael. He was the black sheep. He had gone away from the family tradition.

[CR] No longer a liberal.

[PF] Serve him bloody well right.

[CR] Teach him a lesson.

[PF] Everybody else had a good chance of winning.

[CR] Do you think his father felt that way?

[PF] No. They didn't actually say that. It was the banter. His mother was a bit that way.

[MF] Ah! Not my mother.

[PF] When Michael was in the first results and he'd won, it followed that everyone else would win by enormous majorities. All through the next days there were these terrible results: Dingle had lost in Dundee, and John lost in Bodmin and then the worst was grandfather in Tavistock. He just shut himself up in his room. He wouldn't talk to anybody for about four days afterwards.

Paul had no specific memory of Michael in 45, but 1953 was another matter:

> My mother rang up and said, "You uncle's being fantastically generous. He's giving you his tickets to the coronation. So Julie and I went and were bored absolutely stiff. I just remember Jill opening the door back at Roslyn Hill[2] still in her dressing gown after half past five, and they were both smoking hugely then. I remember thinking, "God this is dissolute, really degenerate, the whole situation here. We had gone to the coronation and here were these people who just laid around all day and enjoyed it. I was completely shocked by this.

Then there was the time when Jill took Paul to see Nye Bevan. Jill made sure Paul was heard. "Shut up," she would say to whoever was arguing, "let the boy speak!" Paul said, "I was only 15 and I didn't want to speak " "It all rings true," Michael said, "except that he didn't want to speak." Paul, who claimed to have no settled opinions at that age, protested, "I was very shy."

Obviously fond of Jill, Paul remembered a time they were all together in a car arguing, and Jill whispered in Paul's ear, "Michael thinks he can win an argument by how loud he shouts." "Indeed," Michael muttered. "It's no good. He won't win," Jill assured Paul. "The Bevan thing," Paul remembered. "I sat there tremendously embarrassed by all these people and all I could remember about Nye was he fondled Jill. He

---

[2] Michael and Jill rented a large flat on Roslyn Hill Road in Hampstead in the early 1950s.

was a groper. I remember thinking, "It's my auntie, leave her alone." I wanted to know how Jill reacted. "I think she'd worked out that you don't defeat sexism just by getting on your high horse. One of the ways of doing it is by humour. That's how she would [cope]." Michael made no comment.

I carried on as if Michael were not there: "Do you remember Jill and Michael getting into arguments?" Paul did. "They pretty much agreed about everything, but she would argue about the style—the way in which he would conduct the argument." Did Paul remember the famous Michael Foot phrase, "My dear child"? "That was all the time," Paul said. "It wasn't so much that he disagreed with her. It was usually when she was in danger of giving away some cabinet secret, especially when I was around because I would be leaking it to *Private Eye*. But I would be the last person in the world to leak anything. But just the thought that I ... "

"Very good cooking," Michael said. "I didn't cook anything," Paul said. "The potatoes," Michael said. "Just right." I pressed Paul on one more issue: his disagreement with Jill and Michael about the Balkan wars. Paul took an internationalist view, condemning nationalists on both sides. Michael kept saying to him, "You saw the bloody film" and Paul kept saying, "Of course I did." "Do you want to have it out again?" I asked him. "We tried to educate him," Michael said, "but we failed." Perhaps Paul should see the film a few more times, I suggested to Michael. "You wouldn't have suppressed it in your bloody state, I hope. If you had that power?" Michael asked Paul. "Your bloody state!" Paul repeated, laughing. "Trotsky wouldn't have suppressed it," Michael said, hardly stifling a laugh. Paul had a capper: "Trotsky, by the way, had a brilliant line on the Balkans—the best of all: 'You start going down one nationalist road you end up with royalism,' [Michael growled] and that sort of thing. That's my position, really."

A question about Paul's last contact with Jill elicited his memory of her writing a letter about Michael's antics at the Byron Society a propos of Benita Eisler's new biography. "Terrible book," Michael grumbled. Jill described how Michael grunted throughout Eisler's talk. I interrupted:

A friend of mine in New York who knew I was working with Michael—I belong to this group of biographers at NYU—called me up and said, "Too bad you missed the meeting. ... Eisler said Michael had stood up and said, [Paul broke in, 'Worst book ever written,'] before she had a chance to speak.

"It was very mild," Michael said placidly. "Jill didn't say it was mild," Paul noted. Paul described how well Jill seemed to cope with her last illness. She was still concerned about friends like Francis Wheen, whose book on Marx had received a negative review which so incensed Jill that she made Michael write a letter in protest. "Francis is a really good friend. He's terribly decent," Paul observed. "A wonderful chap," Michael chimed in. "Happens to agree with us on Yugoslavia. Just thought I'd mention it." Paul retorted: "I think you can be allowed to be wrong on the Balkans."

Jill and Michael created their own world—one that Paul witnessed in the mid-1950s when they moved to the Abbey Road flat. Paul would walk up the stairs (the flat was over a ground floor garage). Entering the flat, Paul would see a box of a hundred Gold Flake that Jill and Michael smoked between them in the course of a day. Michael was Paul's big hero:

I used to bring my friends from Oxford round to Abbey Road. But then they were going through the withdrawal of the whip [when Michael was on the outs with the Gaitskill party leadership]. He used to come home very late and Jill would say, "Just sit there. He'll be back." So we'd sit there and chat away. Michael would come back and go straight up to the bedroom and we would hear him and Jill discussing everything that had happened during the day. When he came down, he made it quite clear he wanted us to go away.

"Indeed," Michael muttered, saying he did not engage in such "inhospitable manners."

Paul and Michael began discussing the war. By 1939, Paul was saying, "you could not have sustained a position against the war. Orwell was against the war originally." But after he returned from Spain in 1938, he had changed his mind. "Where were you?" Paul asked Michael. "AhAhAh, much earlier," Michael explained:

[MF] *Tribune* was founded in support of Spain, changing party policy against the nonintervention and so right from that moment [1937] we were backing the Spaniards and recognising there was a threat of war from Hitler.
[PF] It's not the same. You could take the side of democracy in a civil war, but if you're going to have a war of nations fighting each other, then the issues may change.
[MF] No.
[PF] I just want to know how the argument develops.

You were all against war and for peace—the Peace Pledge Union and all that ... Then the argument develops that you're all in favour of the war.

[MF] The whole thing was the Spanish Civil War.

[PF] But I'm saying that's a different argument.

[MF] I know, but what I'm saying is that what changed the whole thing was the Spanish Civil War.

[PF] And I'm saying that's a different argument.

[MF] I know, but ... it was all tied up in the resistance to fascism.

[PF] The problem comes when you're supporting Chamberlain and Churchill ...

[MF] We weren't supporting Chamberlain, we ...

[PF] No, no, no. When you're supporting the nation going in against the Germans, that's a different argument.

[MF] A bit of a different one ...

[PF] Which is why you gave me that book ...

[MF] All done for your education, some way or other.

[PF] I respond to the educative thrust. The fact is the situation is so serious, so powerful are the Nazi forces, we join up with those who want to defend a capitalist country.

[MF] What you say is true. There was some equivocation in 1935.

[PF] They were saying, "Chamberlain in our enemy."

[MF] I fought in that election [1935] and in that election it is true that we were not so perfectly clear.

What this argument was about, really, was that the Labour Party in the mid-30s held back from the idea of a war against fascism and where exactly Michael stood then, I'm not sure he ever made clear.

Paul's point was it wasn't just the appeasing Conservative Party that had underestimated German strength and determination to dominate the world stage. The Labour Party shared the blame for sticking to its preoccupation with the evils of capitalism. It had taken persistence, but Paul had got Michael to focus on the pre-Spanish Civil War period. In 1935, Michael had worked on a book for Stafford Cripps, *The Struggle for Peace*, supplying notes. Much of the material was "good old anti-imperialist stuff," Michael said, "attacks on the British empire." "You mean the British empire was a bigger enemy than the Germans?" Paul said. He was getting at something, of course: the major shift in mood after Munich, and not just the Spanish Civil War, as Michael would have it.

65

The next day I joined Michael and Moni (married first to Michael's friend, James Cameron, and then to Denis Forman) on a jaunt to The Gay Hussar, Michael's favourite rendezvous. On the way, Moni, who is Indian, spoke of Jill's idealisation of India, an attitude Michael shared. Jill wanted to believe in a Fabian India, Moni suggested, a vision that Moni found outdated but touching. It was not the socialist paradise Jill and Michael made of it, but Moni lauded their idealism.

Moni described one of their trips to Kashmir during the coldest part of the year, when no one they wanted to meet was there. "You don't have central heating in India," Moni pointed out. "Worse than Moscow," Michael concurred. But at the time neither he nor Jill complained. Moni told me about how faithful Jill was about visiting James Cameron in hospital. "She was very fond of Jimmy," Michael said. Later Moni said Jill did not particularly like Cameron and felt that in some way he was a bad influence on Michael. But Jill was the kind of person who responded with great compassion to people in distress. Here was more evidence that Michael seemed not to realise that, in fact, Jill did not care for cronies like Cameron or Mervyn Jones and that many of them had no liking for her.

At the Gay Hussar we had a brief discussion of a new biography of Indira Gandhi. Moni spoke against it, not because she had read it but because she had read negative reviews and because Sonia Gandhi had opposed it. Later Michael would take the same line, which I thought rather a poor show in a journalist and biographer. In some matters, Michael and his circle took a kind of partisan view of the world that boded ill for my own biography. Moni, in fact, would later intervene, imploring me not to publish the 'Lamia' story.

Moni corroborated many of Julie's stories about Jill's exasperation with Michael. Like his brothers, Michael expected women to wait on him. Moni quoted Jill: "She always used to say, 'My God, everything is done by the women!' She did not approve of this. The mother and the daughters do everything for the sons and brothers." Michael spoke up, "That story she [Jill] got from my sister-in-law Ann, my brother John's wife." Later, I called Ann and she corroborated Moni's story.

Michael, rising to the bait, said, "I often told Jill my mother was a better feminist than Jill gave her credit for." Michael noted that both his mother and father were staunch backers of votes for women. He remembered how warmly his mother received the women speakers who came to the house "and all that kind of thing. The way she'd talk about them all." Moni was not having any of it; "I don't think she [Jill] meant politically, but the day-to-day domestic stuff." Not only was this a good point about Jill, it revealed the *huge* void in Michael's perceptions of his marriage. What it meant for a woman, a wife, to cohabit with him day-to-day never entered his consciousness. He simply had no conception of women's domestic work. He avoided the subject by extending fulsome compliments to women for serving meals and attending to the great man's daily needs.

Moni apologised for contradicting Michael, but he seemed not at all offended. "Quite right to broach the subject," he said. "We haven't talked about it before." Indeed, I could see that he loved Moni. She was charming and engaging. Her sharp, critical mind only enhanced her appeal. Michael showed a kind of exuberance in her presence that I had not seen in the company of others. I understood why Jill, at one point, thought of Moni as her replacement. Moni's words "bring back lots of conversations on the subject," he chortled. "The whole of that subject we'll have to go over again; that is, the subject of the unredeemed male chauvinism of the Foot family. It's true of some of them—not me, but the others! My brother Hugh." "Yes, she mentioned him," Moni said.

On the way back to Pilgrim's Lane, Moni got on to the subject of Jill's travels. Jill disapproved of the sumptuous accommodation British diplomats allowed themselves. "When you both went to Athens for some function and you stayed as the guest of the ambassador, she could not believe the lavishness." Michael agreed: "It was ridiculous."

This episode reminded Michael of travelling to Teheran just after the war. Ernest Bevin dispatched Michael and a

Tory named Anthony Head (it became known as the Head and Foot expedition) to get into the Soviet-controlled part of Iran:

> It was a wonderful trip—tremendously exciting to go there at that time ... But the pain in the ass, the chap there who was the second-in-command was a caricature ... He said, "You can't meet those people. They're Communists." But the whole point was to get a report about the other side! He wasn't interested in anything to do with the bloody country. He was solely interested in promotion ... and how this terrible new Labour government—Bevin—was stopping their promotions and wasn't dealing with it properly. The Tory with me was as horrified as I was. ...

One of the top people [in the government] there said, "You know we're in an awful situation now. We haven't got an air force. We haven't any proper military force. We haven't got any soldiers. We haven't got any sailors. But we've got one secret weapon." We said, "What's that?" He said, "We're very good double-crossers" and they did double cross the Russians [who withdrew from the country in May 1946]. "We brought back a very interesting report, but Ernest Bevin who sent us off wasn't even interested to hear. He was like that, you see. He was so egotistical."

Michael and Moni agreed that the Iranians and the Egyptians, products of very developed cultures, were the most adept Middle Eastern countries at playing this sort of duplicitous game.

66

At breakfast Michael told me the Elizabeth Frank biography of Indira Gandhi had created quite a stir:

> Apparently, it's got some things in it that are quite stupid. It's just distracting from the merits of the book, some gossip stuff about whether she [Gandhi] was having an affair with somebody in the office there and things which ... It's rather put me off the book, I must say.
>
> [CR] The review I read was very good.
>
> [MF] I read that first, too, and I thought "that's a good book." The chap who did it in the *Guardian* was quite sensible. He's a real expert on India and all that ... but what I read last night I'm afraid that, especially Sonia—we got on with Sonia very well, and we were quite interested in the part Sonia would play [after Mrs. Gandhi's death]. Maybe her not doing it [getting into politics] was right because she's had some terrible failures since she's done it. She's aroused a great deal of anti-foreigner feeling in India: can't have an Italian running our ... really xenophobic feelings combined with anti-feminist feelings, and the mockery is even worse than any other thing. But the last time we were there, when we met [Robert] McNamara, she was just deciding whether she was going to ... become the leader of the party. She was very anxious about it. Having done it she can't really retreat.

Michael's passion for India was inextricably connected with his romance with Mrs. Gandhi and her family:

Right from the beginning we stayed in Indira Gandhi's house. We met Rajiv and Sonia. Whatever else he was he was a wonderfully good-looking chap, delicate hands. He was much more interested in Sonia and the family. He didn't want to go into politics at all.

Michael rarely noticed—or at least he seldom commented in detail—on anyone's physical appearance:

It was only when his brother was killed, his mother—he had to do it. I think he was much better than people have given him credit for. Jill was sympathising with her [Sonia]. The Congress party was pleading with her to come out and play a part—"We will win the election." But she was still holding back. The other Congress leaders were not of any caliber.

What bothered me, after my own sessions with Michael, was his rather Puritanical response to Frank's biography. He had not even read it, yet he was already condemning it. How could a journalist and a biographer base an opinion simply on soaking up some negative press comment and the word of friends? I asked a question that did not seem to have occurred to him:

[CR] You don't think Sonia might be overreacting to this biography?
[MF] Well, she might be, I suppose.
[CR] That's my experience. Often families overreact.
[MF] You bet. That might very well be. Much of the biography is pro-India. But I didn't realise it's got this

stuff in it ... this lover in the office. Now it [Frank's book] also says that at an early stage in her life Indira was not going to return to India. She was going to come here ... and that it almost happened. Now ... she's [Frank] defending it, saying some people talked to her along those lines. I never heard it.

But what did that prove? Surely Michael could see that his friendship with Indira could not, in itself, weigh against the researches of a serious biographer. I later read the book and saw no reason to dispute Frank's account, which, after all, was a report, not a flat statement of fact. But to Michael and his ilk, any suggestion that Indira, who had spent the war years in London quite happily, would even have considered a life apart from India was anathema.

Michael, by his own admission, was a hero-worshipper, and even when he admitted his hero's faults, he could not seem to then re-factor his hero worship. Rajiv, for example, had accepted enormous bribes, Michael admitted. That was "very sad," Michael added. "I couldn't believe it at the beginning," but Suraj Paul, one of Michael's principal Indian backers, had disabused Michael of his illusions.

67

Later that afternoon, I interviewed Kathy Seary, who had come to work as a housekeeper for Jill in the early 1970s. Kathy described what happened after the controversy over the cenotaph coat:

[KS, quoting Jill] "Now we're going down to John Lewis's to buy him [Michael] a coat." So we bought him

this lovely, navy blue coat. And he looked dreadful in it.
It was a longer coat, you see, and it didn't suit him at all.
He looked better in a shorter coat.

[CR] Did he have an opinion about the coat?

[KS] He didn't like it. He said he wouldn't wear it.

[CR] Did she take it back?

[KS] Yes, she did.

[CR] Do you remember her buying other clothes for
him?

[KS] No, she did not buy a lot for him. He liked to
buy his own in a shop in Hampstead. He bought that
"donkey jacket" there.

We departed for dinner with Peter and Celine. Kathy and
I walked out onto Pilgrim's Lane toward the bus stop. I
mentioned that Michael was still taking busses. "He loves the
busses," Kathy said. "He used to walk down here [we were
approaching a bus depot] every morning and get the No. 24
bus to the House of Commons." That was our bus too.

At dinner, Peter, an architect, explained his effort to make
improvements in the Pilgrim's Lane house—usually thwarted
when Jill engaged shoddy workman. Michael, like Mr.
Magoo, seemed oblivious to the ramshackle state of his home.
Blissful in his deafness, he didn't hear the incredible racket his
neighbour's child made. I heard not only the raucous sounds
of play, but also a barrage against the wall that made me
wonder if some sort of child's squash game was in progress.

Peter brought up Salman Rushdie, a rather contentious
subject among Michael's friends. Moni, Peter said, could not
understand why Jill and Michael fawned over him. "They
didn't need him," Peter said. Celine admitted that Rushdie

could be quite charming. I said my impression, based on recent press reports, is that Rushdie was "quite silly." "Very silly and selfish," Peter added. "And Jill and Michael were sycophantic. That was the long and short of it." It did not occur to me, then, but perhaps this view of the relationship explains why, the fatwa over, Rushdie did not care to resume his relationship with Michael. Endless praise can begin to pall.

Celine brought up the shabby way Rushdie had treated his second wife, Elizabeth:

> I said, "Michael, this man ought to be shot. This lovely woman moves in with him in circumstances that are absolutely unbelievable. She gave him a child and now he's off with some model." I said, "Michael what would Jill say?" "Oh," he said. "I think she'd be very tough on him. "You should be tough too. You should tell him he has behaved very badly.

Peter and Celine believed that Jill and Michael overrated intelligence and talent. They would forgive almost anything from those they admired.

Peter and Celine also thought that Michael deluded himself about Julie. When Michael asked for their reaction to Jill's memorial event, Peter told him, "Well, the only person who really caused a ripple of irritation right throughout was Julie." Michael wanted to know why. "She spoke very well," he emphasised. "It was insincere," Celine said. "From the fiction department," Peter added. Michael shrugged off their reactions: "But people like Julie." "No," Peter responded, "they put up with her because of you." Mrs. Seary admitted that she had been so offended by Julie's praise of her mother —that she wanted to walk out, staying only out of respect for Michael.

Talked turned to Michael's risky adventures on London streets. "I'm terrified about his crossing the road," Peter said. "He holds them [traffic] up with his [walking] stick," Mrs. Seary pointed out. I mentioned Michael still took busses. Peter described an incident in which Michael had gotten on a bus, started reading a book, oblivious to the fact that here was some kind of wildcat strike, and spent nearly two hours on the bus. "He takes pride in his bus knowledge," Peter said. "They [the bus drivers] will sometimes stop between stops to pick him up."

Celine brought up Jill's frustration with Michael during his retirement. When he returned home early one day— around 4—she wouldn't talk to him, Celine remembered: "She wouldn't offer him a coffee or tea but just complained that he was back to bother her. He bent over to give her a kiss, and she said, 'go over there and read the newspaper.'" Poor man, Celine thought.

Celine and Peter doted on Michael. They brought out sides of him that probably would not have been expressed otherwise. They took him out to interesting restaurants, beyond his usual Hampstead haunts and the Gay Hussar. One night they ended up in Hackney at a Turkish restaurant and then at a nearby Karaoke Bar. "People in the public, who were sort of good socialist folk," Peter remembered, said, "HI MICHAEL! HAVEN'T SEEN YOU ON THE TELLY FOR A WHILE." Michael watched someone croak out a song. He turned to Peter and piped up, "I can do better than that," and he did, although he sang the words faster than the music.

Celine and Peter thought that Jenny took Michael's lapses too seriously. So what if he had recently showed up at the French ambassador's residence in his house slippers. Peter proceeded to describe one of Michael's anarchic speeches, given during his visit to Bermuda:

> We were on the edges of our chairs because Michael was the keynote speaker in Black History Month. Michael mentioned that Byron's great friend, Thomas Moore, had been here. He was on the edge of the precipice. Then suddenly he would say, "Jerusalem!" He'd weave into the topic a plea for moving the United Nations in New York to Jerusalem. "Bermuda's been a place where all kinds of great pronouncements have been made. Wait until the end, I'll give you the details."

Michael had everyone laughing. Later at a Labour Party conference, a Bermudan who had heard Michael speak came up to him and as Michael was about to speak, Jenny broke in. A dismayed Peter recalled the Bermudan saying to him, "who is that woman who bosses him around?" Michael was having a good time, Peter noted, and Jenny "tore him away, thrust him into a car and drove him home. That's what happens. He's powerless. He knows he can't get home unless she takes him."

Celine wanted to talk about how Michael had handled Jill's last days. He slept on a small living room sofa next to her when she could no longer negotiate the stairs to their bedroom. She didn't want to sleep alone. "Poor Michael," Celine kept saying. "Michael was dead tired. She would have him go up and down. 'Get me water, some milk, another pillow.' He wasn't fed because Julie wasn't feeding him." Celine said to Jill, "You can't do this to Michael. He's an old man. He needs his sleep." Jill countered, "you don't know Michael. He can perch anywhere." Celine did not think Michael would outlast Jill. During this diatribe, I could see why Julie said her mother found Celine irritating and also why there was such animus between Celine and Julie.

On the way back to Michael's, Celine turned to me in the car and said, "I think Jill told me towards the end that he was losing it a bit. Not quite as crisp intellectually as he used to be." The next day I left for home.

July 2001

68

On this visit there was much talk of my Gellhorn biography, which had just appeared and had received excellent reviews, with a few very negative ones, including a personal attack on me by one of Gellhorn's friends, the journalist John Pilger. Michael wanted to know why. "Well, he said I wrote a salacious book," I told Michael. Of course, it was nothing of the kind. Michael's response was "Dirty sod. I tell you, I've got very strong feelings about him. The way he's behaved over the breakup of Yugoslavia. It's absolutely outrageous. Pilger bilge, I call it. But we have to be careful about it because Paul is a close friend of Pilger." I said, "Paul may not have a good opinion of me anymore if he's been talking to Pilger." Michael dismissed the idea.

69

On this trip I was able to speak with one of Julie's friends, Lizzie, who had lived for a time with Julie in the mid-1950s and had kept up with Julie and her family since then. Lizzie described visiting Jill during her last illness. It was typical of Jill to want to hear all about Lizzie's life, rebuffing Lizzie's efforts to learn more about her health. To Lizzie, Michael seemed fragile but as garrulous as ever. Jill said, "Michael do be quiet. I don't want to hear you about Byron. I've heard it so many times. I want to know what Lizzie has been doing." Lizzie had come with flowers and Jill whispered, "Lizzie would you put these in water because Michael doesn't know about such things."

Lizzie's earlier memories were of a jokey Michael teasing her (he called her Dizzy Lizzie) and Julie when they were girls, "What are you two little chicks up to now? What fellow do we have calling at the door this week?" Lizzie added, "He never talked to me about politics because I didn't know anything about politics. He always seemed to be in his head somewhere else. I absolutely adored him. He couldn't do anything wrong for me." Like Julie, Lizzie was repulsed by Michael's eczema and asthma. "I had actors and film stars in my head and I could not understand Jill, obviously beautiful, being with this unattractive man. But later when I grew to know him and love him I could understand completely—his charm." His humour, in particular, made him seem sexy—as did his pleasure in being teased.

70

Back in Hampstead, I quizzed Michael about a journal Jill had kept during their first trip to India, in particular Jill's disenchantment with their traveling companion, Jennie Lee, who seemed full of herself. "A bit of that," Michael commented dryly. I read him another part concerning Jill's take on his own behaviour: "I see Michael all the time throughout the visit with his tentative subtle questions to the ministers. His appreciation of their humour and theirs of his, his suppressed irritation with Jennie and Michael English, his speech at Calcutta philosophical but much appreciated and with plenty of laughs, his horror of Jennie's rich friends in

Bombay who complained of income tax and talked of low castes." Michael muttered, "That's right," and then spoke up: "The chap, Michael English, we were there, you see, because it was a tour, an official trip, arranged by this chap—I'll get his name in a moment." I read other bits from her journal-style narrative, noticing that Michael simply would not comment on Jennie Lee, concentrating instead on the oafish English.

"For our anniversary," Jill continued, "Michael chose a rosewood walking stick which cost only three rupees. It is very beautiful in its simple way, and I insisted on paying that small amount as a token wedding anniversary present." Michael sort of chuckled, "That's nice. I've got it somewhere there, I think." Jill reported that several people expressed their hope that Michael would become prime minister, adding "I think he would make a most acceptable and excellent foreign secretary, but what a hope with Callaghan hanging on."

Michael did not think becoming foreign secretary was a realistic possibility. I tried to get him to say more: "That would have been a hell of a thing. I would like to have seen that, Michael." He thought leader of the House of Commons was as good a job as foreign secretary. "On the question of the bomb," said Michael, returning to the issue that trumped just about any other in his mind, "people say you should have done more when you were in the bloody government. I'm not saying they haven't any case at all, although we were so interested in other things and getting on with them. I knew if we raised the question of, you know, unilateral disarmament in the Callaghan government, there was no hope. And so we didn't raise it."

Michael's career as a government minister made him a target of the tabloids. The *Daily Mail* ran a series of articles claiming that during a hospital stay Michael had received special treatment. But Michael accepted only the care available to other NHS patients. "I didn't like taking libel actions because I'm a journalist," he noted. Indeed, he had had to defend himself in libel actions that resulted from his articles. But when the tabloid continued to publish false stories and refused to retract them, Michael sued, forcing the paper to pay him £6000 and issue an apology. "They went to every kind of length to prove that I was wrong ... They couldn't get the nurses to say anything ... They're swines [the tabloids], you know."

71

Michael liked to quiz me about what was happening in the States. He had made relatively few visits there—only four in all. He vividly recalled his first visit to New York City in 1933, the founding meetings of the UN in San Francisco in 1945 and the Army-McCarthy hearings in 1952, which he watched on American television. He had also visited Julie in the 1970s when she was married and living in Indiana. He had no idea how little influence newspapers exerted compared to other media. "When I first went there [New York City], the place was so exciting, you know. Going down Broadway and seeing topical plays and the fights and arguments about the Depression."

Michael's comments punctuated a very jolly dinner topped off with some of Julie's delicious cake. I mentioned that she had lost weight since I saw her in April, but that she had paid a terrible price for it, using cigarettes as an appetite suppressant. Michael decided to call her. He got her answering machine and left this message:

Julie, if you're not there, we were just saying there's a new report about smoking. Anyone who smokes can't cook a decent cake. They poison their cakes with smoke and I'm afraid you've poisoned us. We think your cake was wonderful, but we want no more smoking please. A special message from us, if you can sort it out. It's the unanimous opinion here that you must give up smoking right away.

"There you are," he signed off. "After that, I don't see how she can possibly continue smoking," I said. "She's going the other way," Michael replied.

72

At breakfast, Michael regaled me with memories of Beaverbrook, who hosted Michael during his convalescence from the terrible auto accident that left him lame. Jill and Michael had gone on to Marrakech, which Michael quite enjoyed, especially when Randolph Churchill showed up, suffering from an illness. Randolph was a rather irascible figure, Michael acknowledged, but "we were nice to him when lots of people found it difficult to be nice to Randolph." Their jolly reunion "assisted our recovery," Michael observed, "although it may have finished off Randolph," who died shortly thereafter.

"Your politics was no barrier?" I asked Michael:

[MF] Well, you see, on some things our politics were not so different. We were both furious anti-appeasers and anti-Chamberlain.

[CR] But he did want to take your parliamentary seat.

[MF] Actually, he was so unpopular ... You can't imagine the rudeness of Randolph Churchill. He could be terrible.

[CR] But he was never rude to you?

[MF] He was rude to his local Conservatives, the people who were backing him and all the rest ... By the end of the campaign, they would not come to see him off at the station. Jill and I would see him off.

Although Randolph certainly attacked Michael during political campaigns, they often joined up for a drink at the end of the day.

After breakfast, I mentioned the conflicting accounts I was hearing from Julie and Celine: "Celine says, 'Don't trust Julie'," and Julie says, 'Don't trust Celine.'" "You'll have to make up your own mind about such things," Michael observed.

A letter from Brian Brivati, Gaitskill's biographer, led Michael to describe an incident at Porto Fino. On holiday there, Michael and Jill ran into Gaitskill, who was accompanied by one of Michael friends, Maurice Bowra, who had taught Gaitskill at Oxford. "We couldn't walk properly because every time we'd be cut by Gaitskill," who was evidently still sore about Michael's harsh criticisms of his party leadership. Gaitskill and Co. would go off in another direction when they saw Michael and Jill approach. No word was exchanged between the two men for two days. On the third day, "Bowra came out to us, crossed the road and said, 'I can't let this go on any longer. I think they're behaving stupidly toward you—whatever the arguments you have. I've told him I can't be a party to that because we're old friends.'"

Michael and Gaitskill never did exchange words.

73

We were about to embark on a journey to Michael's home ground, Plymouth.

Over dinner I asked him about a newspaper clipping I had found. His mother was quoted as saying his switch to the Labour Party was sincere but misguided. "Yes," Michael said confirming the report. "I should have told them before, you see. But somehow it slipped out without their knowing."

Jill was quite envious of Michael's upbringing, especially the large family which was so mutually supportive. She never had that experience of community and of belonging because her parents had divorced when she was an infant and her mother had led a peripatetic life, with Jill sent away to boarding schools.

The next day we set off for Plymouth, our first stop a stay at Michael's niece's home. Ally was very welcoming, although her husband Owen seemed startled when I took out my tape recorder. I explained my working methods. He asked what would happen if Michael did not like my biography of Jill. I laughed and said that might mean we wouldn't be friends anymore and he'd kick me out of his house. Owen look bemused.

Later that day Julie and I got into a conversation about authorised biography after I told her about Owen. "It [authorised biography] verges on autobiography," she said. "Yes, it does," I agreed. "You're not going to be able to put in the shit," she declared. But she fully understood my position. "There have been a number of cases," I pointed out, in which biographers had signed agreements with estates stipulating they could not interfere "because the biographer is afraid that as in a romance, when the family falls out of love with you, then you're stuck. But I just think that changes the atmosphere, to face Michael with a contract and say, 'Sign this.' I couldn't do it." Julie agreed, "I don't think that would work with Michael. He would put his back up."

Julie then proceeded to fill me in on family background, her account rising, as usual to a level of candour that troubled family members but was invaluable to me. Her portrait of the Foots ripped the veil of propriety off the account in Mervyn Jones's biography of Michael. Even so, Jones's account had been received with what I consider to be rancour—as I discovered whenever I brought up his name in Plymouth.

"Michael's father was a teetotaller," I said to Julie, getting her started. Yes, but the only one among the Foots. Michael was very fond of his surviving sister, Jen, an alcoholic. He would hold her hand and gaze at her. Now in a nursing home, she had trouble with her memory but seemed gentle in sobriety. In her cups, she could get quite stroppy, Julie said. "All the brothers drank themselves stupid." Michael was closest to another sister, Sally, an alcoholic who had drowned. "She lived in squalor ... the animals lived in the house with her and that meant a horse ... She was lovely but an animal lover to extremes," Julie reported.

> [CR] So far as you know, has Michael ever had a serious problem with drink? Clearly he likes to drink.
> [JH] I wouldn't call it a serious problem. He certainly used to drink enough that he would be drunk when he went to bed.

She remembered episodes when he got the staggers and drinking jags with Julie's husband Mike, a generous host who was forever topping off Michael's glass. "They would end up having an argument ... shouting simultaneously, their voices getting louder and louder and Jill and I would go out into the kitchen. Then they got ugly, quite aggressive with each other. Have you ever heard Michael get angry and raise his voice?" At that point I hadn't. "It's none too pretty." There would be banging fists and more shouting. Michael had a temper which could be terrifying, Julie said.

The next day I questioned Chris, Michael's nephew, about the Foot brothers. Chris was a genial and gentle man and probably wary of me. The Foot brothers were "all different," Chris began. Mac (Hugh) was the exuberant one. "Really!" I exclaimed, "more than Michael?" I had always assumed that Michael outshone his brothers in this category. "Much more," Chris affirmed. "He was much bigger for some reason." Mac liked to instigate trouble. He was rather like a naughty boy. It was like being back at school," Chris said. He was too young to remember how Michael reacted to his brothers at family reunions at Pencrebar the family home. Chris simply envisioned the long tables with food and kissing aunts with powdery faces. Michael just blended in, visiting his family with Jill, a part of the gathering and yet somehow also apart—or so I envision him.

Owen drove Michael, Julie, and I around Plymouth while Michael expatiated on his father's political career. "He was the No. 1 anti-appeaser down here in Devonport and Cornwall. The bloody Tories used to go for him more strongly than any other single person. He used to pay them back! Huh!" Curiously, though, Isaac was great friends with Lady Astor, even though she had been part of the Clivedon set, notorious for its pro-German bias, a fact Michael never mentioned.

Evidently Isaac Foot admired Lady Astor's feminism, the way she stood up to the jeering male Parliamentarians, especially Winston Churchill. Isaac also believed she was always mindful of Plymouth's welfare. Her husband, in fact, had promoted the Plymouth Plan for an ambitious rebuilding of the city after the devastating German bomb attacks. This vision of public works certainly appealed to Isaac and Michael. Jill featured the latter in *The Way We Live* giving an impassioned speech in favour of government investment in the city's revival.

Michael became a tour guide, describing Plymouth as having the most beautiful natural harbour in the world. The famous Barbican, he noted, would have been destroyed if opponents of the Plymouth Plan had prevailed. He repeatedly extolled the sunshine—the best in the world. At lunch, I said I had a question for him: "Is this the *best* sunshine?" He didn't respond to the teasing. Instead, he explained why Plymouth had not become—as he vowed it would in *The Way We Live*—the best city in the world: Some parts of the plan were not implemented and others did not do much to fulfill Jill's vision of a city of neighbourhoods organised around village greens. She wanted an intimate feel, a human scale for urban life. Those who argued against the plan's advocacy of wider streets were "right in a way," Michael conceded. Those in favour of going back to narrow streets were treated like reactionaries, but in retrospect Michael had to say they had a point. Such urban renewal—as it was called in the States—actually laid waste to communities, destroying their organic networks of home, family, and work. But the new Labour government, pressed to create new housing opted for housing estates and high rises that Jill would later attack in her film *Who Are the Vandals?* (1967).

Later in the day, Julie, Owen, and I accompanied Michael to a sitting for his portrait. The painter was a book collector and the conversation turned to Rousseau's *The New Heloise*. "Several of my ones," Michael noted, "when they read *The New Heloise*, it made them change— Byron, Hazlitt, and Shelley." The talk segued to Scottish enlightenment philosophers, whose books also were in the painter's collection. But the painter had an agenda: he wanted Michael's help establishing a lottery to support a library. The scheme had considerable support, the painter emphasised. Michael listened sympathetically but did not commit himself. "Can you say a bit more about the lottery—your feelings about it?" the painter asked. "Now," Michael began slowly, "not a lot of people are against it, you know, but I suppose the reason I'm against it—my father, you see, was a great anti-betting, anti-lottery ... But I also think that most of the things we should be asking government for help with should be tested on their merits and do it on that basis rather than having some intermediary, a lottery, doing it."

Back in the car, Michael regaled us with an election song. Unfortunately, I had my recorder turned off. Turning it on, I said:

Know any more songs about Lord and Lady Astor?
[MF] Just the one.
[CR] Let's hear it again.
[MF] Who's that knocking at the door?
 Who's that knocking at the door?

If it's Astor and his wife,
We'll stab them with a knife,
And they won't be Tories any more.

We had resumed the Plymouth tour, arriving at Devonport Guild Hall, where Nye and Michael had spoken in '45. Michael pointed out areas left and right that had been smashed in the war. The rebuilding had not gone well. It was an awful area, Michael admitted. We passed the dockyards and Albert Gate while Michael recalled the great meetings in the Guild Hall.

Since Jill's death, Michael's attachment to Plymouth and his family had become more important, even if he did not sentimentalise or reminisce much. Jenny Stringer would put him on a train to Plymouth and then call Ally to tell her where exactly Michael was seated so that she could be there to assist him when he arrived. Shortly after Jill died, Michael had told Ally, "The fun of life is gone."

He had made a remarkable recovery from that low moment and certainly his remaining family in Plymouth contributed to his restored spirit. We spent a few hours gazing at family photographs. Michael pointed out pictures he had taken of his sister Sal. They had grown up together. He'd show the photographs to his sister, Jen, seated beside him. How much she could remember was hard to say. I asked Michael:

So who was the best talker in the Foot family?
[MF] My brother John.
[CR] Really? Not you?
[MF] No. Good God. My brother John, my father—he was better than all the others rolled together. He could

do it in all the places—either in the pulpit or on the political platform. He didn't draw any sharp distinction between the two. He was fighting the bloody Tories in both places right up to the end.

There were lots of pictures of Cornwall, of Cheesestring, for example, where the Foots holidayed. Michael took several of these—"not the greatest feat of photography," he remarked. "That's Dingle!" Michael exclaimed. "He has a tubercular arm—not as athletic as the rest of us."

"I can actually hear what you say now," Michael suddenly spoke up. "I've got the double lot in," he said, referring to his hearing aids. He could not put them in by himself. It took considerable fiddling. I inserted them once. Usually Molly or Jenny put them in. His hearing improved marginally, but he touted the NHS's good work. Later, he would wear only one hearing aid and then often none at all. One-on-one I think they functioned reasonably well, but in crowds or groups the hearing aids seemed to produce only a confusion of sound.

74

"Whoopee!" Michael said as his barbecued fish arrived. "Look at that! Amazing." A meal was never just a meal; with Michael Foot it was a celebration. Nearly every mouthful got its own cry of satisfaction. I remembered, though, that on the boat he had been excited about the fishing and then sobered by seeing the fish pulled on board. He was going to eat it, but for that moment he did not like staring death in the face. Now, even with the whole fish—head and all on his plate, he devoured his delicacy without a qualm. While we talked, Michael put his head down and dug in. All he managed to utter, again and again, was "now, now, delicious."

Later I questioned him, "You're not really against fishing, are you Michael?"

"Well, not really, but every now and again I'm shaken." Even after what I told you about Benjamin Franklin? "Yes," he insisted. I had told Michael the story from Franklin's autobiography. Although he was a vegetarian, Franklin had been lured by the wonderful smell of sailors cooking fish aboard ship and had forsaken his principles, pointing out that he had watched the fish opened up and saw inside them smaller fish. He reasoned that if the bigger fish could eat the smaller fish, he could eat the bigger fish. "Good excuse that is," Michael conceded, but he had read Brigid Brophy's brief in favour of vegetarianism and been persuaded (mostly). "My father was a seaman," I said to Michael gravely, "and it would be hard to convince me."

"Some apple pie?" Owen asked me. "I'll take the burnt part." "Are you having me on?" he asked. "No, " I said, "but I know it's hard to tell when I'm joking." "If he was joking," Michael said, "I'd be happy to have his burnt part." "Too much," Michael said, looking at my piece. "Just a quarter." He usually ate small portions.

He passed on coffee. "I think I'll have a little sleep, if you don't mind," he said. "No whiskey?" Owen asked. "Not at this hour. Disgraceful," he muttered in mock disgust. Michael asked the time. It was late afternoon, but no one specified the hour. "Michael always wants to know what time it is and his sister wants to know how old you are." Jen must have asked me that question ten times. "The two of them have it covered," I said. "Do you worry about time?" Ally asked Michael. "No, not really. Jill did not give a damn until the last minute."

"Really," I said. "Now this is something I didn't know. Let's hear more about this." "It wasn't of great significance, one way or the other, in my opinion," Michael answered. "Well, actually, the story goes like this," Julie intervened:

My mother was very punctual, but Michael likes to get to the train at least two hours before departure and she did not feel that was necessary and Michael would be standing at the front door saying, "Come on, my child." She would look at her watch and say, "We've got another hour and a half."

"You better tell him about the Russian embassy," Michael spoke up. Julie didn't know that story. "What, did she try to seek asylum?" I asked. There were always jokes about Jill's Russian ancestry on her mother's side. "No, she turned up two hours early at the Russian embassy—the great big posh one. She knocked at the door. Nobody opened it." "This was when he was a spy for the KGB," Julie suggested, alluding to the stupid articles that had appeared in Murdoch's *Times*, linking Michael with Soviet agents. "Did you have a code name, Michael?" someone asked. "'Boot,'" wasn't it," Ally offered. The shaggy story got shaggier and I never did learn about the great event at the Russian embassy. Instead, Michael took out after Conrad Black, Canadian owner of the *Telegraph*, a "raging right-wing Tory worse than our own breed" and that was that: he went off for his "little sleep. It's just wonderful what you've done for us today," he said to Ally and Owen. And it was. "If I don't see you kids again," he added, "behave yourselves."

75

The next morning at breakfast Michael told us about his pursuit of his first love, Marie-Jean, a French girl, who visited

Jen in Plymouth in 1934. When she returned to Grenoble, he pursued her. "Did you find her?" I asked. "No, I didn't. She got on to another chap there. I had never heard of Stendhal. I was ignorant. Subsequently, I knew every inch of Grenoble after reading Stendhal." I mentioned that Vesna, Jill's Croatian friend, found something French about Jill. "No scrap of Anglo Saxon," was Michael's only comment. "So you can read French?" Ally asked. "Just," Michael said. His sister Jen knew it better and he had enlisted her in his search for his French love. She did not find Marie-Jean and Michael celebrated his 21st birthday in Paris with his brother John.

After three days in Plymouth, it was time to return to London. The trip confirmed that the single important influence on Michael had been his father, who had also referred to his wife as "my dear child." I mentioned this fact to Julie, who remembered Isaac, the 'pater familias', rising at dawn and turning on the radiogram so that Bach blared through the whole house. "No chance of sleeping through it," Julie said without any air of grievance. She felt welcomed by Isaac and the whole family, finding a home and a sense of rootedness so different from the peripatetic life she had led with her mother during the war.

On the return trip home in the car, Michael reminisced a bit about his brothers. I asked him if he had thought of studying law as they had done. "Never," came his quick reply. Reading law was a dreary enterprise and then it took years to get established—none of it appealed to Michael.

I suddenly asked him, "Why do you think you lost the election in 55?" A long silence ensued. "Not quite sure," he replied tersely several minutes later. Surely he lost because his views were out of sync with Plymouthians, a rather

Conservative, even stuffy bunch, in Jill's opinion.[1] He did not dwell on defeat—a healthy attitude, no doubt, but I had to wonder if his failure to examine election results indicated a certain wilful blindness to political realities. Did Michael's exuberant rhetoric grate on an electorate confronting postwar shortages, the shrinkage of the empire and housing problems? Labour was out by 1951 and perhaps the only surprise is that Michael lasted until 1955.

76

Back at Pilgrim's Lane, Michael and I talked over our trip. He was very fond of Chris and Sue and I said they had charmed me. Chris had been Jill's favourite and had described her as his mum away from home. Chris, like so many other younger Foots, had spent time at the Pilgrim's Lane house. Michael was curious about how I got on with the others and I told him it had been a very pleasant trip indeed, with fine meals and lots of cordial drinking. "Ah," he mused. He wanted to know how late I had stayed up. Usually until 12 or 1, I told him. "Late as that?" he said. Anything after 10 was now a late hour for him.

We got onto the subject of Barbara Castle again. Michael was determined to stay in her good graces. Thus he had turned down the request of an unauthorised biographer for an interview about Barbara, knowing that Barbara would not like him to cooperate with anyone she had not sanctioned.

I understood his loyalty to friends, but I put it to him that

---

[1] In Jill's biography, I performed all sorts of little touch-ups at Michael's request: smoothing out, for example, Jill's references to Michael's Plymouth constituents as "sticks in the mud." Michael laughed and said, "They are to some extent."

there was "another argument":

> **[MF]** Yes, go on.
>
> **[CR]** When someone tells you "Please don't talk to this biographer who is writing a book about me," that person is asking you to not talk about what is a part of your experience. From a certain point of view, it is a form of censorship.
>
> **[MF]** Yes. You bet. Mostly my sympathies are naturally on the side of the writers.

Michael thought Orwell was rather arrogant in forbidding a biography. He also thought publishers were quite nonsensical in calling Michael Shelden's biography of Orwell authorised. Michael did not like Sheldon's book because of its treatment of Sonia Orwell, who had been a close friend of Jill's and Michael's. "He had no compunction about what he said about her." Michael added, "Wipe Shelden off the books." Declaring war against the term authorised biography, he said, "So you're not writing the authorised biography of Jill." But he was on my side, he assured me. "Carl, I'm glad you're doing it. It's the best thing, from Jill's point of view."

"Did you follow the controversy about Orwell supplying names?" I began. "Yes, I did," Michael responded quickly. "And it was a great pity that he did it." Michael did not think his friend should have cooperated with the government. "But he wasn't trying to get these people surveilled. He was just saying, 'Lots of these people are soft on Communism and you should know about it.' He was telling friends who had formed a kind of propaganda unit inside our foreign office to combat Communism. There shouldn't have been such a thing established and he should not have been disposed toward it as he was."

77

June Purvis, a scholar of the suffragettes, was my next interview. She had worked in Jill's impressive collection of materials on votes for women, and the two women had become friends. And June had kept in touch with Michael, so much so that he was keen for me to have a sit-down with her, which we did at Pilgrim's Lane. June remembered sitting in a restaurant with Jill and Michael. Michael's money had fallen out of his pocket onto the floor. As the waiters were picking up the money, Jill told June that Michael had not let Jill stitch up the holes in his trousers, so every time he went to pay for a meal ... Evidently this had happened on several occasions. "He's always stuffing his pockets with things!" Jill complained. But June saw a loving couple in tune with one another, manifesting an intimacy fostered by long years of understanding between them.

June recalled spending a week at Pilgrim's Lane studying Jill's papers. Jill would fix them breakfast. Michael would always put his plate on the floor for Dizzy to lick up the leftovers. "Julie remembers that the dogs were not trained." June agreed. I remembered Michael telling me that Dizzy had eaten Paul Foot's sweater. "Paul was afraid of the dog," Michael admitted. "Every time he came to the house he came with a torn sweater. Very anti-dog for some reason, the only member of our family." "The positions that man takes," I commented. "An anti-dog internationalist."

Later that day I had a session with Michael attempting to identify names in Jill's correspondence, much of which (after getting a tip from Julie) I found stuffed in a cabinet in Michael's bedroom. There were no envelopes and sometimes no dates or last names. Michael had to bring the documents up close to his good eye and peruse them for several minutes, muttering "I'm not sure ... Now ..." Then, occasionally, he would shout, "Ah!" when he had puzzled out who the author was. 'Pamela,' turned out to be Enoch Powell's wife:

> We were in the House of Commons at the same time.
> Sometimes our views would converge for different
> reasons. During the debates about the House of Lords—
> we had hardly spoken to each other before that—we did
> invite him here [to Pilgrim's Lane]. She [Pamela] was at
> Eaton Place and used to invite us there quite often. But
> it was all completely separate. We never had anybody
> else at those dos because we didn't want to interfere with
> the possibility of saying what we wanted. Enoch was
> an interesting chap in many ways. He wasn't a racist, in
> my opinion. Some people said he was a racist ... because
> before that "rivers of blood speech" [an anti-immigration
> tirade] there was a massacre in Africa just two or three
> years before. He denounced that in the most furious
> terms in the House of Commons. It was a brilliant
> speech... It was impossible for a racist to have made
> such a speech. Some people thought it very strange that
> we would have any kind of conversations because they
> regarded him as a racist. They said he should never have
> made the speech—and he shouldn't have whatever his
> motives. We never discussed that speech. And when his
> wife looked as if she might raise it, he would say, "Here,
> we have our friendship and we don't talk about such

things." We had many interesting meetings with him—something like ten years.

Michael did not say it, but what he and Powell had in common was a love of Parliamentary debate. Indeed, they had entertained the House for many days debating a bill about the reform of the House of Lords. Powell wanted no reform at all and Michael wanted to abolish the Lords. As different as those two positions were, they provided a meeting point, since neither man wanted the government bill to pass.

Sometimes Michael would get engrossed in the letters, many of them 'thank-you' notes for dinner parties Jill had arranged. Often, in good weather, her guests dined under the pergola in the garden that made Pilgrim's Lane such a paradise for Michael. "I don't want to leave it," he said, reading another thank you note.

These sessions were not only slow-going; they were disheartening. Michael had no gift for summoning the company of the past. All that seemed left, in most cases, was just a faint afterglow. Like Boswell feeding Johnson names and issues, I tried, when I had the background information, to stimulate Michael to greater feats of memory. But this technique rarely worked, so grooved had his mind become with a small number of anecdotes and impressions. I remember the biographer Jeffrey Meyers saying to me, "You won't get much out of him." Meyers had interviewed Michael about George Orwell, who had worked closely with Michael at *Tribune*, but even the persistent Meyers, in the end, felt he had gleaned little.

I left London the next morning.

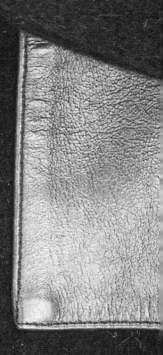

Michael remembered a party at Pilgrim's Lane to launch his book on nuclear proliferation and disarmament, *Dr. Strangelove, I Presume*, during which the criticism of Blair burgeoned while Jill and Michael tried to temper the acrimonious argument.

January 2002

78

Recently Michael had encountered Salman Rushdie at a party given by Geoffrey Robertson, the lawyer who had secured Michael's libel judgment against Rupert Murdoch's *Times*. Jill and Michael had installed a new kitchen with the damages. Spotting Rushdie, Michael approached and said, "Salman, let's have a meeting sometime soon without any kind of reference to Elizabeth [Rushdie's estranged wife who remained Michael's friend]." Rushdie agreed. "That was just before Christmas," Michael noted. Rushdie said he would call Michael. But no call had come. Michael rationalised by saying Rushdie might have rung up while Michael was away for the holidays (Michael had no answering machine or fax). "What I'd like to do—if it's okay with you—is you should have a talk with him." Of course I was agreeable. I wrote to Rushdie, mentioning Michael's fond memories of him. I never received a reply.

Michael spent the rest of the morning making calls on behalf of Mark Seddon, editor of *Tribune*. Mark was running for a parliamentary seat. It was delightful to hear Michael not only touting Mark but also, in a genial way, quizzing his callers about their experiences in the Labour Party. "It's nice to talk to you," he would say. "I thought you wouldn't mind if I rang. Thank you for letting me talk to you."

But I managed to get him to make a call on my behalf to Tony Benn:

"Tony?" Michael spoke into phone in an unusually quiet manner.

"Michael Foot here. How are you? Can I wish you a happy new year?. I'm ringing about someone who's writing a biography of Jill and I wondered if he could come and see you. He's a fully qualified biographer, well prepared. He's written some wonderful stuff before and he knew Jill and he would very much like to see you. What? Carl Rollyson. I think he did write to you in the last week or so ... He can speak to you now maybe? Yes, he's with me now. He could come any time that is convenient for you over the next two or three days. Not Saturday. Sunday morning, you say? Have a word with him now. He's very reliable, you know. He's read Caroline's book, of course [Tony's wife had published a biography of Keir Hardie]. So here he is."

I took the phone:

"Hello Mr. Benn ... Yes, yes. I know your wife's book ... I'll be here until the 19th. 11 on Sunday would be delightful. No. 12, right. I'll be coming from Michael's. By underground, yes." I got to know Michael and Jill while researching my biography of Rebecca West. and Jill was quite helpful. Yes, I'd love to meet you. You can always reach me here. Thanks very much. Bye Bye."

I turned to Michael and said "That was easy." "That's good," Michael said. "He's just completing his diary he says. His diaries are more elaborate than any individual who has ever lived. He records every word."

Before dinner we had our usual round of Scotch, chips, and olives.

[MF] "I think it's better with the olives, don't you?"

[CR] "Good contrast with the chips—crisps, Americans call them chips; the British call them crisps. You can't call them chips. What you call chips Americans call French fries.

[MF] Yes. So if you ask for either of those in your bloody country, you'll get the wrong thing.

[CR] Yes. So be careful next time you come.

[MF] Hm.

Having exhausted this important topic, Michael told me about Geoffrey Goodman, a political crony and organiser of the Aneurin Bevan Society. Michael wanted us to meet and talk about Jill's contribution to a collection of essays on Bevan. We were going to meet at The Gay Hussar.

Another friend Michael wanted me to meet was Brian Brivati, who was working on a condensation of Michael's Bevan biography. Brian was one of those "new husbands," Michael pointed out, by which he meant that Brivati did some of the cooking and minding the children. "Like me," I said. "I do the cooking." "I see," Michael considered. "Then how does your wife get on when you are away?" "That's why she does not want me to leave home," I said. Michael had forgotten that I had made him an omelette. "I should remember that better," he said. "Yes, you should," I said. "I remember what you said, 'Fancy that, a biographer who makes omelettes.'" I reminded him: "We were very tired at coming back from a trip, and so you decided to risk it."

We spoke of other innovations—the fax machine, for example. Michael listened politely and though I offered to buy him one, emphasising how easy they were to operate, he could not be convinced. The wiring in the house had not been upgraded—God knows how old it was. Of course, he had plenty of people to help him and he had no interest in speeding up his existence. He did have a video cassette recorder and player, but he relied on Damon to operate it.

In the kitchen at seven we watched Jon Snow deliver the Channel 4 news. This was a nightly ritual Michael never missed if he was home. A report on Tony Blair's visit to India provoked this outburst:

Some people say: "Your attitude toward Kashmir is quite inconsistent with your attitude about Croatia and Bosnia. If they've got a right to self-determination, why shouldn't Kashmir have it?" Of course it's a powerful case. But there's some very big differences.

A phone call interrupted his argument. But he eventually got round to it again:

Sometimes Jill would say to me, "If Croatia has a right to vote for her independence, why not Kashmir?" It looks as if that case is clear. But if you go back to ten , twenty years or so, people in Kashmir have not voted to go with Pakistan and have not voted to become a Moslem state. They wanted to stay in the Indian state and have better rights... but not to clear out of the Indian union because that would destroy many other rights they have. So the leader of the Moslems in Kashmir is Abdullah, a

Moslem. The first time we went to India we stayed with Sheikh Abdullah in Srinigar the last year or two of his life. He didn't want to take the state out of India. So all that makes a very different story ... Tony Blair's trying to take the edge off the intensity of the crisis [one of those periodic confrontations between India and Pakistan over Kashmir]. That may be the most necessary thing to do in the circumstances. But I do fear that he should make it a balance: we have to pay as much attention to the chap in Pakistan. It's not fair to the Indians who are running a democratic society.

Michael was much attached to Kashmir, "one of the beauty spots of the world." And he empathised with Nehru's and his daughter Indira's attachment to that place. "The sunshine and the mountains covered in snow. You can see the mountain tops."

Talk of Blair stimulated Michael to say, "Some of our people are in my opinion too critical of him. Some of them say, 'Oh Gordon Brown is much better, you know.' I doubt that there is all that much distinction between the two." Michael remembered a party at Pilgrim's Lane to launch his book on nuclear proliferation and disarmament, *Dr. Strangelove, I Presume*, during which the criticism of Blair burgeoned while Jill and Michael tried to temper the acrimonious argument. "We'd just been down to Checkers [at Blair's invitation] and people said, 'Oh, that's had a terrible effect on you.'" Blair had courted Michael, of course, and their history was a fascinating one, since Blair had joined the party and run a losing campaign for a parliamentary seat during the debacle of Michael's leadership. Michael had then predicted a brilliant future for Blair. It sounded prophetic, but of course, Michael would have said as much of anyone Blair's age who campaigned on his side during that devastating year. "Now, the thing I'm sure Jill would have applauded about Tony Blair is that he doesn't run away. He doesn't leave it to someone else. He gets in and sometimes he makes a mistake ... but he's very different from the way other Labour leaders behaved ... as compared with Harold Wilson."

Angela, a temporary replacement for Molly (on holiday), brought cheese and grapes but Michael rarely took dessert and this time he turned away her offering with a request for "one grape." The phone rang again. It was Mark Seddon, wanting to consult with Michael about Mark's campaign for a parliamentary seat. "A good boy," Michael said as he rang off.

Michael was still mulling over whether he would attend a football match on Saturday. He expected his friend, Peter Jones, to ring about a four-hour trip to the game. "But they can't win if you're not there," Angela broke in "And then there is your responsibility as one of the directors of the team," I added. To this he gave a typical high-pitched scream, which I always took to be a kind of riposte to ribbing. "I think it's called the burdens of office," I said.

But Michael was still fixated on Kashmir: "The danger, I think you see, is [saying] it's half dozen of one or another. That's not fair to the Indians. They've got a damn sight better case than that. That's all washed aside as if it's the Indians who are refusing to meet."

Michael had been a member of the Indian League since he was 18. "So when I first came to London—just about 1933 or 1934—I met Krishna Menon, and we were friends right from then. A real body fighting for Indian independence, putting the case very well ... He played a very big part in what happened in Africa and other parts of the world. All that will be washed away if people say Pakistan has as good a case as India."

Suddenly Michael asked:

How about another drink, Carl? A stiff whiskey?

[CR] No, just a stiff coffee. You go ahead. I don't want to stop you.

[MF] No, I can't drink coffee at night.

[CR] No, another whiskey.

[MF] Well, it's conceivable. What's the time now?

[CR] It's only 10 after 8. You can't go to sleep yet.

We spent the rest of the evening watching Jill's film *Blue Scar*, set in Wales. The documentary aspects of the film, Michael noted, were well done, as were the scenes of Welsh singing. But he seemed rather shaken that his memories of it did not square with his response now. He turned to me and said, "It's not very good, is it?" I had to agree.

79

The next day I lunched with Tom Hancock, a town planner and architect whom Jill had befriended. He took her ideas quite seriously, admitting she had influenced his own views considerably. Indeed, he did not shy from Michael's view that Jill had been a kind of mentor to Hancock, who was a generation younger. Michael even went so far as to speculate that Tom had been in love with Jill. Hancock never said as much, but it was clear from talking to him that his affection for Jill ran very deep. As always, Michael reacted to male interest in Jill with pride, not jealousy. That other men were attracted to her only ratified his own choice of a mate. It made him feel victorious, in a curious way, when other men admired his wife.

I asked Tom one of my favourite questions: how did Jill react when Michael called her "my dear child"? He remembered that "Jill nudged Yvette [Tom's partner] and said, 'You mustn't get married.'" Yet Tom could see Jill working on her relationship with Michael. Relationships, like her home, like architecture—like everything in Jill's William Morris world—ought to aspire to be aesthetically pleasing. Michael, I knew, admired this aspect of Jill, but did he attempt to reciprocate—that is, to work on their relationship as she did? I don't think so. At best, he did so intermittently. I remember watching Jill on a television documentary, saying flatly that although she thought when she met Michael he shared her vision of a more beautiful world, she had deceived herself. In the end, she concluded, he had very little of William Morris in him. Quite true: he had little sense of pattern and took no interest in the garden except to extol its beauty in vague terms. He had no visual gifts. He was a man of the word, but I know from my own experience that a man of the word can remedy his shortcomings and can make himself *see*. Wives are very good at getting their husbands to do just that, but at some point Jill concluded that Michael was helpless in this regard.

Jill's gift for making her world a work of art was surely one reason why Tom Hancock found her so attractive. "Did she sacrifice her own career?" Tom asked. I explained the complications: the downturn in the film industry, the reluctance to hire women directors, her commitment to Michael and making her third marriage work and the devastating rebuff from Michael Balcon when Jill tried to resume her directing career. I told Tom how I had read to Michael Jill's letter to

Balcon asking for a job. I related why I thought Jill had been broken by Balcon's brush-off. "Since then Michael has begun to see himself as an obstacle to her career." "You're rotten," Tom said, laughing. "I know," I said, "but that's what biographers do. They break your heart. He's learning things as I learn things."

Tom paused and then said:

I remember making a comment to Jill just before the leadership election in 81. She said she was trying to persuade him to stand. I said, "For God's sake, he must stand. No one else can possibly keep the party together and he's the only person who's really loved by everyone in the party—left to right. His time has come. But she was very apprehensive.

I wonder if Jill realised that Michael's time had ended? It seemed to me that by 1981 he had lost his edge, one that he still had when he narrowly missed becoming leader in 1976 after Wilson resigned.

Tom thought Jill's anxieties had to do with how life would change for her and Michael. "They had a modern marriage," Tom reflected, "one that people dream of but rarely achieve. That people can be open and have a degree of freedom and respect, and not be kind of ... what's the word? Chained together." "Possessive," I said.

As lunch ended, Tom proposed to drive me back to Pilgrim's Lane. I had told him Michael was eager to see him (they had not be in touch for a few years) and Tom seemed just as keen to resume their friendship. Soon after we arrived, Tom reminded Michael of the time he had driven Michael to

Tredegar. "Tre-de-gar," Michael corrected. "Tre-de-gar," Tom said. "Tre-de-gar," Michael insisted. "They will think you're a foreigner." "They said as much, didn't they," Tom laughed. "Yes, they did," Michael agreed.

Just then the phone rang. It was journalist Geoffrey Goodman confirming a meeting with Michael at 4:30 the following Monday. Afterwards, I was supposed to meet both of them at the Gay Hussar for an early dinner. Michael asked Geoffrey about Mark Seddon's prospects. Did he have a chance of getting adopted as a Labour candidate in a Wales constituency? It sound as though Geoffrey was telling Michael that Mark was indeed in the running. When Michael hung up, he explained to Tom that there was a by-election. "You're not going there, are you?" Tom asked. "I'm not," Michael laughed, "but I'm hoping they'll get our friend, Mark Seddon. ... It's quite a long shot. You know the Welsh quite often put up their own candidates. So you asked if I would stand. Those days are over."

The exchange that followed between Tom and Michael revealed just how aware Michael had become of his failing powers:

[TH] I thought you might go on the stump for him.
[MF] On the stump I can hardly speak ... anymore. But there you are.
[TH] I'm not sure about that.
[MF] Why?
[TH] You exaggerate.
[MF] I'm not exaggerating at all. I can hardly ...
[TH] I don't suppose the flow of rhetoric is what it was.
[MF] Well, I'm doddering along. Several people can testify to that.

Michael then changed the topic, asking when we would again meet for a meal. He would joke about his rickety constitution, but I never heard a word of self-pity and never saw him depressed, even during some very long days together. He really would do what he could for Mark even though it would strain Michael's current capacities. Michael was a gallant campaigner—not just a politician, but a human being who tried to make every day an event. He would rise as high as possible to the occasion, drawing on whatever last reserves he had. He was not a man to hold anything back. The heroic way he confronted each day was what made it such an honour to be in his company.

Tom is the one I remember asking Michael directly about the extraordinary fact that Michael had included me in his household:

> **[TH]** I was asking Carl how you can put up with someone in your house.
> **[MF]** What?
> **[TH]** This chap [Tom indicated me].
> **[MF]** Why?
> **[TH]** I just think your personal privacy and space ...
> **[MF]** What?
> **[TH]** This writer comes and invades it.
> **[MF]** Nice big house. It's been arranged for such things.
> **[TH]** Generous spirited, I think.
> **[MF]** All designed by Jill.
> **[TH]** That's right. It all depends on how well he behaves.

It was a remarkable thing to do and Michael was right: it

had been designed for others to enjoy. So many members of Michael's family had stayed at Pilgrim's Lane. Paul Foot wrote a book there. All of Julie's children had lived with Michael and Jill at various points in their youth and so many others—like me—had enjoyed extended stays, basking in the Craigie/Foot hospitality.

But my residence at Pilgrim's Lane was different, Tom understood. I was a writer and my material was Jill and Michael and I had become part of his daily routine. What Michael offered me went well beyond what Tom called "generous spirited." Paul Foot and others argued that by accepting Michael's hospitality, I had indebted myself to him. He had a claim on me. They, of course, were not privy to the conversations I had had with Michael about how I had to maintain my independence as a biographer. No matter how many times I had reiterated that position, no matter how many times Michael acceded to it, my place in his entourage certainly gave every appearance of *dependence*. I was like that biographer in Clint Eastwood's *The Unforgiven*, a part of my subject's retinue, the very definition of biographer as follower.

I was not fawning. Indeed, I teased Michael a good deal and talked openly with Tom and others about my critical perceptions of Michael. I was not guarded in the least and made no pretence of sharing Michael's views—with him or with others and yet, how could they not think of me as an acolyte? In the end, whatever I wrote, as far as they were concerned, had Michael's imprimatur—or I wouldn't be living at Pilgrim's Lane. To put it another way, to truly be independent would be tantamount to betraying Michael, and that would be exactly the charge sheet that Paul Foot and others would compile against me. I would resist their interpretation, but I did not then—and do not now—feel the least bit surprised at the attack. I had been asking for it, so to speak. What did surprise me, though (and this reveals how even with all my experience as a biographer I was still naïve enough to think Michael saw it my way) was how quickly Michael would turn on me when he felt I had violated his *amour-propre*.

After Tom left, Michael said: "I think we did talk possibly about you writing a book about me afterwards."

[CR] Oh yes.

[MF] But Francis Wheen is asking whether he can do that. And so ... It's not absolutely definite. But if he's willing to, I'd be very pleased that he should do that.

[CR] He's a good writer.

[MF] Yes, and he's a very good friend of Jill's too. He did two books—one on Tom Driberg, a very amusing book and one on Karl Marx. Anyhow, it's not absolutely sure. But if he does, I'd like to say yes. He's not covering ...

[CR] I'll tell you how I feel about it. I feel the more books about Michael Foot the better.

[MF] Okay. [Michael laughed]

[CR] So I think that's terrific. I think that anyone you think could do a good job should do it.

[MF] Well, that's very good of you. In any case, that's a nice response.

[CR] Let me tell you something, Michael. It never occurred to me—not because it isn't a good idea—to write a book about you. The idea was always to write a book about Jill.

[MF] Right.

[CR] And Julie was very keen to nail this down.

[MF] Yes.

[CR] I think that she's gotten some enjoyment and benefit out of my doing this book on her mother.

[MF] Of course she has.

[CR] And I think she wants to keep up the relationship.

[MF] That's right.

[CR] And she was saying, "Well, what about Michael?" I said, "Michael Foot is a terrific subject. I certainly would be interested in doing it." Then she sort of jumped the gun. I know she talked to you about it. My feeling was, I wasn't going to say anything to you. I was going to do Jill's book and perhaps do a book about you. But I'm not in any big rush.

[MF] Yes.

[CR] If Francis Wheen wants to do a book, I think that's wonderful.

[MF] I think so too. I'm very gratified that you should think of it that way. I think your book—as I've said to you, I'm very pleased that you're doing it and couldn't be more pleased and I think that Jill would take the same approach I have. But she would also be pleased about Francis Wheen.

[CR] Well, he's here and he knows you.

[MF] Of all the letters I got about Jill, Francis Wheen's was really ...

[CR] One of the things I dislike is biographers who try to tie up people's lives. And I would never do that.

[MF] Well, there we are.

Michael had begun this conversation gingerly. He clearly thought I might be upset about Wheen because Michael had given me some encouragement. I really wasn't upset. I had never troubled myself about doing subjects other biographers were already working on and could not see how I could object to someone doing the same to me. Later I would learn that Michael saw the situation quite differently. If he encouraged one writer, that ought to mean that another would be disadvantaged or even shut out. Much later, he would not treat me with such consideration and that would anger me—not because I felt I had a claim on him, but because it seemed to me he was not being true to his own principles. and perhaps I already had in mind the notion that I would write a biography like this one—unconventional and unsparing, a book that would fare best if it was begun and completed not only after my work on Jill was finished, but after Michael himself no longer was around to respond to what I wanted to be my story.

I intended to talk with Wheen, not about his desire to write about Michael but only about Jill. If he brought up the subject of a book about Michael, I would have repeated what I had said to Michael. But I supposed that Michael himself would convey my response to Wheen—if only through Paul Foot, who was Wheen's close friend. For whatever reason, every time I called Wheen he stalled and when we finally did speak for a few minutes on the phone, his tone verged on being hostile, relaxing only when I asked him a few questions about the warm way Jill reacted to Wheen's children when they came to Pilgrim's Lane for a party.

Michael's talk with me about Wheen did, however, strengthen my desire to write about him. I felt I had a unique and privileged point of view and my pride as a writer was aroused. I'm not speaking of a competitive instinct. I was simply in possession of material that I knew I would one day develop. It really didn't matter whether Wheen—and later, another historian—would make appeals to Michael that he found attractive. What, in the end, did disturb me is Michael's belief he could veto my project.

80

Over breakfast we had one of our periodic discussions of Disraeli.

> **[CR]** But given your politics shouldn't you be supporting Gladstone?
> **[MF]** Well yes, my father, you see, was a Gladstonian Liberal and remained enthusiastic.

Somehow I could never get Michael to focus on why he felt so much affection for Disraeli. Clearly he was attracted to the literary figure, but what about Disraeli's imperialism? Michael, in effect, suggested that Disraeli did not take imperialism seriously. If not, what then? What did *that* say about Disraeli? Didn't it ratify the suspicion that Disraeli was just an opportunist? But it was hard to make any headway against one of Michael's favourites.

Michael was more interested in discussing the press and how it played up stories like the so-called Blair/Brown rift, which Michael thought much exaggerated. Books on politicians in mid-career seemed to Michael supererogatory.

81

"Now when you talk about Milton Shulman, I think we ought to do it, but I've got to be slightly apologetic," Michael explained. Shulman, a writer who at one time was close to

Michael and Labour Party politics, had turned apostate and he had not seen Michael in years. Talking to Shulman was a kind of breakout for me—as the interview with Tony Benn would be, since both men were highly critical of Michael. Michael suggested, "It would be very nice if we could do it with the two of them [Shulman and his wife]." This was exactly what I did not want to do. How could Shulman unburden himself with Michael in the room? And what Shulman's wife would be like, I had no idea. But certainly I would never find out if the interview became a social occasion for reconciliation. I doubt that Shulman would like that anyway. How could it be comfortable for him to consort with a friend from the past whose politics now seemed so antiquarian? Although I had had only a brief phone conversation with Shulman, I could tell that he regarded Michael fondly but as a relic of a socialism that seemed—at least in retrospect—unreal.

"I've got to do it decently. I've got to give them a meal. If I fed them tomorrow? See what they say." Michael wanted the Shulmans over for lunch. "They did know Jill," he said tentatively. "Oh, very much so," Julie added, just joining our conversation. "Very much so?" Michael looked at Julie. "Yes," she insisted, "He and Drusilla were always at dinner when we lived in Roslyn Hill [in the early 50s]." "That's what he says in his book," I added. Memories of the Shulman friendship had evidently faded in Michael's mind.

I told Julie that Tom Hancock had asked me why Jill had not been able to keep Michael better dressed "It was an uphill struggle," Julie said. "I don't think she worried about that at all," Michael said quietly. "She did," Julie corrected him. "She was," I said. "It's in her diary." "She was very concerned," Julie continued, "at how you appeared in public." "Ah," he said in exasperation. "She used to enlist my help in the early days," Julie said: "Go and tell him to change his shoes." Michael interrupted, "That's a lot of balls." I laughed. "What Julie says is absolute balls," Michael reiterated. "You knew one Jill, and I knew another," Julie retorted.

[JH] I knew a side of her that you didn't know. You can't know all sides.

[MF] I knew most of it.

[JH] I knew her before you did.

It was all very funny at the time—and not so funny later on when Julie's Jill made her appearance in my book. "I wonder if you'll recognise her [Jill] from Carl's book?" Julie asked Michael. I laughed again. "It will be really interesting," Julie remarked slyly. Michael did not reply. I thought then—and am even surer now—that Julie had a much better grasp of the dynamics of Jill's biography than Michael did. He really could not see outside of his relationship with Jill.

"Anyhow, don't you have any of that nonsense that Jill wouldn't like a book done [a biography of her]," Michael told me. "I could live with that," I replied. To Michael it was very important to believe that Jill had given her blessing to my biography. But how could he speak for Jill? Julie had told me that Jill had great reservations about such a book when it had been proposed to her. "It wouldn't make any difference, anyhow," Julie argued. She understood that I would have gone ahead anyway, regardless of what I might think of Jill's reaction to my efforts. "It would make a difference if she thought that, Julie," Michael insisted. "Susan Sontag didn't want hers done. Martha Gellhorn didn't want it done. A good book came out of that," Julie noted. Michael countered: "That's something quite different. You were saying Jill didn't want a book written about her. That's balls, absolute balls." Julie told him straight up:

You're deceiving yourself. We spent a whole evening, a whole dinner, talking her into it.
[MF] Sally [Vincent]?
[JH] She liked Sally, so it wasn't because of Sally. She said, "My life's not interesting. I don't like talking about myself," she kept saying.

This scene had taken place at Pilgrim's Lane during Jill's last illness shortly after Sally had done a very fine profile of Michael and Jill.

The relentless Julie brought Michael up short again: "You and my mother were not in accord on the subject of books. You are romanticising her. She was very worried about having the library floor strengthened." Michael had to concede: "She was right about that." "Now you tell me," I said to Michael. I suddenly pictured myself crashing through the floor one night, buried among the piles of books that made up the columns surrounding my bedside. Then Michael relapsed, saying Jill "had exactly the same ideas about books as I had. Partly learned from my father."

After listening to the back and forth between Julie and Michael, I said: "I now realise how I'm going to write this biography. It will be in two columns: one for you and one for Julie. It's going to be a two-column biography." Julie laughed and Michael said, "That's quite a good idea." Indicating Julie, Michael said, "Sometimes she's got good ideas, but ... " Julie filled in the gap: "Only when they agree with you." Michael turned to me: "Sometimes she's absolutely cracked." To Julie, he said: "You know that, don't you?" Julie asked asked him: "are you ever cracked?" "Yes," he responded. "As long as we agree," Julie laughed.

82

In Tony's Benn's downstairs office in Holland Park, we took out our duelling tape recorders and had at it. After some preliminary questions about when he first met Jill, he said he wasn't sure what Jill thought of Michael's running for the leadership. I explained her conflicted feelings and then Benn said:

> The trouble was he was elected by people who didn't really agree with him because the left was so strong that they he thought he was the only leader who could defeat the left. He was put there in a position to do something that was contrary to his real beliefs in order to survive. It was a short and difficult period. He's really a writer, Michael, a polemicist and I don't think this sort of day-to-day stuff was his prime interest really ... He's in good shape ... He rambles a bit.
>
> [CR] He was rambling when I met him in 92.
> [TB] Yes I think that broadly speaking is true. He has a lot to say.
> [CR] And more than once.

Although Tony Benn had not been close to Jill and Michael, he had been in their home many times, including the period of the "husbands and wives dinners," when both men were in the same Labour cabinet. They had had such a long, conflicted, political relationship that I wondered if Benn might have an insight into the Foot/Craigie marriage, especially since his wife Caroline had written a book about Keir Hardie and had consulted with Jill. So I broached the topic this way:

[CR] Jill had her own opinions and had had her own career. There must have been times when she was frustrated, when she wanted to speak out ... and there's Michael. He's the political figure; she isn't. Did you ever see any of that?

[TB] I sensed it, really. I looked through my diary—I have an uncut diary—the published diary is only about ten percent of the full thing. I looked through it. There's not a lot about what Jill said. She didn't like Harold Wilson very much. She detested him. You could see she was very supportive of Michael, but ... he moved from being a passionate—well, originally, of course, he was a great polemicist in the 30s, then editor of the *Evening Standard*, expelled from the Labour Party during the war and when I first came in he was out of Parliament and then he came back again in with Nye's seat and when he became a cabinet minister he became very, very loyal to Callaghan. My wife, Caroline, extremely shrewd too, thought that Michael, far from organising a left cabal, which we all thought we were, was really sort of keeping the left quiet on behalf of Callaghan. ... Then of course having been the great nuclear campaigner—bitterly disappointed by Bevan's speech about going naked into the conference room—it really broke Michael—then, of course, as leader of the party had to support the developing party. In the 83 election he was in a difficult position, because two previous leaders of the party denounced the manifesto on which Michael was fighting the election. A lot of re-interpretation of history needs to be done because the left got the blame for everything, but actually Roy Jenkins—the gang of four who set up the SDP—and that's never referred to as a factor by anybody ever, although 10% of the Parliamentary Labour Party left the party. Michael as the leader of the party shaped unity as the great theme. By then he had really alienated himself from the left, and Jill, I think, would have been a bit ambivalent about that.

Michael shared Benn's animus toward the SDP, but he saw the SDP, in part, as responding to the divisiveness that Benn himself had fomented by taking on the mantle of the far left— an infuriating move because Michael (Benn was quite right) had always been the left's darling. I concurred with Benn that Jill was a bit farther to the left than Michael. "I suspected so," Benn said, "but I never embarrassed her by asking her."

Benn mentioned that Jill had been very critical of him for not remaining loyal to Michael. "Actually, I voted for him in 80," Benn noted. "Neither Healey [who became Michael's deputy] or Silkin did. Michael was very, very angry with me for standing [against Healey for the deputy leadership]. I think he's forgiven me for that now," Benn said. That had been my impression, too, although at the time of Benn's standing Michael and Jill regarded Tony as a divisive force in the party. Joining with Healey was a way to bridge the gap between right and left in the party and Healey, in the event, proved to be a loyal lieutenant.

Benn also expressed considerable affection for Michael, "a

historic figure and highly regarded and he's never said a word about Blair, although I can't think he's terribly happy about the old Labour/new Labour division. Blair set up a new party. He [Michael] can't be happy about the nuclear program and the absolutely pro-American line. Privatisation."

Mentioning Michael as a historic figure led Benn to say that Michael's reputation was quite separate from his period as party leader. "He'll be remembered primarily as a writer and historian." Benn played variations on this theme throughout our interview. Later he and Michael would have another falling-out, on what issue I cannot remember. Benn noted that Caroline, his wife, had liked Jill very much, especially after consulting Jill about the Keir Hardie biography. "There's a line in your wife's book," I told Benn, "about how political biographers often don't pay attention to the wives of political figures. Jill heavily underlined that passage in your wife's book. That obviously struck home." Benn commented: "Well, two very able determined and intellectually strong women who are married to men in this peculiar business known as parliamentary politics. It is a very difficult role."

Benn expressed surprise when I mentioned Jill's flirtatiousness and the many men who made passes at her while she was married to Michael. Then he said, "Biographies that expose sexual activities are a bit boring. I'm not very much in favour of destroying people retrospectively because of their sexual exploits. For all I know Michael may have had other dalliances, though I never thought so." I said there had been some. I saw no point in not saying so, since my biography would deal with them. "It's the story of a wonderful marriage. It had its ups and down."

Boring? Surely Benn meant dealing with the sexual life

of politicians was distasteful to him. I decided to describe that long passage in Jill's book about Elizabeth Garrett's authorised biographer, who had been enjoined not to write about Garrett's private life:

> **[CR]** And Jill does not agree. We want to know what these people were really like. These were flesh and blood people, not political engines and I want to know what Elizabeth Garrett's marriage was like, the full flavour of how she came to her ideas. Michael knows my books ... and I told him "You have to be comfortable with this. I probably am going to learn things that disturb you or even embarrass you."
>
> **[TB]** Well, Michael was so fond of her [Jill] that nothing you wrote would disturb him so long as it was true.
>
> **[CR]** I think that's right. He said, "It's your book."
>
> **[TB]** It's like a painting. It belongs to the artist, not the subject.

83

After the Benn interview, I returned to Pilgrim's Lane to give Michael a report. I told him that Benn had concluded that the husbands and wives dinners were really Michael's effort to monitor the left. "Ah well," Michael said. "He had much more experience than I did. He had been in the previous bloody cabinet. In my opinion, our cabinet behaved much more faithfully in carrying out Labour Party policy than his did." Well, of course, that wasn't Benn's point. Even if there was no collusion between Michael and James Callaghan, certainly Michael, a fierce loyalist, would have wanted to steer the conversation along Callaghanian lines. Or was that what he was telling me in an oblique fashion? To Benn, the husbands and wives meetings were about keeping the left together; for Michael the dinners were about keeping the left inside a cohesive cabinet, which to Michael was no sign of disloyalty to the left at all but rather a way to make the left and the government more effective. In a way, this division of perception explains a good deal about why Michael and Benn could never work together effectively after Michael became leader: their ideas of the left's role and how it could be strengthened clashed. Benn thought Michael was repudiating his earlier firebrand leftism, as did Barbara Castle.

Michael was amused to learn that my interview with Benn included our duelling tape recorders:

> **[MF]** So he put his machine in front of you like that, did he?
> **[CR]** Yes.
> **[MF]** Did you joke?

Not really, we just treated it as a matter-of-fact procedure, I told Michael.

84

Later we had another one of those periodic sessions of my quizzing Michael about Jill's correspondence. I quoted a gracious letter from Yehudi Menuhin: "I would have loved to stay longer to have tired the sun with talking and sent him down the sky." Menuhin had a home in Highgate not far from Pilgrim's Lane. "That was his bloody wife interfering," Michael said, in response to the letter. Jill had been furious with Menuhin's wife. Jill wanted to know more about

Menuhin's history as a child prodigy. "But every time he began to answer, this woman would interrupt as if we were interested in what she was saying about it."

Menuhin's letter captured very well what it meant to spend an evening with Jill and Michael at Pilgrim's Lane:

> All the more was that a stimulating evening [Menuhin wrote] and that glorious food exceptional for us both and if I were obstreperous I'd beg forgiveness. It is long since I have added to my over-regulated regime the luxury of giving opinions, debating, and challenging with those whose brains and minds will so clearly throw the ball back at me either for me to field or hit square on the nose.
> **[MF]** Ah huh [Michael hummed with satisfaction]. That's the stuff!
> **[CR, reading Menuhin]** "It was bliss, in fact."
> **[MF]** That's wonderful, very fine! That's Jill! That's what she provoked!

I introduced another letter, this time from Peggy Ashcroft, one of Michael's companions on the Aldermaston marches. He had seen Peggy playing Desdemona in the famous production with Paul Robeson in the early 30s. Peggy had been interested in producing one of Jill's plays, but nothing had come of it.

A letter from Marjorie Abse (Leo's wife) expressed what many others said: "Not just the meal. The atmosphere was so very consoling. I loved looking at your house, the dog Dizzy, the fire, the contentment."

Another note, from Alan Brien and the late Jill Tweedie, helped Michael recall a trip to France they had all taken together. It was very dangerous to travel with friends that way,

Michael pointed out: "We argued all the way." Alan was quite worth seeing, Michael said. "He'll be glad to talk. We'll have to provide him with something."

I quoted a love letter Michael had written to Jill from Jamaica (circa 1946, when Michael was visiting his brother): "The only thing missing is that you're not here. Sweetheart, I've already told you ten million times already ... One day we will come here together. Never again must we have holidays apart. I think of you my darling and think of how you're getting on with all your struggles."[1] Michael exclaimed: "That's a pretty good letter, that one! You can print that." I agreed it should go into her biography. "Right. I should think so," Michael said, "I'm amazed. I really am pleased."

A letter from the Silkins (John and Rosamund) evoked memories of trips to Glyndbourne: "John was chief whip for a while and was a very good friend to me. But when I stood as leader, he said he didn't think my health was good enough to do it. Both of them died before us." Michael imparted the last bit of information without even a hint of irony. Certainly he looked frail—even by the late 1970s—but that appearance was deceptive. His health was excellent. He took long walks on the Heath until the early 90s when he retired from Parliament.

I read Michael a long four-page letter Jill had written to an editor objecting to the errors in the *Observer*'s profile of Michael. It read like an in-house biography, revealing in remarkable detail how Jill had constructed her own account of Michael. She started with the Cenotaph controversy. Michael had not worn a "boiler-maker's jacket" which showed disrespect for the Queen. He wore, instead, a "smart, short

---

[1] Jill was having arguments with UN bureaucrats about a documentary she was shooting for UNICEF.

overcoat from Jagers. His suit was fresh from cleaners and not rumpled." Michael had put in a gallant performance, although he would never become, she admitted, a Beau Brummel. She scotched the story that Michael had been offered a post in the first Wilson cabinet (1962-1966). On the contrary, Michael maintained a consistently independent position as a government critic and desired no office. The impression that Michael was somehow out of touch with his parliamentary constituents simply was not true. He reported regularly to the people who had elected him and the idea that Michael had no contact with workers other than during a brief stint as clerk in a Liverpool shipping yard was false. "He had intimate dealings with workers at Devonport" and similar relationships with steelworkers and miners in Wales. He had worked hard to form bridges between workers and management as part of his attempt to preserve jobs and the local economy. Indeed, Michael's shift from his family's Liberal politics had to do with his experiences among labourers in Liverpool and did not reflect the influence of Stafford Cripps and other politicians.

Perhaps the sorest point was the profile's harping on Michael's friendship with Beaverbrook. The two men had quarrelled often, Jill pointed out. Michael had quit working for Beaverbrook, finding it "unendurable." They had reconciled after tempers cooled, but even then Michael consistently attacked Beaverbrook's policies.

Jill seemed especially put out that the article should portray Michael as a sort of London socialist. She and Michael actually preferred their cottage in Tredegar and liked to spend the holidays there with working class friends. She certainly downplayed their connections to what she called "Hampstead intellectuals."

Michael seemed to relish Jill's brief on his behalf, making what I took to be approving noises. The article also tried to make Michael seem insular, with few contacts in American labour unions and little interest in traveling abroad. Jill pointed out their friendship with the Reuthers [Walter Reuther had been head of the United Auto Workers for many years], adding "We've travelled abroad almost every year of our twenty-five year marriage." She listed the countries Michael had visited: Germany, Palestine, Morocco, Persia, Finland, France, Italy, and India.

Why should "he [Michael] be portrayed as an eccentric rather than a family man?" Jill complained. He had been a good stepfather to Julie and took great interest in Julie's children and liked the company of young people. This I knew to be so, having observed it on many occasions. Indeed, it seemed to me that Jill and Michael went out of their way to cultivate young people and to listen to what they had to say.

When I had finished up, Michael chuckled and said, "pretty amazing." Michael mentioned that Jill had been very angry with Clive James, who wrote about the 83 election. "I don't know if that [Jill's response to the profile] was ever printed," Michael said. "That's what I'm wondering," I replied. "I'm not sure she sent it. I just found a copy of it in her papers. She may have written it and decided not to send it. I don't know." Michael let the letter speak for itself, showing no real interest in taking up her points. He did very little in the way of self-exculpation at any time. He never seemed to brood over the past or feel resentful, except for a few choice targets such as Rupert Murdoch or David Owen.

Michael associated Jill's long letter with the 1983 election. He thought again about what a hard time she had of it. He did defend himself in so far as he thought the Labour Party would have gone bust if he had not assumed the leadership. Even after the disastrous defeat, the party lived on to fight another day, as far as Michael was concerned. He did not minimise his responsibility for the defeat—except to agree with Tony Benn that the SDP had played a major role in weakening Labour. Michael thought of himself as indispensable only in so far as he felt that only he had kept the party from splitting so badly that it would never recover. "There was no clear alternative, was there?" Michael considered the possibilities:

John Silkin and Peter Shore. Both of them might have— Peter Shore especially—could have done it better ... but when they came round ... they said that she [Jill] put me up to it. But she was as much interested in keeping the Labour Party together as I was.

Certainly Neil Kinnock and others put it to Michael that no one else had such a hold on the affections of the party.

85

Jenny Stringer came over before dinner in time to hear Michael's complaints about a newspaper article attacking Blair, "saying he shouldn't be going round the world dealing with problems. He should stay home. That's talking like a Tory." Jenny raised Michael's ire by implying Blair was indeed seeking to divert attention from problems at home. "That's not fair," Michael protested. "He'll come back and sort the railways out and the NHS, won't he?" Jenny taunted him. "You can't say he doesn't take responsibility. He does. What the previous ones—Wilson, Attlee—they pushed it off." Jenny said Michael had got her point wrong: Blair was "pretending to play God." Michael lightened up and took her comments to be a retreat. So she wasn't objecting to Blair's trips abroad? He was trying to stop her from sounding like a Tory, he reiterated. "I'm sorry I ruined your evening," Jenny said. "No, it was quite exciting," I assured her. "Thank you anyhow," Michael said to Jenny. "I won't mention the B word again," Jenny promised. Michael mentioned Jenny's "rage." "Stop by anytime when you want to talk about politics," I said.

86

We sat down to dinner. "Jenny was quite fired up this evening," I said to Michael. "She's always like that," muttered Angela, who was bringing food to the table. Michael said nothing. In full Boswellian mode, I tried again: "Tony Benn said that Tony Blair did not change the Labour Party. He reinvented it." Michael said nothing, concentrating on his food. I said Blair was much admired in the U. S., where it had now become virtually impossible to implement any sort of liberal or progressive agenda. "Now, how much Blair understands about that, I'm not sure," Michael said. Gordon Brown had more experience in America, Michael pointed out. Michael knew quite a bit about Brown through a mutual friend, the journalist Jon Snow, who often holidayed in America with Brown. "Some people in the party attack Gordon Brown for having followed the policies of the previous Conservative government even more than Tony Blair. ... The two of them [Blair and Brown] agreed ... " Michael didn't finish his sentence, but I knew he meant that Labour under new leadership would not raise taxes. "Is Barbara Castle still criticising them about pensions?" I asked. "Even more so," Michael reported.

87

The next afternoon, I asked Michael about the recent change in the Conservative Party leadership. He had little to say, observing that Labour did not "tear its heart" over the current disarray on the other side. He noted that John Major had recently criticised his own party for taking such an adamant stance against the Euro. Mention of Major predictably led to this comment: "Some people talk as though he was a very good prime minister. We thought he was very bad, especially on the whole question of what they should do in Yugoslavia." Major failed to take any kind of decent action, as Brendon Sims had pointed out in a recent book, Michael said.

"I'll just a have short, sharp sleep," he concluded.

88

We met Geoffrey Goodman for an early dinner at the Gay Hussar. "You don't mind if I run this machine, do you?" I asked Goodman. "Not at all," he said. "Nothing to hide." "And everything to reveal, I hope," I said, laughing. "I'll kick you under the table, Geoffrey," Michael spoke up, "if there is a problem." "I'll have a broken leg," Geoffrey said. "Yes," I agreed, "from the leader." "He's been complaining about my going off to football matches," Michael said, referring to Geoffrey.

I suppose I would have been better off seeing Goodman alone, although I doubted he would tell me anything he would not want repeated to Michael and I was curious, anyway, to see how Michael behaved with a crony. I asked Goodman when he had first met Michael. It was 1949, when Goodman was working at the *News Chronicle* and covering the Labour Party conference in Blackpool. All these characters—

Woodrow Wyatt, Tom Driberg and Michael "made quite an impression," Goodman observed "and Nye," Michael added. Actually, Goodman pointed out, he had met Nye slightly earlier when he asked Bevan for an interview about the NHS. A "cheeky young reporter then," he had accosted Nye on the street. "Who are you?" Bevan asked. Goodman told him he was a *News Chronicle* reporter. "Well, it's not as bad as some of the other bloody papers." Goodman eventually became a major fixture in the Aneurin Bevan Society.

Goodman recalled Michael's Abbey Road home just before the 1964 general election. Geoffrey marvelled at Jill's ability not merely to serve delicious meals, but to "deploy the table." She was a master organiser. "Whether she organised Michael or not, I don't know. It's up to him to say," Goodman suggested. "She tried to," I said, "people say they notice some differences now. So maybe we can attribute the former Michael to her." "Well, he's reaching the age of maturity now," replied Goodman. "Senile," Michael said quietly. "Not that, never!" Goodman rejoined.

After Geoffrey's wife, Mougit, joined us, we discussed the menu. Michael passed on my teasing suggestion of a "Serbian-style" chicken. Mougit mentioned that she had been "awestruck" when she first met Michael and Jill. "And did you get over it?" Michael asked. "Yes," she replied to our laughter. "Because it was so easy. They were so easy."

I brought up the pronunciation of Callaghan's name. Michael emphasised the 'g'. So did Tony Benn. But in the States I had always heard it pronounced with a silent 'g'. The difference, I was told, was between English and Irish pronunciations. Which did we suppose Callaghan favoured? Mougit asked. Michael said last names had not been used in cabinet. Mougit said Michael had just revealed a Cabinet secret and violated the Official Secrets Act. Michael laughed and could not say how Callaghan pronounced his own name. "Maybe it depends where he is," I suggested. "A very apt reply," Mougit said.

Throughout our lunch the Goodmans and Michael kept coming back to Frank and Nance Cousins, frequent guests at Abbey Road. "A truly wonderful lot," Michael concluded. "Next to going out with Nye. Much more enjoyable than any other kind of political discussion." I'd never heard Michael value anyone's company in quite that way. In 1956, while Jill and Michael were living at Abbey Road, Cousins had been elected general secretary of the Transport and General Works Union (TGWU). "Frank Cousins never knew Nye so well," Michael noted, "because they just didn't quite ... If Frank had come into the management of the TGWU a bit earlier, the whole shift of the party might have been better. But they didn't quite fit."

Mougit quietly mentioned the "influence of the wives. Jill always stressed that a good deal." Geoffrey observed that Nance was a formidable character who would "round on Frank and say, "You're talking rubbish."" She was more radical than her husband. Jill would support Nance and both of them would attack Harold Wilson: "By God, Jill and Nance between them they pretty well tore Mr. Wilson bowel to bowel. The chap over here [Michael] had the job of saying, 'Well, that's not quite true. Give Harold credit for this or that.'" I asked why Wilson set them off. They didn't trust him, Geoffrey answered. "They thought that he was ... "playing two games, [Michael finished Geoffrey's sentence]. Putting one line to us and another to other—and he did."

We paused after that reminiscence of the shifty Harold while we chewed and ruminated. Then Geoffrey told the story about Dizzy chewing up one of their children's toys and how thoughtful Jill had been about sending a replacement, which their daughter cherished. "What happened when you had parties?" I asked Michael. "What did you do with the dog?" Michael said, "The dog joined the party." "He was a very prominent figure then. There wasn't any difficulty about that. He misbehaved occasionally. Also, I'm very sorry to say he made an enemy of Una right from an early date ... He chewed up a nice thing of hers. So Una took some time to forgive him, I must say." Of course Michael could not resist retelling the story about Paul and Dizzy. Referring to Paul's penchant for writing about people who had been unjustly incarcerated, Michael said to him, "You framed my dog!" Several people had urged Michael to get another dog (Dizzy died shortly before Jill did). "I don't think it would be fair to the dog," Michael said. "And I don't think the dog would be as good as Dizzy. It would mean I would walk more. That's something to be said for it." Michael told the Goodmans about my two Scotties, Holmes and Watson. "Two males, are they?" Michael asked. "Actually, one is a female,." I clarified. "Ah," he cried:

[MF] You shouldn't call one by a male name."

[CR] Well, she doesn't mind whatsoever.

[MF] How do you know?

[CR] She loves it. Watson is the female.

[MF] Dogs are very sensitive on these questions.

[CR] She loves it. Holmes is the alpha dog. It worked out.

Mougit claimed Jill would agree with me. Geoffrey concurred. But I don't think we altered Michael's dogmatic view. Geoffrey rejected the idea that Jill had somehow pushed Michael into running for the leadership. "She just thought Michael was the best for it [the leadership]," Mougit suggested. But it was not the office itself that she craved. He was too good for the office and for the British people, Geoffrey averred, expressing a sentiment I had heard from many of Michael's friends. "It wasn't going to happen," Geoffrey added, given the "scene." Michael did not comment, except to mutter, "Anyhow."

Lunch was over and as usual Michael insisted on paying for all of us.

89

Tea with Michael Holroyd and Margaret Drabble. Drabble had her own take on "my dear child." Times had changed: "No husband would now call his wife 'my pet.' It would be an insult to animals and to his wife," Drabble said. "'My child, my little one'—it was generational. It did not strike me at all oddly ... My grandfather used to address my grandmother as "dear chick."' They thought nothing of it. It was an endearment. He obviously had respect for her. She was quite brusque with him sometimes: 'Sit there. Don't get in everyone's way.'" Holroyd agreed: "She was not edited."

Michael celebrated his 70th birthday with Drabble and Holroyd. Jill mentioned that she had not planned anything special and that "Michael was cross." Drabble recalled suggesting to Jill: "'Well, why don't you come to supper with us.' And he came, and I got a cake made. But he was in a bad temper because he thought something more should be done. It was very, very last minute. Melvyn Bragg came. We had a funny evening. It was her [Jill's] idea, basically." When Jenny Stringer read Drabble's comments in manuscript, she asked me to take them out. Jenny had worked with Drabble on the *Oxford Companion to English Literature* and they were friends. I never heard directly from Drabble, but Jenny assured me that Drabble wanted it out. I gave way, eliminating the business about Michael's being cross. But you can see how the politics of biography work: all this fuss because Michael's minder didn't like the tone of this little scene. On the big issues, I would not budge, but with these little sideshows I surrendered. Michael acquiesced to Jenny's concerns. I don't think my scene upset him, but for the sake of Jenny, Paul Foot and a few other people, he did not mind sacrificing my text.

Jill exercised a sort of domestic discipline over the unruly Michael, Drabble and Holroyd agreed. "I used to like to see Michael and Dizzy on the Heath," Drabble said. "That was his region. They had made their escape." But the overriding impression I received from Drabble and Holroyd was of the texture of Michael's life, graced by Jill's garden and dinner parties under the pergola. "Does he still have that tankard?" Drabble asked. "There were little touches like that that made you feel at home. It wasn't pretentious." Michael might look "ordinary" in public—to use Holroyd's term—but "at home everything took on an aesthetic quality."

I asked one of my other standard questions: "Can you think of anyone else like them? Who cut across the literary and political ... " The Priestleys? Drabble ventured. Peggy Ashcroft? Earlier, journalist David Leigh had proposed Harold Pinter and Antonia Fraser. "We are more segregated now," Holroyd observed. "Vacuum packed."

90

While Michael was out at dinner I took Peter and Celine out to repay them for their earlier hospitality. Celine gave me her reading of Michael: "If I had a hundred years, I wouldn't understand him. He should be more aware than he is and maybe he is, but I don't understand ... " Peter interrupted: "But you know he kicked over the traces with his west country Methodist upbringing and his brothers never quite went as far as he did and I've always had the feeling that Michael is surprised that he went as far as he did go."

Celine brought us back to the crux: "I can't quite understand whether Michael is a saintly person or a weak person." "That's a good question, Celine, a very good question," I responded. "I would say he is both," Peter remarked. "He is very forgiving and it's not just because it's the easy way out. Too often it has not been an easy way out. He can be very tough. I've heard him refuse when somebody's asked him to do something he doesn't want to do." But Celine would not give up. "I can't quite comprehend ... " "We're seeing him from a narrow domestic perspective," Peter cut in. "It's putting up with nonsense on such a massive level," Celine said, referring to how Michael was paying Julie's way on holidays, giving her Jill's Henry Moore painting and in general providing her children with funds he ought to be husbanding for his own retirement. Both Celine and Peter saw Julie's family as draining Michael dry. Celine thought Michael made "good people look like fools. Do you understand what I mean? He treats the bad people and the good people on the same level. I don't know why we bother." Certainly Peter and Celine expected no other reward, which was why I found their testimony worth considering. Celine seemed to be wondering who really mattered in Michael's life.

Her puzzlement provoked me to share mine with them. I told them about asking Michael to set up an interview with Callaghan. Michael agreed but never seemed to find the right moment to contact Callaghan. I thought of just doing it myself, but I thought my chances of seeing him were much better, of course, if Michael approached him. A year went by. Michael kept saying I should wait until he had spoken with Callaghan. "Finally, this trip Michael did pick up the phone and called him," I said. "He didn't get a yes or a no but rather 'I'll call you back.'" A day later, the phone rang. Michael was out, and I answered. It was Callaghan. He said, "Is Michael there?" and I said no. Then I introduced myself. He said, "I'm very embarrassed. I hardly knew Jill Craigie. I really don't know what to do. I want to see Michael, but to bring you all the way here to talk about Jill when I really have nothing to say." I said to him, "Look, you've spoken to me about Jill. We've had our talk. I can tell Michael in the nicest way I know that we spoke and this seemed to be the best way to handle it—to have a conversation on the phone about your memories of her." He said, "Would you do that?" Of course I would, I told him. "It's the best way to handle it." Michael came home. I said we had had a very nice talk about Jill. Michael was relieved. Perhaps he knew all along that Callaghan had nothing to say. But with Michael, I never really knew. "Maybe he doesn't know himself," Peter suggested.

91

The next day over breakfast I teased Michael about Paul's book on Shelley. Why hadn't Michael written on Shelley rather than Byron? Well, Paul had written about Shelley first, Michael said. "That was the reason?" I asked. "Partly," he replied. "Paul has some derogatory things to say about Byron," I noted. "Yes, they've all been banished since, on further discussion," Michael assured me. Paul and Michael had appeared jointly at the Byron Society and at the Arts Council in Plymouth. Michael said they had had a "good time," but I pressed on: "Does he think that Shelley is a greater poet than Byron?" "No," Michael assured me. "He doesn't think so at all. He's converted the other way around in my opinion." I laughed. "Better ask him," Michael advised me.

Paul had become convinced, Michael assured me, that Byron had a sharper wit and a better sense of humour than Shelley. As with Jill, Michael always tended to suggest he won the argument with his interlocutor, while off handedly suggesting there were still a few minor disagreements. "I'm sure they all thought that Shelley was a better feminist than Byron. However ... " As Michael paused, I wonder who "they" was. I think he meant Paul and Jill, who tended to share a greater understanding of women's issues than Michael had, although Michael claimed Jill had a "very considerable influence" on his Byron book.

After dinner, Michael told me about how journalist Anne Robinson, her husband John Penrose, and Moni Forman and her husband Denis had combined together to work out a scheme to make Michael comfortable in his retirement. Michael benefited from what is sometimes called a reverse mortgage, one that allows the homeowner to take equity out of his house in order to assure a steady stream of income. "I wouldn't be living in this house now if not for that." The group, along with Jenny Stringer, earned Michael's gratitude, since they got nothing out of it. "Just to be nice to us," Michael said. Celine had said that at one point Julie had tried, in effect, to obtain ownership of the house. Exactly what happened I could not determine, because Jenny and Julie—whatever their other differences—combined to deny there had been a problem. But Anne Robinson (no longer in Michael's orbit) would fill in a few facts later and even Michael obliquely adverted to the trouble with Julie and how it had disturbed Anne *et al*: "Sometimes they were not too pleased—arguing about what Julie may have done in a previous kind of thing we had on. We had a previous kind of arrangement to help Julie [to buy her flat in Stoke Newington]. Sometimes they were critical of Julie. Not with any great reason, in my opinion." This kind of comment from Michael infuriated friends like Celine, who simply viewed Julie as a parasite—as did Anne Robinson. Julie had had a falling out with Anne and Michael also seemed down on her. He had no respect for *The Weakest Link*, Robinson's starring vehicle and could not understand why it was so popular. Michael objected to Robinson's autobiography, which he thought made Jill out to be a subservient wife. He also disliked what he called Robinson's "glorified gossip column." The final charge, though, was Robinson's view that Barbara Castle had "stolen the show" at Jill's memorial event. Michael conceded, though, that some people had said as much to him. "You can understand how Julie would be offended. On that argument, in the main, I'm on Julie's side. I think it's a great pity they [Julie and Anne] had the argument."

After laying out some careful groundwork—telling Michael that I thought the falling out between Julie and Anne had led both to revise history, to find in one another's past behaviour reasons for not trusting the other person — told Michael I had not yet interviewed Anne, but that I would. "I think," I told him, "that Anne Robinson thinks that in some sense Julie was exploiting you. That's why there's very bad blood here, why these two women are angry at each other ... suspecting each other of low motives. I don't think I can get the whole truth from talking to either one." Throughout my analysis, Michael muttered what sounded like assenting noises. He did finally said "Yes" when I added that the accusations would continue. "I'm sorry that is the case," he concluded. I said, "I feel I have to listen to her [Anne] if I can get her. She's so busy." Michael agreed: "I think so too," adding "and we had some nice expeditions with her—to Sissinghurst." Michael raised his voice: "John Penrose and I have never had a quarrel. He's done nothing but good to me."

92

Over several days Michael took time out to read to me as he read to Jill, usually picking up a volume of Montaigne in Florio's translation and dwelling on a favourite passage, many of them having to do with love. Michael was attracted to what he called Montaigne's "fiascos in love-making. He was the first person to dare to write about it." This from Montaigne's famous essay on Virgil: "I've often lacked luck but also sometimes enterprise." Michael's voice dropped on the last half of the sentence, making me laugh, and continued: "God keep from harm the man who can laugh at this" — Michael seemed to make up this line. Was he incorporating my own reaction into his reading of Montaigne? "These days love calls for more temerity, which our young men excuse on the pretext of ardor. But if the women considered the matter closely, they would find that temerity comes rather from contempt. I used to be scrupulously afraid of giving offence and I am inclined to respect what I love. Besides, in these negotiations if you take away respect you rub out the drama. In this I like to have a man somewhat play the child and the timid slave. If not altogether in this, in other situations I have something of the stupid bashfulness that Plutarch thinks of."

Listening again to this recording of Michael recite these passages, I am struck by the sort of man Michael thought himself. Montaigne, Michael supposed, spoke for all men. Montaigne was universal and Michael was a universal man. Nothing Michael had done—no matter how foolish or wise— embarrassed or especially impressed him. His behaviour was part of the human condition and this awareness of his own humanity gave him, I believe, a profound peace such as few human beings experience. Michael might not be capable of saying all I wanted to know about him, but then who has ever had such a capacity? Perhaps Montaigne came closest and this is why Michael revered him.

Michael was as open with me as he knew how to be. It was not enough, but then what biographer has ever been satisfied? "Both wisdom and folly will have all they can do to support me and help me by their alternate services in this calamity of old age." Michael looked at me, "You see, you don't know anything about that. Read with Jill, February 14, 1964," Michael said, quoting his own words on the book's flyleaf. "I don't say I read to her everything, but a lot of it." If the reading sometimes wearied her, how could there not have been other times when she realised how much of his heart he was sharing with her.

Gore Vidal pleased Michael when Vidal told him that the Virgil essay was one of his favourites. Vidal had visited Pilgrim's Lane around the time of the 1983 election and the two men shared their love of books and of Venice. The Vidal meeting fit into Michael's genealogy of literary affinities, which stretched back from Hazlitt and Byron to Swift to Montaigne. Read his book on Byron and you'll see it is a celebration of the scholars and writers who congregate around great literary figures. Nothing disturbed him more than a scholar who did not acknowledge his colleagues. On one of our outings in Hampstead on Flask Walk we stopped in at a bookstore and Michael bought a copy of one of his favourite Hazlitt biographies for me.

93

Over breakfast, Michael had more to say about Enoch Powell, a brilliant parliamentary debater second only to Aneurin Bevan. "He would sometimes prove too much. He was so confident in his own argument that he could not carry it beyond. But every sentence was well formed and the ideas were brilliant." Powell had also earned Michael's respect because he had written an honest and moving biography of Joseph Chamberlain. Powell had set out to write a book about a hero but in the end exposed Chamberlain as a fraud, instead presenting Gladstone as the true hero. The drama of Powell's own struggle to reveal the truth received Michael's accolades.

Talk of Powell led Michael to an even greater Conservative hero, Disraeli, and his Tory biographer, Robert Blake. "When he [Blake] started writing it, Disraeli was still the great hero of the Tory party. The Tory recovery was going to be along the lines of Disraeli's ideas. That was the kind of feeling when I was at Oxford." But Blake discovered that Disraeli "couldn't tell the truth and that on some of these issues, he was quite prepared to tell terrible lies in order to promote his own position." Now what was Blake to do? Michael asked. Michael reviewed Blake's biography and befriended him. Blake thought Michael wrote nonsense about Disraeli being a subversive, revolutionary figure. "I used to send him postcards: "Further proof of your revolutionary friend." Disraeli had no respect for the truth and would say anything that might prove advantageous to himself, his friends, and his family. Blake was really shocked, Michael repeated. But Disraeli's duplicity delighted Michael, who saw his hero as simply using the Conservatives for his own political ends— perfectly acceptable behaviour to Michael, of course, since he had so little respect for Tories.

Michael's third story of the morning concerned arranging a meeting between Dylan Thomas and Arthur Koestler. Both men had been drinking and Thomas was in an aggressive mood. Koestler, often an obstreperous drunk, hardly acknowledged Thomas's presence. This nonevent went on for about two hours and when the men emerged from a nightclub in Piccadilly Circus, Michael invited them to his flat at 62 Park Street for another drink. Still ignoring Thomas, Koestler challenged Michael to a game of chess. They often played and Koestler always won. Thomas turned to Michael's books and spotted a copy of Koestler's *Darkness at Noon*. He started reading it, but then began writing in it—"some kind of insult to Koestler and then Koestler looks at it and writes a reply. That carried on for quite a time. After a while Koestler went off into the night and Thomas stayed that night with me and he left—as he very often did—his shirt behind." I said, "A pretty valuable copy of *Darkness at Noon*." Michael said, "You bet. I was very pleased about it, but then lo and behold somebody stole it." Later I told Michael that when I worked on his biography, I would post an author's query in several publications requesting that the person who stole his copy of *Darkness at Noon* please return it to Michael's biographer, no questions asked.

Molly came in. She was preparing Michael for a trip to Jamaica to see his nephew Oliver. "I'm sorting things out for your suitcase. You'll leave them in there, won't you?" I laughed. Michael was not the tidiest person. Molly's tone reminded me of a mother I once saw in a restaurant watching her child. After the child sauntered out, her mother called after her, "You're not touching anything, are you?" In fact, Molly had hidden the suitcase so Michael could not get at it. "You don't need to worry about it," she assured him. I laughed. Molly laughed. Michael got suspicious when Molly said Julie had provided a new suitcase (the old one was falling apart). Molly enumerated the items she had packed for him, ending with, "You just leave it to me." Then she offered this alternative: "Or I'll take the suitcase and go to Jamaica and you stay here." Properly mollified, Michael said, "Okay, thank you."

94

Over dinner with Julie, who loved intrigue, she told me that Molly had said to her, "Marie, is it? is coming for lunch." "Oh," Julie said. "It's his girlfriend?" Molly whispered. Julie gave Molly a knowing look. "Well, then, I better make myself scarce," Molly said. "Don't you dare," Julie said, wanting to have a full report. When Molly brought Michael and Marie lunch, she went over to Michael and said quietly, "Do you want me to leave?" "Yes," he said. Molly went upstairs and later told Julie, "He's never done that before" and it was true, Michael was very relaxed about having people around at all times. I can't ever remember him asking me or anyone else to leave the room during a telephone call or when a guest appeared.

Dinner with Julie also revealed a nicer side of her relationship with Michael [JH]. He used to watch out for me when I was much younger—behave in a fatherly way—when my mother wasn't looking. I got into trouble with the union [Julie was a news photographer then]. I had been out of work and had to go back to work. The union said, "No you can't. Your dues aren't up to date ... Michael said, "Let me know how much it is. I'll pay it, but don't tell your mother!" Many a time he helped me out and I was never to tell my mother.

Julie did not say why Michael did not want Jill to know. But I knew. Jill always thought of Julie, a child she had brought into the marriage, as her responsibility. Jill found it intolerable to think that Julie had become any sort of burden for Michael.

95

Over breakfast with Michael, I engaged in our favourite sport: teasing Molly. Michael (still hard of hearing in spite of the NHS "deaf aids" he touted) did not hear Molly ask him if he wanted another croissant. I told him in a loud voice, "Molly says, 'No more croissants for you!" She would always laugh when I carried on this way and Michael would refuse the bait. "She says she wants to keep the Elgin Marbles here, so that she can see them whenever she wants." This was one of Michael's hobbyhorses: the Marbles belonged back in Greece. "I'm hoping to go today [to see the Marbles]," Molly said. I said to Michael, "Make your choice: the Marbles or the croissants."

Michael's sense of art—let alone politics—coalesced around the Marbles. Why wouldn't the British government want to make the world a more beautiful place, not to mention doing the right thing? This talk led directly to Byron and Greece and the poet's anti-imperialistic politics. "What he saw was the oppression of the Greeks," Michael declared. Then of course there was the socialist Papandreou and the restoration of democracy after the dreadful period of the Colonels. Michael mentioned Melina Mecouri's campaign as Minister of Culture to restore the Marbles to Greece. Michael attended a press conference with her at one point, emphasising that returning the Marbles should be the policy of any Labour government. He never thought their return would happen quickly, but he was dismayed that the issue still had not been resolved.

96

The next morning I gave Michael a preliminary report about the documents I had retrieved concerning Jill's marriages and divorces. When I told him Jill first married in 1933, his response was, "amazing." Why he said that, I can't be sure, except that I don't think he had ever tried to work out the order of events in Jill's life before she met him. "How old was she then?" he asked.

[CR] She was born in 1911.

[MF] No.
[CR] Yes.
[MF] 1913.
[CR] 1911, Michael.
[MF] No.
[CR] Yea, the birth certificate is there.
[MF] No.
[CR] It is. It's in the public record. 1911. I'll show you
Friday. I'm getting a copy Friday. I looked it up. It's there
in the book.

There was quite a long pause, during which Michael cleared his throat. "I'm amazed," he said. "Family Records Centre," I told him. "Well, they made a mistake." "No, Michael." My tone was rather like the sort a parent might use with a recalcitrant child who knows better. "It's a recorded birth certificate," I said, almost laughing now. "It's also on her death certificate." We would have to have a lot of records that were inaccurate. "Well," he said grudgingly:

[CR] No, it's 1911.
[MF] I really don't ... I'm amazed. It was on her last passport. It was wrong.
[CR] I found three of Jill's passports and they all say 1911.
[MF] Do they?

I reiterated all the evidence. "Good heavens," he whispered.

Later Jenny told me that she knew Jill had been born in 1911 and not 1914 as all the obituaries stated. She hadn't told me, she explained, because she wanted me to find out for myself. Celine also knew—not the specific date, but that Jill was older than Michael (he was born in 1913). I again had to wonder at Michael's powers of self-deception.

[MF] So ... So ... if that's so ... If she got married in 33 ...

[CR] Yep, she was 22 years old.

[MF] I see. Otherwise, she'd be ... Yes, I see.

[CR] So when she died she was 88. Not 85, like the newspapers said. You see, I don't believe everything I read in the newspapers.

[MF] No. Nor do I. But ...

Now he was done with it, finally, I thought, incorporating Jill's real age into his calculations.

Julie obtained Jill's wedding pictures from 1933 from her aunt, Jill's first husband's sister. I showed them to Michael. "Well I'm damned," he said. "That's Jill and her first husband," I said. "Well, I'm damned," Michael repeated. "So what's he called?" Michael asked. "Claude Begbie-Clench. That's Julie's father," I explained. "Did Julie ever know him?" Michael asked. Such questions again brought home how little Michael had inquired into the past of the mother and daughter who had become his family. I gave him a rundown. "That's very fine," he said, looking at the pictures again. He wanted me to identify the other people in the pictures, which I did. Looking at Julie's "Begbie uncle," as we began to call him, Michael said, "What a moustache, eh?" It was one of those ostentatious curled-at-the-ends jobs. "What date is that?" "1933." "Well, I'm damned."

I showed Michael a picture of Claude Begbie-Clench as a boy. "Good looking chap," Michael said. "Jill had that, I suppose," Michael muttered.

> [CR] No, no, it's all from the aunt in Italy.
>
> [MF] Ah!
>
> [CR] Jill kept nothing.
>
> [MF] I see.
>
> [CR] Jill kept ... the only thing of Jill's I could find [dating from] before she married you was about three letters from Jeffrey Dell, scrapbooks about her movies and no documents, no letters, no birth certificate, nothing because Jill's life started with Michael Foot. I think that's how she saw it.
>
> [MF] She had a great respect for Jeffrey Dell. ... She was a fair-minded woman, Jill.
>
> [CR] When people would ask her about her life before you, she did not give very many details.
>
> [MF] Well, that's another matter. I never asked for them. Now you say 1933, she first married. When was the second marriage?
>
> [CR] I don't have a date yet. I'll have the date for you Friday when I pick up the marriage certificate. I can tell you approximately: 1937.
>
> [MF] Was it really?
>
> [CR] Maybe as late as 1938.
>
> [MF] Well I'm damned.

Not asking for details was a part of his trusting nature, of course; he was willing to take people as they presented themselves. The result, however, was a sort of mythifying. For Michael Foot, the romance was clearly not in the details.

97

At lunch I asked Mark Seddon how he had met Michael. Mark had known Michael since 1983, when as Labour Leader Michael came to Norwich to appear at a union-organised people's march for jobs. Mark had been delegated to meet Michael and take him to St. Andrew's Hall, a historic site where meetings supporting the French Revolution had been held. The "election on the ground," as Mark put it, was a huge anti-Tory wave. The other election occurred in the media, where Michael was depicted as a "hobbling old pensioner." Mark and Michael had become closer when Mark became editor of *Tribune* around the time of Michael's 80th birthday (1993). Mark's other close association with Michael involved *Tribune*'s editorial line on the Balkan wars. When the journal came down on Michael's side, supporting the Croats and Bosnians, *Tribune* lost subscriptions. For Michael, Mark pointed out, what was happening in Croatia and Bosnia was a replay of the Spanish Civil War, with the Serbs standing in for the fascists.

We talked a good deal about the house at Pilgrim's Lane. Mark visited often. He mentioned Jill's articles for *Tribune*. This surprised me—not that Jill had written them, but Michael had made no mention of them. I noted that I could not find a single filing cabinet. No effort had been made to organise any of their papers (well, Jill had hired someone to do some assembling of her correspondence, but this was a rudimentary effort). I said that the only way to find Michael's reviews was to search out the book in question in his library. He would stuff clippings of his work between its covers. "How refreshing," Mark said. They had no thought of posterity. "No pomposity, no pretension," I added. "No covering of their tracks. None of those things you associate with people in the public eye."

Did Mark ever see Jill and Michael argue? "Banter, lots of back-and-forth," he replied. "She didn't like going to South Wales, did she?" Mark asked. "Oh, she loved it," I said—"according to Michael at any rate." Mark was surprised: "She did? That's interesting because people there seemed to think that she didn't." I could only say, "Maybe Michael's exaggerating. But he said she liked it [Wales and the Welsh] much better than the people in Plymouth—more outgoing." "Well, there is a lot of truth in that," Mark said. "More friendly."

Was this another one of Michael's myths? "You heard it from people in Wales?" I asked. Seddon answered: "One or two. It's sort of entered into folklore. There is still this thing in South Wales which is still operating, still monocultural. There is an interest in, but also a suspicion of outsiders. So for some of them, I would imagine, what is this glamorous woman coming down here? Is she patronising us? Which she wouldn't have done." Later, I would learn from Glennys Kinnock and friends close to Michael that his view of Jill's utter comfort in Wales was over the top. It struck me that even someone only slightly on the sidelines had perceptions—for example, concerning Jill's relationship with the Welsh—that Michael could not imagine.

Later that day, I went over to journalist Jon Snow's home for an interview. He hosted the Channel 4 news hour. He knew Michael, of course, through covering politics. But their friendship really began when Jill called him up and invited him over. After all, through the telly, Snow was already a fixture in the Foot household. Although Snow did not want to imply Michael had single-handedly accomplished the feat, he certainly thought Michael was the driving force in ensuring that Salman Rushdie had government protection during the fatwa. Jill and Michael had what Jon called "safe parties" for Salman, "to keep him engaged with the rest of the world." The drama of it, the "battling of some invisible enemy," thrilled Jill. It was the "great defence of the word" that drove Michael.

"Salman was liberated" by this kind of soirée. "The detectives were absolutely paranoid. This was the middle of Hampstead. Their curtains would be very firmly closed." Jill had great affection for Jon. He loved her, Jon said and she treated him virtually like a son. It was at one of those soirées that Jill blurted out the story of the Koestler rape. "I don't think she meant to," Snow added quickly. But "she had been waiting to." Michael just sat there, silent, Jon recalled. Somebody said something about Koestler and it was as if the plug had been pulled from the dam. "We sat there, poleaxed," Jon said. "She was contorted about it."

Jon recalled how Jill had become obsessed with making *Two Hours from London*. He did not see how two octogenarians could possibly pull it off, but if they did, he told Jill, it would be sensational. Jill gave Jon progress reports on film production. Still, how could Jill manage to get Michael—whose verbal style was "all over the shop"—to deliver the right sort of voice track for a film? "It just isn't his skill. He is inapplicable to the television age." But Jill eventually toned down Michael's style and got him to speak in a more modulated fashion and Jill got Jon and a roomful of others to preview the film and talk it up.

Jon attended the first showing of the film with his "heart in his boots," worried what to say if the film proved a failure.

But it was very moving—even more so because Michael, "a dear old man," was shown off at his gallant best. Nevertheless, "it was a diatribe. They were so vitriolically pro-Croatian." I understood Jon's point. The film never mentioned Tudjman's thuggery.

I asked Jon about how Jill and Michael behaved at home. She was in charge, he said. "She both lionised him and was exasperated with him ... What she said went. The Bosnia film proves it. I don't think Michael could have done the film with anybody else." She ran the dinner table conversation, making sure only one line dominated the gathering. "If something was going on at her end, she'd suddenly stop things and say— she'd be worried that Michael was having a conversation that she wasn't getting a bit of the action ... " How did Michael react? "He never showed any resentment," said Madeleine Colvin, Jon's partner, who now joined our conversation. Jon agreed.

Later on, we discussed the nature of the Foot/Craigie marriage. Jon mentioned casually that there had been infidelity on Michael's part and then proceeded to tell me about the "vampire lady," whom Julie had brought up earlier. A friend of Jon's had hosted Michael, who turned up with the "vampire lady". "They definitely shared a room, I can tell you that," Jon said. Was Michael then misleading me on the platonic nature of his love for Marie? I never got a better answer out of him.

I mentioned the to-do over Jill's birthdate. "Michael is a man who very much edits his world," Jon said. I brought up Julie's comment that her mother would be horrified at the idea I was doing her biography and that Michael, in turn, was horrified that Julie should say such a thing. Both Jon and Madeleine instantly agreed: "Her mother would absolutely not want a biography. She wouldn't even want it without warts."

We then discussed Jill as a political wife, agreeing that she did not thrust herself into Michael's public life. "She let the boys get on with it," Jon said. "When Neil [Kinnock] came along, Glennys was an absolute structural part. She was so presentable and so political and so out front, but Jill was never talked about at all in that context." Michael was "such a political loner" throughout the 1960s, Jon observed, "I was surprised to learn he had a wife. He carried on in the left, *Tribune*... If you didn't know, if you weren't on the inside, you saw him as an isolated figure. He wasn't cabinet. He was that voice out on the left when all the others were in government. It's only in the 70s that he starts getting into office." I suggested, "And then it's too late." "Yah, yah," Jon agreed. The discussion led to a rather bleak conclusion: Michael's political career was a failure.

Jon mentioned that he did not visit Michael more often because Jon felt inadequate. Michael tended to endow Jon with a breadth of knowledge that Jon did not possess. I suggested that Jill and Michael "projected into you."

[JS] They do.
[CR] You become the great ...
[JS] Yah, yah. I ring up and she says, "You were marvellous last night" and you think, "Don't say it."
[CR] That's Michael. He's a supporter. He's a partisan.
[JS] He's a partisan, an absolutely sumptuous human being.

And that about summed it up for Jon Snow.

99

On my return to Pilgrim's Lane, I quizzed Molly about the "vampire lady". She had some sort of degree in witchcraft or the occult, Molly thought "She paws him," Molly said "and it embarrasses him." But Molly thought her "a nice girl. I liked her."

When Michael came downstairs, I told him about finding a thank you card from a guest who had compared Michael and Jill to Thomas and Jane Carlyle. "I think it was meant as a compliment," I said. "I'm sure it was," Michael agreed. But Michael agreed he was quite different from Carlyle. Michael had read a good deal of Carlyle, especially lauding his book on the French Revolution, which Michael's friend, A.J.P. Taylor, read every year. Michael's father was especially fond of Carlyle because the writer had rehabilitated Cromwell.

I told Michael Jon Snow had given him high marks for ensuring Salman Rushdie's safety. Michael responded, "I thought he [Rushdie] was going to get in touch with me before Christmas, but he hasn't." Jon Snow had told me that he believed Rushdie felt badly about the way he treated Michael and that is why Rushdie stayed away. But this was speculation, as Snow seemed to realise, adding that Rushdie ought to feel guilty. Michael never ceased making excuses about Rushdie's failure to call him. Michael still thought Rushdie's wife Elizabeth was the wronged party, "but that doesn't mean we [Michael and Salman] shouldn't have a sensible conversation."

100

From time to time I would try to press Michael about what Jill thought of his work. Did she have a favourite book? His Bevan biography? I suggested. He agreed, but characteristically he had virtually nothing to say that revealed in detail what she thought. Celine said Jill had been intimately involved in planning and sometimes even editing Michael's work. I never found any support for her contention in Michael's talk. Like many wives, she served mainly as his sounding board. Michael reminded me that Jill had complained that his essays about his heroes in *Debts of Honour* included no women and he later rectified that problem. She had also given him the title of one of his other essay collections, *Loyalists and Loners*.

The conversation trailed off into Michael's usual topics until I interrupted:

Here's my other question: Tell me about the "vampire lady" in Bristol.

[MF] Who?

[CR] Julie calls her the "vampire lady" in Bristol.

[MF] Ah, yes. Marie. Dr. Marie Roberts. She writes about vampires. She's a Gothic expert. Julie doesn't know anything about that. She's not a vampire. She's alive and kicking, I'm glad to say.

The next day Michael set off for a holiday in Jamaica and I returned to my home in Cape May County, New Jersey.

March 2002

101

When I arrived at Pilgrim's Lane, Michael told me over lunch in the kitchen that he had arranged for us to visit Tredegar. We would stay with Alan and Megan Fox, staunch supporters of Michael in his constituency and good friends to Jill. Damon was going to drive us. Perhaps because Michael knew I would not be making many more trips connected with Jill's biography, he had also arranged for Jill's Croat friend, Branka and her husband to come for a meal at Pilgrim's Lane, and he invited me to a *Tribune* dinner benefit.

"I wasn't sure you'd be here tonight," Molly said to Michael, trying to plan her day. "I will be now. Puts you back, doesn't it?" he teased her. I laughed. "No, no, honestly," Molly said. She laughed. "Well, there you are," Michael said. We were very fond of Molly. She cooked delicious meals, never intruded, and seemed to like the kidding. She was a consummate professional. "You'll have a rest now, Michael?" she inquired. "I will," he said, but he continued to talk.

A little later Molly came in for a consultation about what clothes to pack for the stay in Wales. This time she was worried that he would insist on his a worn-out track suit. Under her breath she said, "I shall be removing that in the middle of the night." "What? The which?" Michael asked. Molly now could not stop her laughter. She sounds now, as I listen to her, like a naughty girl. This time, she spoke up, and repeated her insubordinate statement. Michael had his mind on other subjects and didn't respond to her.

Michael was coughing quite a bit but insisted he was in perfect health, having just fought off a bad cold. "I get a bit overtired sometimes. Some nights I don't sleep as well as others, but otherwise ... I've been down to Plymouth a few times." These trips were for football matches. "We're coming to the end of the season and still doing well. It's a tremendous performance."

102

Molly came back into the kitchen, saying in a very worried voice, "I think Margaret Thatcher has died." She had heard part of a report on the radio. We turned on the tube and watched a jumble of commentators speculating on Mrs. Thatcher's future. She wasn't dead but incapacitated in some way. Michael could not make it out. "So what are they saying?" he asked. Molly and I gathered that Mrs. Thatcher had had some sort of stroke that made it difficult, if not impossible, for her to speak.

"Now, if it does happen," Michael mused. He cleared his throat: "I must be ... say something. She sent me quite a nice letter, you know, when Jill died. If Thatcher has passed on, what will I say?" I said that though she could not talk, the Tories were worried that she could still write. "They were very rude to her, the Tories," Michael said:

Almost all my dealings with her were pretty awful. If she conks out ... "

[CR] I guess you have to say something. You can't say,

"No comment."

[MF] They quoted me quite wrongly ... when I came back from Jamaica the other day. I went to this party for Francis Wheen's book [on Marx]. I went and sat on a chair—at these places I can't stand up and so I sat there and a woman came up to me—I gather from the *Telegraph*. It was just the day before Princess Margaret had died ... The woman said something like, "What do you think about [Princess Margaret's death] and I said, "I don't give a bugger about such things. I'm not giving any interview to you and she printed it. I should have been more careful. But there's some truth in that. The bloody Sunday *Times* reprinted it. But Jill was very shocked by Princess Margaret—when we went down to Windsor for a weekend when they had a do [when Callaghan's government fell]. Jack Jones was there and Princess Margaret came out and said, "Who is Jack Jones?" He was the most prominent labour union leader in the country. She didn't say, "Can you tell me who is Jack Jones?" Dreadful, you see. But I shouldn't have said that.

103

At dinner, Branka reminded Michael of how he and Jill in effect took on the British Foreign Office, which put out the line that the Serb attack on Bosnia was just part of a civil war. On the contrary, as Stevan Dedijer, a Serb resident of Dubrovnik argued, the Serb assault, was no different from the World War II fascist attacks on Yugoslavia. Branka, Quintin (her husband, Michael, and Jill formed part of a group that resisted others on the left who similarly contended there was no side to support in the Balkan split-up. Michael even went so far as to link the Major government with the World War II appeasers, calling them the "guilty men," the title of the famous pamphlet attacking Chamberlain and his ilk that Michael and other Beaverbrook journalists had published during the war. That Major & Co were not willing to intervene and stop the Serb advance was a disgrace, Michael avowed.

Molly came in and we went over the itinerary for the next week: our trip to Wales and a visit from Elizabeth West. She would be coming over for dinner. "I can hear better," Michael said, explaining why he liked to have people come to Pilgrim's Lane.

104

Over breakfast, we discussed the news. Nothing new about Thatcher. Michael began to reminisce about her years on the public stage:

Just at the beginning of the new troubles in Ireland ... Bobby Sands was on a hunger strike. Bobby Sands was a young IRA member ... threatening to kill himself ... Now he was also asking for so-called prisoner-of-war status ... Otherwise he was going to starve himself to death. So John Hume, very nice chap, member of Parliament for the town up in the North, a Catholic town ... came to see me just after his election and said, "Can't we do something to stop this—Bobby Sands killing himself. But if he does, it's going to set back the whole business of trying to get a settlement there. Can you look and see whether something can be done. I know we're not going to agree to prisoner-of-war status and I'm not in favour of that"—a brave chap John Hume, himself a Catholic, but he was quite prepared to take risks. "But there could be some alteration in his diet, or something else about the way he is treated, an alteration of circumstances that might stop him killing himself. Can you put that case to Mrs. Thatcher? I said, "Well I will put it to her as you put it to me and I'll see what we can do. I'll put it on behalf of the Labour Party as a sensible way out of the situation." And so I then asked to see her.

At what Michael called "an entirely private meeting," he was accompanied by Don Kincannon, Labour's spokesman on Irish affairs. Kincannon had been in and out of prisons, taking quite a lot of risks himself, Michael pointed out. "He was a great big towering chap who made a huge great target." Thatcher had with her William Whitelaw, her second-in-command, "a nice decent chap who had also been in the Irish office." Thatcher also had two civil servants by her side.

Thatcher listened to Michael's case. To him, she seemed more interested in impressing the civil servants than engaging him in dialogue. She said she did not expect that Michael would want to put the terrorist's case. His point was that Sands's death would only worsen the troubles; keeping him alive would at least offer some hope of reconciliation. Thatcher seemed to imply that Michael was afraid of the IRA. "Don't talk to me about being afraid of these matters, this chap Don Kincannon he walks into the Mays Prison at the risk of his life and so he's come along to put the same case," Michael said to her. "Then in her book on that period, she has a very brief reference—a footnote—in which she says she was very surprised that I came along and put the case for the terrorists. Just like that, you know."

105

We arrived at the home of the Foxes, Alan and Megan, in the afternoon. "So the book now is going to be devoted entirely to Jill?" Megan asked. "Yes," I assured her, "and he [I nodded toward Michael] only comes into it when it is relevant." Everyone had a good laugh. "I'm finding lots of things I didn't know about her," Michael said. I don't think I had ever heard him actually say that before. "There have been some surprises," I agreed.

Michael began talking about the smaller Welsh communities that were failing economically. "They say it is difficult to get water to them. But people are living there. Why the hell should they move?" he demanded.

Just like Nye Bevan, Alan came from a family with a father who went into the coal pits at fourteen. Alan was a fount of Welsh history and commentary on Michael's role in Tredegar. No longer a mining community, or a steel works, or even a tin plating enterprise, Tredegar now had to "re-invent itself," Alan said. "So when Michael and Jill came, there were still mines and steelworks ... " "Certainly," Michael broke in, citing the facts and figures.

We discussed what we would do the next day: see the miner's cottage that Jill had fixed up for their home in Tredegar and visit the Aneurin Bevan memorial—a handsome rise of land, now graded so that one can easily climb to the top and see the surrounding countryside from the same perspective Bevan had when he addressed his constituents on the eve of poll.

Alan and Michael diverted themselves for quite a while

discussing Donald Dewar, Michael's tenant at Pilgrim's Lane and a great figure in Welsh politics. Michael had spoken to me about Dewar many times. "Makes me laugh, Donald Dewar," Michael said, recalling how Dewar never seemed to spend money on anything. But it was Alan who made Dewar come alive: "He had a strange face—a sort of pinched ... like a miser's face. He was a caricature of himself sometimes but a very endearing man. He was crusty but really nice." Michael added: "A mystery man, you see."

In four days it would be Neil Kinnock's 60th birthday, said Alan, a great friend of the Kinnocks. Alan, I had noticed, often appeared in biographies about Kinnock. "You can give him some tips on dealing with older age," Alan told Michael. "I went to the launching of the book about Neil," Michael said. Had Alan read the new Kinnock biography? Michael wanted to know. "I read the bits I'm supposed to be responsible for," Alan replied. "Ah!," Michael pounced, "You mean you look it up in the index?" Michael's voice was rising the way it always did when he was having a bit of fun. "You looked yourself up in the index. You read the pages? That's a confession! Like a bloody politician!" Alan started to speak, but Michael overrode him, "That's quite a confession, don't you think? Ah!" Alan said he had skimmed parts of the book. "Ah!" Michael cried out. "Indeed!"

I was looking through the new biography as Alan and Michael jousted. "Maybe I can start an argument here," I interrupted, beginning to read aloud:

It has been suggested that Foot regarded Kinnock as the son he never had. There was, Alan Fox recalled, a special rapport between them, a father-son thing. Foot

rejects any such notion: "Balls! The only member of
the Kinnock household with whom I have the slightest
fatherly relationship is with Stephen."

"Yes," Michael said. As I read, both Alan and Michael were
hooting. I continued:

Kinnock totally confirms Michael's assertion. One of
his greatest attributes is that he can treat everyone,
including youngsters, as equals. Very few politicians have
that talent.

It was quite true. Earlier, Alan's 8 year-old grandson had come
into the room, and Michael had no trouble talking to him
about his interests. "What seems more likely," the biographer
observed, "is that Foot saw Kinnock as—like Bevan—an
authentic product of the South Wales working class." "That's
quite right," Michael agreed. Michael liked Kinnock's passion
for education. It was exciting.

I read another bit to see what the reaction would be:

Where Kinnock saw in Foot the representation of the
principles of the Bevanite left, Foot saw in Kinnock
something still more fundamental—namely, the
embodiment of the world which had given rise to Bevan
and his principles. Of the two it is difficult to avoid the
conclusion that it was the older man who was more
romantic as a cursory glance at their respective careers
will confirm. But Kinnock said spontaneously, "I happily
acknowledge a real love for Michael, for his gentleness,
his humour, his almost superhuman generosity of spirit

and of course his sheer good company. That I still cherish."

"That's half-way toward what I was saying," Alan said.

Then Alan quite abruptly remarked, "The sibling that you scorned." Michael replied very quickly: "I never scorned him," Alan amended: "Spurned him." "Spurned him? You say," Michael queried. "You don't want to say that. I never spurned him, ever." Alan was laughing throughout this exchange and Michael took the teasing well, but I thought there was a hint of resentment underneath. "And plenty courageous what he did," Michael said of Neil. I couldn't, for a minute, figure out what this was about. "On devolution, you see," Michael finally clued me in. Alan and Michael supported the idea of more independence for Wales while Kinnock opposed it. "It would have been much simpler from his [Kinnock's] point of view in relation to the party not to come out against it." Kinnock had to fight "a lot of people in the Welsh Labour establishment," Alan pointed out. "I never had any cross words with him about that at all," Michael emphasised. "I thought he was doing it absolutely out of the best of motives." But Michael did believe Neil had taken too strong a line against the Welsh nationalists and did not accord their position enough respect. "Neil got nothing out of it for himself and got a lot of hostility from people here."

Alan thought Neil's major failing was his verbosity: "If only he had a valve to control the volume of gas. But that was part of his character. You either like him or dislike him." Michael voiced no criticism on this score. Alan thought Neil still sometimes played the part of the "valley boy. Of course, Kinnock was nothing of the kind now, having become such an internationalist in his work for the European community. "What? Valley boy?" Michael asked. At local events Neil still worked the crowd. "There are times when he yearns to be of the proletariat. To be just another one of the boys. He can't be that anymore. He overworks it sometimes." Alan turned to Michael, "*You* never worked a crowd to that extent, did you?" "What?" I told Alan that this was a tactic Michael sometimes used when he didn't want to answer a question, or wasn't ready with a reply. "He does like to be loved," Alan added. "Like to be loved, yes," Michael muttered.

"Still in touch with Master Blair these days?" Alan asked. "What about him?" Michael said. "I am going to ... I was rather surprised to get an invitation to Callaghan's ninetieth birthday in Downing Street. Maybe they are trying to make up toward Callaghan, because they haven't been very polite to him. Soon after the victory [1997], the first one they invited to Downing Street was Thatcher. I think that was an insult to Callaghan. It was a compliment to Thatcher that was not deserved at all."

While Michael excused himself for a moment, I asked Alan and Megan for their impressions of the Foot/Craigie marriage. "Very tender," they agreed, and "boyish" and "girlish."

When Michael returned, Alan asked him if he wanted anything. "A whiskey," Michael replied. Actually, this was the second time he had worked the request into conversation. "I don't drink anymore," Alan said. "Whish," Michael said, using one of his favourite expressions. It seemed to express a faint air of astonishment. Actually, Alan did still drink wine. "You posh lot," Michael said. "I've given up wine now—not quite, but almost. I don't mind whiskey." "Would you want a whiskey?" Megan asked me. "I'm going to join him because he will be upset if I don't," I said, while everyone scoffed.

"Do you want some more whiskey, Michael?" Megan asked. "A touch," he replied. "I can see you looking at the bottom of your glass," she said. We laughed. "If I have another half, I promise you I will stagger upstairs." "Are you having one?" Michael asked me. "You see," I said to the Foxes, "he keeps track. I have to match him."

"Look how she [Megan] gets me drunk," Michael suddenly sallied. He loved this sort of mock outrage that was patently unfair to its targets. "I'm just going to finish this whiskey. You'll still have some tomorrow?" Michael asked. Megan assured him of a supply for the next two days. "Thanks to you all," Michael said. "What bed is he in?" Michael asked pointing at me. "Not the same as mine?" "That's what happens when you have a biographer," I told Michael. "Same bed." With our sleeping arrangements, sorted out Michael and I went off to our respective rooms.

106

The next morning the Foxes brought Michael up to date on developments in Tredegar. There was much talk of the town clock, the largest iron clock in the world and a focal point of the town square. The clock had four faces, so it was visible to anyone approaching the city on foot—as Nye Bevan often did when returning from walks in the countryside.

Michael recalled his many walks in Tredegar: One of the first resulted in a near disaster when Vanessa chased a flock of sheep. With visions of a dead flock, Michael contemplated the end of his political career. Fortunately, Vanessa tired of terrorising sheep. "We lost her once," Michael remembered.

"Wonderful countryside—north, south, east, and west, going out of Tredegar—where Nye used to walk. He was a great walker."

Of course Michael engaged in marathon reminiscences of Nye, telling me about what it was like for him in this part of the country during the Depression. In some cases, unemployment was so high, and the local government was so critical of the country's leadership, the Chamberlain government took over community administration. We walked where Nye walked, standing atop hills and looking over valleys. "The clock!" Michael had just caught a glimpse of Tredegar's trademark. "You can't say it's beautiful," Alan began. "Ah!" Michael protested. It had been put together in sections, with the iron pieces brought to the site by mule wagon. "No other clock like it!" Michael exclaimed.

Michael and Jill had made Tredegar home. Michael remembered his neighbours, the Tags. The husband, an injured miner, had a remarkable knowledge of music, Michael noted, almost better than anyone Michael had ever known. It was curious, though, how Michael repeatedly referred to them as Mr. and Mrs. Tag. The Tags visited Michael and Jill in London and went with them to a concert. Mr. Tag also became a rich source of political gossip.

There was much talk too of Michael's efforts to keep mine pits and steelworks from closing. "How did you and Jill keep in touch with constituents?" I asked Michael. "Did you go around to public meetings?" "Yes, we did. More public meetings in Wales generally than in England—at election times especially." Even more important were the trade union meetings of transport workers, miners and so on. We visited the site of Tredegar's workman's hall, which had previously included a theatre/lecture space seating nearly 800 people. Movies were shown there and a library was available.

Alan took us to "the stones"—the Aneurin Bevan memorial. Michael had brought Mrs. Gandhi to the site, knowing that she would be interested since Nye had been a figure of importance in India. In a drenching rain, she got out and paid her respects. A plaque noted that on this spot Nye spoke to his constituents, "and to the world"—words Jill had proposed as an addition to the original memorial message.

107

"So what made you decide to retire from the House of Commons?" I asked Michael. The question seemed to stun him. "You could have done it sooner, I assume, or you could have done it later." "Yes," he muttered. "I thought I was getting too old, chiefly." Did Jill agree? "Did she want you to do it sooner?" Michael thought she was "content, one way or the other. She didn't mind. That was 1992. I was 79." Quite a respectable age for retirement, I said.

As usual, he had no more to say about his own feelings. His talk shifted immediately to his successor. Michael was not a man to inquire into his own motives—or at least he seemed to take no pleasure in discussing such decisions. He did not even comment on what it felt like to leave an institution to which he had devoted so many of his working years. Although deeply attached to the House, he did not spare a moment for sentimentality.

Michael rarely put himself first, even when it came to work in his constituency. He named everyone who helped him establish events like the garden festival, a huge fundraiser. "You never showed any interest in flowers before,"

Jill had teased Michael. "The final closure of the steelworks is taking place now," Michael said, referring to his longstanding concerns about the government's sale of industries that should have remained nationalised. His most difficult period in Ebbw Vale had to do with public protests over the shutting down of steel plants. He did what he could, but this was a war of attrition that he could not hope to win.

Just then Alan came in with his dog, saying she was quite "sprightly" now that Michael had arrived. "Do you know the Robert Frost poem about the old dog?" I asked. "No, what's that?" Michael wanted to know. "The old dog barks backward without getting up/ I can remember when he was a pup." The title of the poem was "The Span of Life," I told him. "Say it again," Michael requested. "My old dog was learning new tricks all the bloody time," Michael claimed. "My Dizzy, you couldn't stop him learning new tricks. Don't believe all the stuff about old dogs." Alan intervened: "Well, they lose a kind of liveliness, don't they? They get a bit creaky." "Ah!" Michael shouted, "I won't have it!"

Michael was thinking about Tommy Evans, a good friend of Jill's. Tommy was a bit creaky himself, suffering from arthritis. But with Alan's consent, Michael proposed calling Tommy, visiting him briefly at home and then taking him out to lunch for a talk about Jill. This was the Michael Foot way: he felt he could not come to Tredegar without seeing Tommy, but it had to be in such a way that he could show Tommy some hospitality. No wonder Michael was so reluctant just to call people and ask them to see me. "I don't mean to fix it," Michael said, making clear to Alan he was not making any sort of demand, "If it's okay with you, Alan." Of course Alan was agreeable. Michael was the kind of man friends wanted to accommodate. When Alan left the room, Michael said with beautiful simplicity: "I'm very happy about this."

108

When Michael went upstairs for a nap, Alan and Megan discussed the role Jill played in Michael's political life. In later years, she made fewer appearances and Alan thought there was criticism of her in the local party. Megan pointed out there wasn't much of a role for Jill to play. Michael could come down for a fortnight and his time would be taken up dealing with constituents. Alan agreed. There weren't many political structures in place that accommodated women in a male dominated culture. This was just as true, for example, for Glennys Kinnock, whose political career took off only after her husband Neil was no longer leader of the Labour Party. Now she was deeply involved in the European Community.

Michael never mentioned such factors. To me, he always spoke of Jill as a great canvasser and all around political wife. Perhaps one of the strengths of his happy warrior personality was his blindness to how others viewed Jill. The idea that she did not quite fit in would have shocked him. Glennys Kinnock told me Jill was not always comfortable with constituents. She was a London woman who could not quite speak to them on their level. On the other hand, Jill loved political gossip and would often arrive with this question on her lips, "What's the view in Tredegar?" No doubt Jill sentimentalised the Welsh, but that did not mean she could ever feel quite at home in Wales.

Megan remembered getting that sad call from Michael, "'My Jill has died.' He sobbed." They knew she had been ailing, but Michael had always been so hopeful about her recovery.

"I wonder how Michael did when he first came here?" I put it to Alan and Megan. "He had some experience in Liverpool," Alan pointed out. He was thinking of how Michael had converted from Liberal to Labour when he fraternised with dock workers. "And he listened," Megan added. "He would listen when they came with their problems. He would talk with them, not at them." That showed a kind of discipline, I suggested, since Michael was such a big talker. "Aneurin was such a high flyer he was rarely in the constituency," Meaghan remembered. "He relied on his agent while he was up in London and around the world. But it didn't matter because we were so proud of him."

109

Alan was driving us to our meeting with Tommy Evans when Michael spoke up, "If I knock on Tommy's door and say I'm canvassing for Tony Blair, he'll throw me out." This was Michael's way of saying, of course, that Tommy was "old Labour" and not very keen on the changes Blair had wrought in the party. Sure enough, Tommy did not disappoint. "I believed in the nationalised industries," he declared and Blair was continuing Thatcher's dismantling of the welfare state.

We took Tommy to his favourite pub for lunch. "So what did you think of this fellow [I nodded to Michael] coming to your constituency?" "Oh great," Tommy said. "We used to watch Michael on the telly when he was on with [A.J.P. Taylor]." Michael catalogued the various names of men and women who had assisted his entry into his constituency. It did not hurt, of course, that he was doing Nye Bevan's biography and had the cooperation of Nye's agent, Archie Lush.

On the subject of Jill, Tommy took Michael's line. To Tommy, she fit into the Welsh setting perfectly. Tommy and his late wife often came to dinner at Jill and Michael's miner's cottage. "She was very attractive and could twist men around her little finger," Tommy said with considerable delight.

Tommy remembered coming back from a political meeting with Michael and stopping in at a pub. Michael sat on a stool next to a chap "with arms like that," said Tommy, indicating hefty biceps. "I'll have a whiskey," Michael told the man at the bar "and if you have any trouble with this chap [indicating the bruiser next to him] let me know and I'll chuck him out." We all laughed, including Michael. "Michael had made a friend for life," Tommy added. "So Michael always went to the bar first?" I asked. "Always," Tommy affirmed. "We had some wonderful trips then, Tommy," Michael said. It was a good example, without my asking for it, of how easily Michael got on with working class people. Seeing how he got on with taxi drivers, people in shops—anyone who approached him—I admired him as an everyday democrat. Whatever one might think of his political policies, his behaviour made his principles palpable.

Talk of political meetings in Wales led to memories of singing at "The Castle," a favourite drinking spot. "I didn't actually dare to sing, " Michael said. "I had more sense that that!" Tommy noted, "It was a nice change, though [the singing], when your brain is racked up with politics and speeches all the time." A fellow at a piano might call out to anyone who wanted to sing. Michael suddenly broke into song—well, it was more like a chant:

When I brought an apple,
She let me hold her hand,
When I brought bananas,
We kissed beneath the band,
When I brought an orange,
She let me hold her tight,
I'm going to bring a watermelon
To my girl tonight.

"I can see why you were so popular," I laughed. "Ah, well," he responded demurely. I liked his sharp emphasis on "tight." Tommy said, "People were so surprised to see a prominent politician coming into The Castle." Michael added: "Jill used to laugh at all these powerful miners going onto the stage and singing in beautiful tenor voices. They were a great lot."

Tommy had been touched when Jill consulted him about whether Michael should take a position in the cabinet: "She was asking me!" Michael said, "She wanted your permission." Tommy was concerned that Michael might be offered a job just to shut him up. But a really important job? Jill wondered. That would be different, Tommy assured her. "Well, that's all right then," she replied.

Tommy drove Michael everywhere and accompanied him to political meetings. He couldn't imagine Margaret Thatcher behaving that way, caring about the grass roots. Michael often talked about his other driver, Winnie, who was assigned to him when he joined the cabinet. She became, it was clear, part of the family. As with Tommy, Michael was still in touch with Winnie.

Indeed, Winnie confided in Michael. She did not like David Owen. "She thought he was terrible," Michael said.

"Several of the drivers refused to drive for him," Michael said. "Why?" I asked. "He was intolerable. He behaved very badly toward people. It's his natural habit. Very arrogant chap." He made an "absolute botch" of his work in Bosnia, Michael noted.

Tommy noticed a characteristic of Michael's that frustrated me as a biographer. "If you went to someone's house and then you came back and someone said, 'What was it like?' It was no good asking him."

Tommy's criticism of New Labour seemed to prompt Michael's outburst against the kind of accommodation New Labour had made with the Murdoch press. In the long run, such kowtowing would not avail. Indeed, the Murdoch press was already turning on Blair, Michael pointed out. Michael seemed still to bemoan the 1992 election, when he thought Kinnock would prevail against Thatcher. I sensed that in his heart Michael wished it had been the positive turn in the party's fortunes.

Michael was a keen supporter of Alastair Campbell, saying people did not give him enough credit. Campbell had done well by Kinnock, handling the press for him. "It's a bit unfair when some of these people talk as if Alastair Campbell has nothing to be said for him. He's a clever chap, although some of the things he has advised Blair to do are quite wrong. But he does it because he thinks it is what Blair would want. He's the servant of Blair."

110

Damon drove us back to Pilgrim's Lane. On the way, Michael commented on the sights, including one town that had two railway stations: Bodmin Place North and Bodmin Place

South:

> There was a story told that a chap won his fortune and decided he would pay a visit to Japan where he had been told wonderful things were happening ... So he came to the station here and said he wanted to book a ticket to Japan. "You can't do that here, I'm sorry. You must go down to Newport and see what they say." So the chap goes down to Newport about 20 or 30 miles lower and goes to the ticket office ... "You'll have to go to London for that," and so the chap goes to London and he books a return ticket to Japan. He had a nice holiday. Then he comes back to get the return ticket and goes into the station in Japan and says, "I'd like to book a ticket to Bodmin Place." The chap says, "Yes sir, Bodmin Place North or Bodmin Place South?"

Thus it was, Michael said, he learned the importance of those two railway stations.

111

Later in the day, after returning from the Imperial War Museum where I read a transcript of Jill's comments on her career, I gave Michael the highlights. I explained there was this three-year gap in Jill's life. What happened to her between the ages of 18 and 21? By changing her birthdate from 1911 to 1914, she was able to say she was 18 when she got her first job. But in fact she was 21. Jill had, in effect, erased three years from her life. "They're not there," I said.

"I still think she was born in 1914," Michael said.

"I've got the birth certificate, Michael."

He paused ... "I know, well ... " "1911," I repeated. "It's *there*. And it's on the death certificate too. Has to be." He paused ... "Well," but he had no more words. "So my guess is that those years between 18 and 21 were extremely rough years," I ventured. "Rough?" Michael asked. "Rough and tough," I said. "I think that too," he agreed. I continued: "It was very bad. It was almost as if she did not exist. She had no politics, no family, no home, no husband, no career. She really didn't have anything. Therefore it's a big blank. But she makes it less of a blank by changing her birthdate. So that takes care of that, see?" Michael had nothing to say. "There are no photographs of her before 1940 in her papers, nothing from her childhood. Nothing before the age of 30. There's nothing there. Completely wiped out," I noted: "So she gives birth to a new self; she reinvents herself. Not even her biographer can find those three years. Unable or unwilling to say how this news hit him, Michael resorted to asking me about more documentable facts—like when she met her first husband.

112

Elizabeth West, Salman Rushdie's estranged wife, arrived for dinner. She brought a gift of Scotch. Julie had told her not to buy anything too expensive because Michael only drank the cheap stuff. Elizabeth thought this meant Michael did not like single malts. But I told her I had bought him an 18-year-old Balvenie and we had polished off the bottle in less than a week. I didn't say that I had to sort of josh him into doing so. He had several Scotch single malts on his mantle, gifts that he never drank. I pointed to his hoard. I think I embarrassed Elizabeth because she said next time she would bring a much better whiskey.

I asked her if it was all right if I taped her. The machine was going already. She glanced at it uneasily. "It's your call," I said. "He's entirely trustworthy," Michael added. So we proceeded with the machine running. She seemed very tentative and I feared with Michael present she would not say much. But then, without him present, I was not certain she would talk at all. She alluded to Rushdie and asked me if I had spoken with him. "Not yet," I said. "He [Salman] thought of Jill and Michael as the parents he never had."

I mentioned that to become friends of Jill and Michael was to feel adopted. "We both felt very loved. I still do," Elizabeth said. "They really cared about us. Very concerned about how we lived. Were we okay? Jill particularly wanted to know that I was okay." This was all said with no mention of the fatwa, or the pressures Elizabeth felt then. "He loved the love," Elizabeth said, "but it was the combination of the political and the literary—an unbeatable combination."

Elizabeth was quite eager to talk about the impression Jill and Michael made. "The overriding memory I have of Michael and Jill is how much they loved each other. We used to come away from an evening saying, 'Jill and Michael are so lovely to be with. They're happy. They give each other company.'" Michael broke in to say, "The police were always upstairs." This was the first explicit mention of the fatwa years, which up to then, Elizabeth had skirted. "Two of them," Michael specified. "Some of them were quite literary themselves," Elizabeth said. "They liked Michael's library." "A little more interesting job than they had before," I suggested. "They spent a lot of time sitting around, reading," she concluded.

Michael was on his third Scotch and kept talking and then he suddenly said about me, "I'm very glad he's doing the book. Of course we'll censor it." We all laughed. "Now he tells me," I said. "Before he said I could do whatever I wanted." Elizabeth expressed mock shock. "No, he's got absolute freedom," Michael said. Then he started up the stairs, saying to Elizabeth, "We'll have another meeting soon. If there's anything you want to say to me about Salman." Elizabeth said, "I always feel better after I've seen Michael." "So, I'll see you again," Michael made another announced departure. "I've finished my whiskey." This time he did leave for bed.

Although I thought the wary Elizabeth would leave shortly after Michael retired for the evening, she gradually opened up after I told her more about my research. Elizabeth knew about Jill's true age, having heard about it from an Indian friend who also knew Jill and Michael and had had a glimpse at Jill's passport. Elizabeth thought Michael did know Jill's true age, but that he would was perfectly capable of backing her up even when the facts stated the contrary. The gallant Michael would do anything to protect Jill's version of her own life.

When I told Elizabeth that Ronnie Neame was amazed that Michael claimed not to have known about the Koestler rape until Jill blurted it out at a dinner party decades later, Elizabeth said that Jill was furious that Michael refused to break off relations with Koestler. The implication was that Michael knew all along. I had to wonder, because a footnote in David Cesarini's biography of Koestler mentions Jill's bruises, which Michael had asked her about after the rape. Jill had also told Mervyn Jones about them. But in Cesarini, Jill is supposed to have dissembled, not wishing to tell Michael the truth because it would prove an awkward secret for a public man to bear. Later Julie told me that Elizabeth was concerned that perhaps she had been indiscreet.

It seemed to me that Michael often entertained some sort of male bonding. He had overlooked Nye's passes at Jill; he did not confront Koestler; he told Elizabeth he wanted to continue seeing her estranged husband. Was it plausible, for example, that Jill would have told the story of the rape to a dinner party if Michael did not already know it? And what did it reveal about his feelings for Jill if he could not then resist leaking her story in a review of a book about Koestler?

Elizabeth told a Dizzy story that also exposed Michael's accomplished ability to ignore what he did not want to see. Elizabeth had set a fur-lined hat on the floor during one of her visits to Pilgrim's Lane. Later she saw Dizzy playing with what looked like a furry toy. About to leave, Elizabeth picked up her hat, now sopping from Dizzy's thorough chewing. Michael would pretend not to notice, or he would take mock umbrage at anyone's casting aspersions on his dog.

113

At breakfast the next morning I told Michael I was going for a walk on Hampstead Heath. He asked me, "Do you think when you walk? Compose sentences in your head?" I did, I told him. "A good thing to do, in my opinion," he said. "Nothing better for writing than walking." I told Michael that Elizabeth had stayed until eleven. He wanted to know what she said. I was fairly vague, though I mentioned she had talked about the Koestler rape. He did not press. He never pressed me about my interviews. I mentioned that Elizabeth had always found Jill youthful. "She never got old. She had her pains, but she never talked about them." Quite so.

Elizabeth and Celine had mentioned this point about Jill: she never wanted to discuss her illnesses or Michael's. Jill was part of a united front the two presented to the world.

Molly was getting Michael ready for his Plymouth excursion. His travels were always a trial for her because he dawdled and fretted. He often developed diarrhoea before a trip. She cut a pill he had to take into four parts so it would be easier to swallow. He was so anxious and nervous he could not swallow and I could see the panic spreading across his face. He looked like a big baby, really quite helpless, unable to do it for himself. Surprisingly, he never got crabby.

"Never again on election day," Molly said, referring to his last holiday in Dubrovnik. "You were going to Dubrovnik at quarter past five," Molly reminded him. "The taxi was coming with Jenny. Five o'clock you still weren't shaved because you had to see the results. Glued to that television. Not ready to go. A year later I'm a lot wiser. That was a panic, that was. I used to be blonde, when I started here, Carl." Michael seemed oblivious to this speech. He was looking for his jacket. "I thought I had seen the last of children when my lot went off to university," she said to me. She laughed. "Mugs under the bed. I forgave him everything."

114

That evening I talked to Jenny for five hours over dinner. I learned that she had promised Jill she would look after Michael. Jill died the next day. To the end, Michael found it hard to accept that his wife was dying. Indeed, during Jill's last months she had had two heart attacks and Michael had been reluctant to call for help. Summoning assistance, Jenny suggested, would be an admission of a dire situation. Jill was ready to die, worn out by her illness.

On what became Jill's last day, as Jenny was taking Michael home from visiting Jill in hospital, he said he felt uneasy. They returned to the Royal Free, entering Jill's room just as she died. Jenny watched the heart monitor recording Jill's ebbing moments. Jenny shook Michael: "Jill's going! Jill's going! Michael, speak to her." Michael continued speaking to Jill long after she had died. Two days after Jill's death, Michael burst into tears. Jenny thought he was having a sort of purge. He then turned to planning the memorial event.

Jenny also told me she disapproved of my describing Michael's infidelity in the biography. The press would sensationalise it. I understood that this would happen, but that did not mean I should not write the whole life. I did not press my case; clearly, she had drawn a line.

The next day Michael went off to Plymouth and I returned home. Although I would make two more trips to Pilgrim's Lane, it was time to start writing Jill's biography.

June 2002

115

I finally caught up with Anne Robinson and her husband John Penrose in New York City. She was in the heyday of hosting a game show, *The Weakest Link*. In the late 1970s she had befriended Julie while both were working at the *Daily Mirror*. Anne lived in Hampstead and soon she and John began seeing Jill and Michael socially. When Michael became party leader in 1981, Anne lamented his struggle with a hostile press. The criticism was difficult to bear because "here was a man way above the caliber of most politicians, but in a more aesthetic sense. He was a great orator, a great historian, a wonderful writer. It was like asking a prima ballerina to do another turn, one for which [s]he was totally unsuited."

As Michael would later say, Anne and John, as well as Denis Forman and Moni, unraveled the financial mess that threatened to engulf him after retiring from Parliament. "It took a year," Anne said, but "our financial people, to an extent, gave Michael an income." In effect, there was so much equity in the home that a plan was devised to take out funds on a regular basis for his living expenses and certain luxuries like his holidays.

Conversation turned to Jill's wonderful dinner parties. "She'd always make Michael do the coffee," Anne noted:

And you know no two bits of Michael coordinate. So we'd wait hours. But it was a sort of ritual ... [He] always walked over to the sink as if this was a completely new adventure ... and he'd been mumbling and bumbling, but he had to produce the coffee. So far as I know, it was the only domestic thing he did.

But when I asked both Anne and John about how Michael and Jill were together, both agreed the word was "charming." "How did she react when he called her 'my dear child'?" I asked. "She smiled," Anne said. When Jill returned from hospital after one of her last illnesses and said anything outrageous, Michael would respond, "Ssh, ssh, my child." John thought "they were remarkably tolerant of each other. He accepted her rather forceful personality." "I think it was very convenient for Michael that she could say all the things he couldn't," Anne observed. "Problems with cleaning ladies Michael could detach himself from," John noted.

Several times during our conversation Anne mentioned that Jill and Michael saw no contradictions between being socialists and having house help or the modern equivalent of a staff and servants. I suddenly remembered a meeting at the Ivy I had had with a movie producer, who said she thought Michael would not approve of such sumptuous meals. I told her I wasn't so sure. When I told Michael about her comment, he remembered that Nye always said there was nothing wrong with being a millionaire for a minute. "They did enjoy the very best. She spent a lot on clothes, and why not?" Anne said.

Anne asked me about Jill's family. I mentioned her Russian mother. "So she was Jewish," Anne said quickly. Yes, I agreed.

Julie had said so and yet Michael said she wasn't. "It might be rude to say so, but I think she had Jewish mother traits," Anne said. I could never engage Michael on this topic.

Anne remembered Michael's vigour. Walking for two hours on Hampstead Heath with Dizzy and getting up at six in Venice and going for a long walk. She had more to say and offered to send me various notes she had made on her relationship with Jill and Michael, but just then she was called away to another appointment. In fact, this would be our only opportunity to talk or correspond.

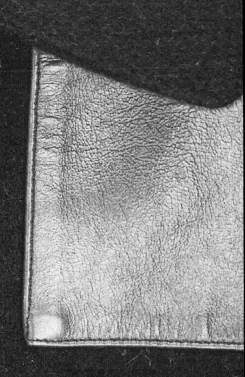

The trouble with Michael—ever since I've known him 48? 49?—He hasn't changed his views one iota ...

September 2002

116

One of the highlights of this trip to London was my interview with Milton Shulman. He could not remember where he first met Michael Foot. Perhaps it was at one of Beaverbrook's luncheons or dinners. Both Shulman and Foot were in the press lord's "best books." Shulman had not seen Michael in a decade. They had last spoken when Michael called him about a program Shulman had done on the radio. At that point, they had not been in each other's company for perhaps six or seven years. Michael called to say how wonderful the program had been. "We must meet again," Michael said. But nothing came of the contact.

"I think that was Jill's impact," Shulman suggested. "Jill always had great grudges against anybody who deserted the socialist field." "Against you?" I asked. "Yes, yes," Shulman was certain that she considered him a traitor since he no longer embraced Labour politics. Paul Johnson was another example of a former ally who had been repudiated. Michael had been so amiable in their last phone conversation that Shulman felt sure Michael did not share Jill's resentment.

"In the early days, we used to see each other all the time," Shulman said.

"The trouble with Michael—ever since I've known him 48? 49?—He hasn't changed his views one iota. How anyone could keep the same ideas through the years of turmoil while everyone has changed their position from left to right and from right to left or to centre ... Michael still says exactly what he said when I first met him." I mentioned to Shulman I had just been reading Woodrow Wyatt's journals, including a scene in which Wyatt encountered Michael for the first time in several years. Michael had been very cordial, and they exchanged pleasantries. But Wyatt wrote: "How could a man as brilliant as Michael Foot be wrong about every issue?" Wyatt was another apostate in Jill's book, Shulman said, because he had abandoned leftist politics. "Jill was outspoken in the background. I felt she was pulling the cords."

Did Jill feel any frustration having to bear the burden of Michael's politics? I asked Shulman. "My wife remembers Jill calling herself a failed feminist. Which seemed to trouble her for most of her later life. She had failed feminism." Michael, on the other hand, seemed to live in a dream world. "It used to be said," Shulman added, "that Michael used to feel that halos came out of the arses of Ebbw Vale miners. Not only could they do no wrong, but morally they were always right. In spite of the winter of discontent, the rows with trade unionists, Scargill ... He still maintained that underneath it all these were heavenly gifted people." Michael held curious anti-English attitudes, as if what the Welsh did was good precisely because they were not English. Certainly, I heard on many occasions his proud boast that Jill did not have a drop of English blood in her. He revelled in her half-Russian, half Scottish heritage.

Shulman asked me if I had spoken with Paul Foot. Shulman remembered many years earlier when Michael had been introduced the 18-year-old Paul, saying, "'He's going to run rings about the Tories. He's going to be a very important figure. ' They always thought he was going to be leader of the party. But he's way out on the left and never changed his mind." "From Paul's point of view, Michael is a Conservative," I told Shulman. "Paul always thought Britain was bound to be a socialist country. Where did he get the evidence from?" After attending socialist conferences, Shulman concluded, "These people will never run the country. It was an illusion." But in his early days (1952), he told Beaverbrook he could not work as an editor for him because he did not want to compromise his socialist principles. Shulman recalled Beaverbrook saying that Michael and his party would never get anywhere, "which is perhaps why Michael's politics never troubled Beaverbrook." Stripped of collectivist pretences, what were the Labour Party leaders? Shulman asked. They wanted power. They were individualists who enjoyed their meals and comforts while expressing solidarity with the workers. Why couldn't Michael see that labour union leaders like Scargill were simply thugs?

Suddenly Shulman said, "Michael used to make great passes at Drusilla, my wife, you know. Whenever they got into a lift, Michael would wait until others got off and then he made his move. He was a great womaniser. Jill was aware of it too. Any woman she thought was going to be a rival was pretty well cold-shouldered out of the way."

117

Alan Brien enjoyed contrasting Jill with Michael:

> She was a very talkative woman. If you sat her down,
> she'd answer a lot of questions you hadn't asked and give

you a lot of information you did not have or would have thought it wiser not to bring up. For instance, we went on holiday with Michael and Jill. ... She would say, "I was extraordinary. I didn't have my first period until I was 18."

Michael was too kind-hearted. Brien told him:

People know there won't be a revolution with you in charge because you won't chop off their heads. The reign of terror will be a reign of reproach.

Brien also said, "I don't see Michael as a particularly observant man." Brien illustrated Michael's obliviousness to appearances and what certain occasions demanded by recalling the last night of their month-long Dordogne trip:

God, we had some rows. I said, "Look, it's the last night, and I think we ought to put on a bit of dog." Have the best bottle we can afford and all that. He said, "Well, what do you mean? You mean with the clothes I'm wearing?" I said, "Well, you know you're wearing that old herring mat of a jacket as long as I can remember. You could get rid of that." He said, "Well, I don't know. I'm so used to that. Nobody else has ever objected to it." So we came down that evening. I was wearing a rather snazzy sports jacket, Daks trousers. I looked really good. Then Jill Craigie looked across and said, "You haven't mentioned it."

I said, "What?"

She said, "You promised that you would get Michael to dress up."

I said, "Oh, I gave up."

She said, "What do you mean? He's dressed for you tonight. He's wearing a tie!" There he was. He had the same jacket and a knitted tie.

I said, "No doubt in Ebbw Vale I suppose you all wear dinner jackets, do you?" He thought that was terribly funny. He laughed for about five minutes.

Brien was one of those interviewees who actually told me what he thought of me. Giving me the address of Philip Oakes (someone else he thought I should interview), Brien said, "You'll like him. You share his skeptical sense of humour."

118

Leo Abse asked me if Michael had suggested I speak with him. I told Abse that his name had come up on a list I had discussed with Michael and Michael said that by all means I should talk to Leo. Abse laughed. "He took a chance, didn't he? There are some people, you know, Carl, you love so much that you don't analyse them. But given my psychoanalytical orientation, I have no hesitation dissecting them." I assured him I was coming for the analysis. "I've no desire to break down too much people one is fond of. However ... " I interrupted: "You have to realise that although Michael is cooperating, this is a real biography. In other words, this is not a saint's life. I'm dealing with their marriage, their sexuality, the politics, everything."

Almost as though he were building on what Brien told me, Abse began by assessing Jill in relation to Michael. Although Michael was Nye Bevan's illustrious biographer, Jill's essay in a book devoted to Bevan, edited by Geoffrey Goodman, was, as Abse told Jill, by far the best piece in the collection. She had a sensibility, an empathy, that made her "see more of the game than any of the more obvious and perhaps more structured people." Jill captured the man in ways the policy-driven Barbara Castle could not perceive, Leo observed:

> I could see trouble brewing when Michael spoke at the launch of [Goodman's Bevan] book. Michael like all of us who are growing old is becoming prolix. He gave, I thought, undue praise to Barbara Castle and I could see this could cause a conflagration without paying the respect that was due to *her* [Jill]. A conflagration did take place.

Abse wasn't surprised, given Michael's history with Barbara —who was, in Abse's view, "the most intelligent hysteric in politics I've ever known." Jill was not a "strident, bellicose, childless woman like Barbara Castle." Patricia Hollis, Jennie Lee's biographer, would later put it more politely, but in effect she ratified Abse's view that Castle essentially behaved like an aggressive male. She had even married a man who performed a wife's role.

Jill was one of those rare women who took maternal caring and concerns into political thinking. "There was something for a man unusually attractive to come into contact with a woman who had commitment but lacked the stridency and aggressiveness that so often characterises women in politics. There was a singularly winsome quality about her." After more than a hundred hours of speaking with Michael, who never seemed capable of stepping back an inch from his marriage and assessing it, Abse's words were striking.

Abse's Welsh constituency was very close to Michael's and Abse's wife, Marjorie and Jill got on very well. Indeed, both women had a tendency to "conflate fact and fiction as only the Welsh can. So … Jill could tell the tale—it had a kernel of truth—but it didn't necessarily happen." Abse found this tendency charming. Drama was a necessary ingredient of life; in Wales nothing was prosaic. People like Jill heightened the mundane. This was a creative side of Jill that Michael never spoke of.

"Jill would tell stories," Abse smiled, then laughed, "which may or may not have been true about certain politicians and their wives but which revealed the yearnings of those people." Later Glennys Kinnock would tell me that Jill served Michael as a kind of antenna, collecting political intelligence from the atmosphere, so to speak. As opposed to Mervyn, who said everyone always spoke of Jill Foot, Leo said he always thought of her as Jill Craigie, "because she had her separateness."

At the same time, Abse observed:

Jill's Romanticism corroborated Michael's Romanticism. She did not put any brake on his romantic attitudes. She was a woman of the film world. and therefore you'd expect the fantasy element I'm talking about. Though I love Michael and I think he is very fond of me, we had the most severe public quarrels—from devolution, where we fought each other to death on the floor of the House, the Falklands where I disagreed with him publicly, to the issue of Ireland. There were many occasions when we marched together and many occasions when we worked together politically … For example, when it came to the leadership battle, you will no doubt get great criticism that she stirred him up and he had no ambitions ... That's not quite right. I think ... she realised correctly that people like Benn and Peter Shore—they weren't worthy. They weren't fit to clean Michael's shoes. She knew the value of her husband. ... Why should Michael play second fiddle to second-class men? You could hardly call Healey second-class, but there was no reason for her to feel that she didn't have someone of greater quality than other contenders ... But he yielded too much ground. He can be too generous to people. It affects his judgment. Bad judgments. It is wrong to think she was a power hungry woman and wanted to be a prime minister's wife. She had different values. She wasn't Tony Blair.

Abse told me about his son, Toby, a historian who had objected to *Two Hours From London*, which in Toby's view idealised the Croats and demonised the Serbs. Jill and Michael lacked all caution when dealing with Balkan politics. They had to take sides. How could they endorse Franjo Tudjman, a notorious anti-Semite? A controversy erupted over how to view the war and Jill's beloved Dubrovnik. Jill and Michael thought "they were living out the Spanish Civil War again," Leo concluded. "They retained a certain adolescent quality ... In a world of cynicism, adolescent idealism may not be such a bad thing."

I knew Leo was Jewish and suddenly asked him if he knew that Jill's mother was a Russian Jew. He was stunned, speechless. He had no idea. Then he said, "Perhaps that is why we got along so well." Then another story occurred to him. He noted that Michael's cheerful tolerance of Leo's dissenting views dissolved only once—on the issue of devolution. The House hushed after a Foot outburst against Abse. Michael mentioned that Abse was a Jew and therefore didn't have the identification with Wales—an astounding comment, Abse observed:

> Considering how tenuous his own connection was ... I have no patience for his romantic attitude toward Wales. I was born there. My parents were born there. But he said it in terms which if anybody else had said it, you'd say it was the most anti-Semitic slur and the House blew up. I let the others go for him. To accuse Michael of anti-Semitism is not only ridiculous ... but he should never have said it. I got up and said I had children who were Celtic Semites. ... The press were all over me after the end of the debate and I very deliberately cooled it. I wasn't having it. I only mention it because of this Jewish factor.

I asked Abse about his analysis of Michael after the 1963 car crash. Abse had written that Michael had returned to Parliament as a more aggressive and effective politician. "Of course he may have been working out his aggression against Jill," Abse speculated. "I've always wondered about that," I said to Abse. "The accident was clearly her fault." Abse said, "My firm defended her." (Julie had told me that if Michael had died there was the possibility that Jill might have been prosecuted). "One can only plead mitigation," he noted. To Abse, it was hard to believe that Michael did not feel "some aggression which he creatively displaced."

This episode led Abse to recount the one time when Michael really let me down. It was to do with the issue of pay [wage and salary restraints]. The government were putting a clamp on pay and the judges wouldn't accept voluntary reduction in their pay. I regarded it as outrageous. You should ask the worker to sacrifice but not the highly paid judges. I discussed it with Michael and I said I'm going to speak against it. He came after me when I started this attack. ... Then he got up and he was drunk. It was the only time. Now why at that period he must have been drinking I don't know. I know I was furious because the Jewish hostility to drink is puritanical. He was very ashamed. After that, he was very careful.

As our interview was drawing near its end, Abse, very much like Alan Brien, seemed to want to take Michael's measure:

> He used to be surrounded by his acolytes. They were nice fellows. He had a group around him, a salon and they didn't stretch him. When he came to me, he stretched me. ... He used to go out to the Gay Hussar— that dreadful place with terrible food. I wasn't in the group. Nice fellows but naïve! I don't think it was good for him to be surrounded by people who were his intellectual inferiors. They were wary of me, but I didn't want to get in with them.

119

I breakfasted with Michael the morning after he returned from another September in Dubrovnik. "Leo Abse says you are too much of a romantic," I said. "Ah, I know," Michael said, even as I was speaking. He didn't respond to the criticism, but rather praised Leo for his courageous stand against devolution. "We were doing it [advocating devolution] to hold the party and the country together. Both Leo and Neil thought we were being affected too much by the nationalists. And they [Leo and Neil] put their views very strongly with no benefit to themselves. They were doing it because that was what they believed."

"Leo's psychoanalytical interests make him one of the most unusual commentators on British politics I've ever read," I told Michael. "Most unusual, I quite agree," Michael said. "He's really big on phallic symbols," I added. "Yes he is," Michael said, "he's still faithful to his Freudianism." In effect, Michael was saying, "That's Leo. He's sincere." But any real engagement with Leo's ideas was not on—Michael implied he preferred his psychology in the form of Stendhal's and Heine's writings.

But I returned to the topic: "What do you think of his idea that after the car crash you became a much more effective member of the House of Commons?" He paused:

[MF] Well ...

[CR] He thinks that somehow that car accident liberated you.

[MF] What?

[CR] It made you more vigorous, more aggressive.

[MF] Now, I'd only just got back there, you see. He's mixing that up with my being a member for Ebbw Vale rather than Devonport. Well, of course there's a big difference. I don't think the car accident made any difference one way or the other.

[CR[Are you saying that in the Ebbw Vale constituency it was easier for you to express your political views?

[MF] That's part of it.

[CR] It [Devonport] was more conservative?

[MF] Now Jill certainly thought that—more than me really.

It was a neat deflection of my questions, since he clearly did not want and would not brook any attachment of his name to a direct criticism of his Devonport constituency in my biography of Jill.

I brought up Leo's Barbara Castle story—that Jill wasn't pleased when Michael praised Barbara's Nye Bevan essay. "Wasn't pleased?" Michael responded. I laughed. "I don't think. I can't recall that at all. I don't think Jill objected to what I said about Barbara at all."

Michael spent much of the morning on Ken Morgan, who I was going to interview. Morgan was a Labour historian and biographer, a pupil of Alan Taylor and a social acquaintance of Michael. "He did the book on Callaghan. It's far and away the best book, better than Callaghan's book." Michael regarded Morgan as Taylor's rightful successor. "He was always nice to us, you know," Michael concluded. Indeed, Morgan was a court historian, never more so than when his official biography of Michael tried to rehabilitate Michael's disastrous period as party leader. Until I met Morgan, however, I had no idea that he was already preparing to write this book. Had he contacted Michael already? Michael did not say so then. But Morgan would play (in Michael's mind) a central role when Michael extricated himself from me and from his assurances that I could write his biography. I had read Morgan's biography of Callaghan and knew that he would never probe the person as deeply as I thought biography required. Morgan wrote what I would call "policy biographies." So I said to Michael:

You know the last time I was here I spoke with Tony
Benn. I told him I was dealing with all aspects of Jill's
life and I was describing to him the kind of biography I
was writing. He said he really wasn't in favour of saying
that much about the private lives of public figures, that
he didn't like gossip in biography. I told him I thought it
all had its place—the whole story. People really wanted
to know what that person was like and Jill in her own
book had said she wished she knew more about the
personalities of some of the women she was writing
about. He said, "No, I don't believe you need to know
all that much" and he was quite adamant. So then I was
reading these obituaries of Barbara Castle and he wrote
one … He mentions you and at the end of the obituary
he just throws in a sentence about how you and Barbara
were lovers. I was stunned. I was astonished because it
seemed gratuitous. I couldn't see why he had put that
in after he had given me this lecture. How can you just
throw it into an obituary?

"First time I've heard of it, actually," Michael said. "I'll send
you a copy," I said. Benn had coupled a comment about how
Michael had not supported Barbara on a particular issue with
the fact that they had been lovers. Michael simply would not
engage in a discussion of Benn on this point.

"Milton Shulman sent his regards," I said, figuring I
might as well change the topic, since I knew Michael could
easily spend the whole morning on well-worn topics. "He
said you called him up when he did Desert Island Disks." "It
was my fault really," Michael responded. "We were going to
meet and I felt shameful not doing it. Nothing against him at

all. He had a wonderful, beautiful wife." I concurred and said that Alan Brien talked about what a beautiful woman Drusilla was. "Alan Brien was quite impressed," I continued. "I was impressed too," Michael wanted it known. "Well, Milton Shulman told me," I said, finding my opening, "that you made at least one pass at his wife." Michael responded:

Well, I see.

[CR] This is the question I neglected to ask you. I asked you what other women you were involved with, but I didn't think to ask you how many passes you made.

[MF] Hmm. Passes. I don't know what you mean.

[CR] Milton said that Drusilla said that you used to wait until everybody was out of the lift and you made a pass at her, which I think Milton thought was perfectly alright because he knew he had a beautiful wife. He wasn't upset at all.

[MF] I see. Passes, I don't know what the definition of that is. [I was laughing during most of this prevarication]

[CR] I guess Drusilla had a definition.

[MF] I think I was best man at his wedding.

He showed no embarrassment over making passes. But then how could he, since he didn't know what a pass was?

I brought up a comment in Edward Pearce's biography of Denis Healey, suggesting Jill had not been the right wife for Michael. Michael needed, Pearce supposed, a wife more like Edna Healey. I told Michael I had called up Denis Healey and asked him about Pearce's comment. Healey laughed and said, "I don't think Edna is Michael's type." Michael listened but did not comment—or rather he performed a typical Michael manoeuvre, shifting the topic to how supportive Healey had been of Michael's leadership, even though they had been rivals and members of different wings of the party. Pearce was a "terrible fellow," Michael did say.

120

I had been wanting to interview Denis Forman for quite some time and did so at his London flat with his wife Moni at his side. I asked him if he was surprised to learn that Jill had married Michael. Indeed he was: "My God, here was this sparkling nightclub girl and she was marrying a member of Parliament!" True enough, although Moni rightly said of Michael, "He was always very posh." Denis associated Jill with the world of film and theatre, but not with the political/literary world that Michael inhabited. This was a thrilling new stage for her, Moni emphasised, because now Jill got to meet power brokers like Lord Beaverbrook and the literati. Michael always emphasised the opposite: how much Jill brought to the marriage, especially her love of art and her exquisite homemaking and design skills. Very few of Jill's former friends carried over into the Michael period. Anthony Quayle, certainly and Ronnie Neame, continued to be important in her life, but the focus definitely shifted to Michael's world.

Now that Jill was gone, I suggested, my biography was Michael's gift to Jill—perhaps meant to make up for all the gifts he didn't give." "Actually, you've put your finger on it," Moni replied, "it's the most important thing for him now."

121

Beginning in the late 1960s, the biographer Ken Morgan visited Pilgrim's Lane on several occasions, and Michael and Jill had stayed a few weekends at the Morgan home. For one visit Michael turned up "absolutely resplendent in a dinner jacket." Morgan remembered a loving, affectionate couple and that Jill seemed to take great pride in Michael's Cabinet work. "She served him breakfast. She was never remotely naggy." Morgan remembered Michael calling Jill "my dear child"—"very curious, that," Morgan said. "He would correct her in public."

122

After my talk with Morgan, I brought the news back to Pilgrim's Lane:

> **[CR]** I should tell you, Michael, that there may be a glut of books on Michael Foot.
>
> **[MF]** Uh. What?
>
> **[CR]** Is Francis Wheen still going to do his book?
>
> **[MF]** Well, I'm not sure about that. It's not fixed at all.
>
> **[CR]** Well, Ken Morgan asked me if anyone was thinking of doing your biography.
>
> **[MF]** Yes, I see.
>
> **[CR]** Because he's thinking about doing it.
>
> **[MF]** I see.
>
> **[CR]** So you may have a lot of contenders here.
>
> **[MF]** Well [he started to chuckle].
>
> **[CR]** You may have to set up some kind of competitive match.
>
> **[MF]** No, not really.

[CR] Anyway, I told him that Francis Wheen had expressed an interest. I told him that I had expressed an interest.

123

We spent a good part of the day and dinnertime as well discussing an article in the *Guardian* comparing contemporary America to imperial Rome. I compared 9/11 to Pearl Harbour. Americans were profoundly shocked that their own country could be so hated as to be attacked in such vicious ways. "After Pearl Harbour, Roosevelt was our hero," Michael said. "A damn sight better leader than we had over here. I'm not saying anything against Churchill, because he was coming round. But put in liberal terms he [Roosevelt] was the chap who was really doing it. He was great."

[CR] Roosevelt didn't care about the British Empire. He wasn't impressed at all.
[MF] That's right. He was damn good. We would not be sitting here if it had not been for him.
[CR] I agree. He's a great man.
[MF] My friend, Connie Ernst and her father were devoted Roosevelt supporters. Most of the war I was with them. The Americans who came were very important to us. Truly great.

When Michael first visited the U.S. in 1934, just after Roosevelt's election, he realised that FDR was also one of the most hated men in America. Michael also happened to be in the U.S. on the day Roosevelt died. "I was in New York. I was staggered, listening to taxi drivers." They told him about what right-wing Republicans were still saying about Roosevelt, describing him as a "traitor." Michael also observed that the ridicule reserved for Eleanor Roosevelt was "still going on." Two days after Roosevelt's death, Michael read an attack on her (called 'The Widow') in a "wretched paper. Terrible, unbelievable venom. Sheer class hatred, I suppose."

I mentioned the sea of change that Harry Truman's administration effected, cutting off further loans to Britain. Michael had voted against the Labour government agreement with the Truman administration, which seemed to him so draconian that it ought to be rejected. But it was the best Lord Keynes could obtain and as Michael noticed years later when Keynes's letters were published, Keynes himself sympathised with those like Michael who believed their country was treated shabbily. Michael's overall view of Truman did seem negative.

124

At breakfast, Michael told me about "a rather anguished letter," he had recently received. He had written an obituary of Barbara Castle in which he referred to an affair she had with William Mellor, *Tribune*'s first editor. "My first job was also with him and so that's when we'd known each other." Michael described the Castle/Mellor liaison as lasting a decade, until he died in 1943. One of Mellor's sons had written to Michael to say, "We're rather surprised because we thought the affair was less lengthy." Apparently the son saw Michael's view of it as an insult to his mother. To me, Michael's comment only illustrated how impossible it is to write any sort of honest biography without offending someone. Michael's response was merely to reply to the chap that they must meet sometime and talk about it.

We then had one of our periodic discussions about the nature of biography. I had been reading Montaigne. I told him how struck I was by this passage: "I have a singular curiosity to pry into the souls and the natural and true opinions of the authors with whom I converse." Montaigne, I added, would much rather learn about what Brutus said in his tent the night before a battle than about the speech the hero delivered the next day for public consumption. Montaigne enjoyed reading about the private lives, the failings, the little quirks of great men. This relish for intimacy appealed to me, I said, because "contemporary critics of biography are so often suggesting that when you write about what seem to be trivial or minor incidents there is no point to that, when in fact they often do reveal personality. Montaigne understood that much better than critics do today." "Yes, you bet," Michael agreed, "You'd have to knock out a lot of Montaigne if he couldn't do that. Perfectly true, Carl. People say you mustn't put any of this stuff [the "minute particulars" Johnson insisted on]. You must use your own judgment."

I then told Michael the Alan Brien story about dressing up for dinner. Michael seemed mildly amused, but he did not dispute Brien's account. Somehow this got us on to the subject of domestic matters. Michael claimed that he used to wash up after Jill's meals. "I've seen a photograph of you with a plate in your hands," I said, dryly. "That was in our Beaverbrook cottage," Michael pointed out, "I used to do the washing up there." "That wasn't just for the photographer?" I asked. "No. But one of the great liberations of America," Michael continued, was the dishwasher. On their 1952 trip to the U.S. Jill had seen a dishwasher and when she returned home she promptly purchased one of her own. Angela brought in some raspberries and cream. "Too much," Michael said.

125

We were coming to the end of what Michael could tell me. I returned home to make calls to a few more sources. I sent Michael chapters on Jill's early life, to which he responded favourably. The trouble did not begin until my final stay at Pilgrim's Lane.

April 2003

126

"Now, I'll go and ring Jennie to see, maybe, if she could do tomorrow. There are some things I'd like to ... " Sure, I agreed. Michael now had seen the entire first draft of my biography. He was upset, although he hardly showed it:

The early parts of it [Jill's book] I read very carefully ... and ... you know ... in a kind of way I was more in favour of it than anybody else. I don't like the idea that I really partly held her up. I think what held her up at the end was the conclusion. She'd got up to 1911 or whatever it was [actually 1906-1907] ... where she stopped was the whole great climax of the ... and so I think that the thought of her having to write the whole of that was a kind of inhibition. She had a kind of block on it.

My biography contained several explanations of why Jill could not finish her book: she was intimidated by new scholarship that drove her constantly to revise what she had already written; she was concerned about the growing ranks of feminist scholars and other historians who would review her work; she was a one-book author who treated the suffragist history as her baby; she was as committed to Michael and her marriage, to her home and family, as she was to her book. Then there was her involvement in making *Two Hours From London*.

The one obstacle Michael could not accept was himself.

Jill complained about him to Julie, to Celine, to Moni, to Anne Foot and to many other friends, family and acquaintances. She wanted him out of the house because he kept interrupting her writing. He believed in her project, no doubt, but he never was able to grasp what even those who were fond of him could see: he was selfish, perhaps unconsciously so, as he was bred by a mother who always put her boys first. Like Carlyle, Michael (albeit in a less peremptory manner) expected his wife's constant attendance. Of course, Jill used Michael as an excuse and it can always be said that writers tend to blame their blockages on others, rather than face their own inability to get on with their projects. I did not make Michael the main source of Jill's problem, but rather portrayed him as part of a complex of factors that inhibited her. Also, I presented Jill's point of view as filtered through Julie and others and my insistence on that approach enraged him, although at this juncture he still managed to control his temper.Michael sputtered as he summoned his defence. I listened for a long while. The thought occurred to me later that he never seriously considered what kind of conditions might have spurred Jill on. Writing came easily to Michael. What Jill needed was for Michael to say, "Look here, you have two chapters left. Why don't you go off to wherever you like and get them done?" Jill might well have objected that she could not cart her archive somewhere else. "Well, then," he could have said, "I propose to go off for a month to Jamaica to visit my nephew Oliver." But he did not like to leave home. When Jill told him, during the 'Lamia' affair, that he should leave Pilgrim's Lane, Michael's first thought was for his books. How could he live without them? Jill had reported as much in a letter to Julie. Michael wanted all the comforts of home and as many people close to him noted, it was Jill who made the sacrifices. That was Jill's choice, to be sure, but Michael could nonetheless have taken responsibility for getting Jill out of her rut by breaking the pattern of a domestic life that suited him but got in the way of her book. Jill still might not have taken Michael up on such a proposal, but it interested me that he never made the offer. It never occurred to him to do so. I know as much because this is a subject we spoke about many, many times. It shocked Michael that I could not simply present his point of view. All other perspectives, especially Julie's, were not only wrong, they had no place in the biography.

When I first met Jill in 1994, she told me she had only two chapters left to write. She said she was stuck. "So how do we go about unsticking you?" Michael could have asked. That was the crucial year. Michael had been retired for two years. Surely it was Jill's turn? I never put this case so baldly in Jill's biography and in the first draft I was not as clear as I should have been concerning Michael's general encouragement of her book project. That aspect I would amend, but my amendment would not be enough to appease Michael. He believed I had betrayed him.

Michael now was going round and round repeating his apologia, "I never had a quarrel with Jill about money, you know," he said, touching on another sore point. "Your story there that she's very hard pressed for money. All that comes from Julie, I'm afraid. But I know a damn sight more about the money she had than Julie." "Well," I began to reply, but he overrode me: "We never had a quarrel about money." My biography never said they did, as Jill did avoid the subject with Michael. "I don't mean to say that she never felt hard up in any way and of course she did sell the two pictures—maybe more—the Henry Moore and the Renoir she had from Malcolm MacDonald, and another ... " But this had been Julie's point: Jill would rather sell her own things than ask Michael for money. He never seemed to consider why that was so, why a wife would not discuss such matters with her husband.

Michael pointed to all the money he had put into the house that had been Jill's to design. He paid for their holidays. "There are several references you make to the money, and I don't like that at all. I don't think it's correct. I think you've got them from Julie." "Well, actually, they are from Jill's letters to Julie," I said, a point I made clear in the notes and the text. "Well, of course the ones in the letters are right for you to quote," Michael demurred. But what Jill said in the letters corroborated what Julie said to me in interviews. "Even if you quote the letters, it's not a fair picture of what happened to this house," Michael then added. But I was keenly interested in how Jill felt about money. He recoiled from the portrait I had drawn from Jill's letters and interviews with Julie that exposed his everyday pettiness about household expenses and money. He did not want this portrait in the biography but Michael's meanness about money (a word, by the way, that Jenny Stringer half-jokingly used to taunt him with) showed how in some respects he was a little man: a little man like Carlyle had been when confronted with his wife's domestic concerns. Michael was a penny-wise-pound foolish sort of man. He could pay for everyone's dinner and fail to give Jill enough money to run the house, get groceries and so on. Jill had found it impossible to engage him on this issue and I was a Boswellian biographer of minute particulars. That money was a form of control Michael exercised was evident to me from comments like Anne Robinson's. She marvelled that Jill did not even know how much Michael made as a member of Parliament.

At this point Michael had no objections to my treatment of the "Lamia" story. "I can't deny that that's what happened. I think you've dealt with that properly. That's that. But all the more so ... and from that time onward as you say in some quotations, relations with Jill were getting better and better." Michael paused and then said, "It didn't happen immediately"—that is, their reconciliations and renewed love for each took months and perhaps even years.

127

My stomach churns as I recall Jenny Stringer's visit to Pilgrim's Lane the next day. I had authored six biographies and was used to criticism. I have always offered my interviewees the opportunity to review their remarks and suggest corrections, although I have never surrendered control over a biographical narrative to any of my sources. Sensing that she came armed, I began to turn on my tape recorder. She objected. I pointed out that I wanted a precise a record of our meeting. Michael had never expressed the slightest qualm about my tape recordings and after I made my point, Jenny relented. Having won that concession, I decided to compromise where I had to in order to preserve the larger truths of the book. I saw no value—not then anyway—in being confrontational. Later, I would have to change my tactics, when I realised that any ground I gave would result in more demands for changes.

Jenny objected to a passage in which Celine described Jill "having Michael going up and down stairs supplying her needs: water, milk, a pillow etc, Celine remembers." Jenny commented: "Well, that's not very nice." She continued to quote: "Celine thought Jill was angry because she was the one dying. He [Michael] looked dead tired." Jenny commented:

Now this is not fair because Michael wanted to do this.
[CR] Well, this is just Celine's impression.
[JS] He never left her side.
[CR] I have no problem taking that out if it doesn't jibe with the general situation.
[JS] It suggests Jill was ordering him about.

I did take the passage out, primarily to appease. Without her interference, I would have presented a fuller picture even if witnesses contradicted each other. The truth is that Jill did order Michael about—not only when she was dying, but many times in the house as well. This I learned from a range of witnesses, many of whom did not know one another.

[JS] Then Celine says [to Jill], "You can't do this to Michael. He's an old man. He needs his sleep." Well, she wasn't doing it to Michael. Michael was wanting to do it himself. I think that's right, isn't it Michael?
[MF] You bet. I thought she was still going to stay [survive].

My narrative never questioned Michael's devotion to Jill during her final illness. But Celine was one of the few frank witnesses who explained the toll Jill's last days took on Michael.

What infuriated me about this sit-down with Jenny is that

I had been asking her for three years to give me her version of what happened during Jill's final days, but she always found a reason to put me off. Now she was doing the fine tuning to ensure that Michael emerged as a Saint. Jill's own conflicting emotions, her anger at Michael for never putting her first came out as she was dying. Her anger did not mean she no longer loved this great man; on the contrary, her anger resulted from disappointment that such a great and generous man had such a flaw. As she lay dying, he was certainly putting her first, but for Jill his effort came too late. This bitter truth was hard to bear. I don't think Michael ever confronted it. In retrospect, I feel rather like James Anthony Froude, who held back the knowledge of Carlyle's impotence and let the world know only in the posthumous publication of *My Relations with Carlyle*. A close reader of Froude's biography can detect a passage where he hints at Carlyle's impotence and a perceptive reader of *To Be a Woman* could, I believe, sense my feeling that for all their loving companionship, Michael failed Jill in a fundamental way. However, to have been as explicit as I am here would have brought the house of Foot down upon me, I have no doubt. Michael did not believe in censorship, so I have no right (reason?) to suggest he would have suppressed my biography, but I also have no doubt that a campaign would have been waged against me by his surrogates. I did not want to end like Froude, who spent a good deal of his remaining life defending himself against the charges of Carlyle's family and friends.

My book then included a scene with Julie at her mother's deathbed. As her mother died, Julie said, "I'm free." Julie told me this, but then asked me to remove the quotation when she saw my text. The comment expressed how much of a burden her mother's judgment had always placed upon her. "That's got to go," Jenny said. "Julie wants it out," I answered. I began to notice how, in the course of this meeting and a subsequent one, even the pretence of giving me suggestions was abandoned. I was now the hired hand doing Michael's bidding. I resolved, right then, that I would have to draw the line.

Michael and Jenny were trying to be helpful, if controlling and Jenny ended this session with a compliment about how I had included some of the tributes to Jill in the letters sent to Michael after her death. Still she continued quoting: "'He feels guilty for not having been with her.' I think Celine must have said that. I don't know what it means." I said it would take more explanation or should be cut, so I would cut it.

Then there was the touchy matter of taking equity out of the house so that Julie could buy her flat. I described how Jenny, Moni and Denis Forman, as well as Anne Robinson and her husband helped Michael and Jill with their financial plan.

[JS] Then you say, "In the process Michael realised that their helpmates had become critical of Julie.

They believed she wanted the house signed over to her." Well, that's not true.

[MF] Never.

Julie had objected to this passage as well, I told them. So where had I got this impression? From Celine and Anne Robinson—the latter, in particular, expressed her suspicions of Julie's motivations. Anne, at this point, was not in Michael's inner circle and could speak with a freedom others could not. Celine never seemed to care if what she said got her into trouble.

Jenny objected to a passage in which I quoted Esther (Julie's daughter) saying that Jill was angry with Michael for "not letting her go." "Is that right, Michael?" Jenny asked him. "No," he said, "I can't remember." "Right or wrong, this is what Esther said," I replied. "I don't think she was angry," Jenny said, "Anyway, you don't have to put it in." I did not reply. "You're going to think about it?" Jenny asked. I laughed and said, "Yes. I'll check with Esther." "Don't do that," Jenny said quickly. "Leave it, leave it." Her tactics were clear: as much as possible confine discussion of the biography to Pilgrim's Lane; when the biography left the house, so to speak, it would be subject to other points of view. "I just want to get it right," I said alluding to my wish to speak with Esther again, "I'll just email Esther." "It's difficult to piece it altogether, actually," Jenny remarked. Indeed and she had contributed to the difficulty. "Don't say I ... I don't want to cause a dispute," Jenny said.

That concluded our first session. I would have another with Jenny alone at her house, when she tried to get me to cut out the 'Lamia' story. She would not have done so in Michael's hearing, because he had already praised my handling of the episode. I did not ask to record her because I knew she would not stand for it. What I learned from her did not change the biography. We spent a good deal of time arguing about my vision of biography and why I believed Jenny was wrong to censor the story of the marriage.

Jenny then objected that I had emphasised the mother/

daughter relationship too much and to Jill's detriment.
"Don't you think," I said, "that readers will see that this is a
daughter's point of view? Are they going to take everything
Julie says as objective, historical fact? Aren't these her feelings
about her mother? How can you be so certain about how
people are going to read this biography?"

Julie did not play by Michael's and Jenny's political rules
and her lack of discretion infuriated them.

Our meeting was not acrimonious, but I did not give any
ground and of course Jenny made no concessions. Then she
took me to a bad Chinese restaurant.

128

I did not tape the last face-to-face meeting about the
biography. Going in I knew how fraught it would be and
somehow I thought the tape recorder would add to the
tension. Instead, as soon as I arrived at Philadelphia airport,
I asked my wife, Lisa Paddock, to drive home so that I could
recount into my tape recorder how I had seen Michael
unravel. This was vital since so much of the account I had
established had been formed of testimonials, that failing to
add my own of this pivotal moment would have served as an
injustice to the uncensored portrayal of the private man I had
been striving to present. Reflecting on the scene, I said:

> I don't think he harbours anger exactly. Julie was getting
> back from Italy and she called: "Should I come and
> get you to go over photographs?" I said, "Well, I can't
> do that because Jenny is coming over and we're going
> to talk about the book." She said, "Maybe I should be
> there?" I said, "I think it's in my interest and yours that

you are." I didn't say this to Michael. I wanted to avoid sitting down with him and Jenny and then having to go to Julie and have to explain it all again. 'This is what they don't like.' I thought, 'I'll be damned if I'm going to run back and forth between contending parties. Just let them have it all out around the table.'

So Julie came and Michael started reading this one passage where Julie says to me, "Have you even seen Michael's anger? It can be really frightening. Jill was frightened of his anger." That's when he went ballistic. "This is outrageous. Leave the house!" Julie just sat there, kept her composure. She said quietly, "I just said she was ... " "SHE WASN'T AFRAID OF MY ANGER. WE NEVER HAD ANY QUARREL!" He went on and on in a rage. Jenny kept saying, "Maybe I should go. Maybe I should go." I just sat there and then I said, "Michael, Ursula Owen described how frightening your anger could be." Well, that was somehow a different matter, he indicated. The thing that really offended me was that at one point he was in such a rage he said, "THIS IS COMING OUT!" I wanted to say to him, "Michael, I thought this was my book?" Well, it is coming out because Julie said to Michael, "Well, if you feel that strongly about it, take it out." She didn't take back what she said. I didn't see why she should. It took him about two days to calm down.

I told Lisa about my meeting with Jenny and her efforts to get me to cut out the 'Lamia' story. Jenny would work on Michael, I predicted and in a few months, I expected to hear from him that he wanted the 'Lamia' chapter out of the biography. Indeed, Paul Foot sent me a letter demanding that the 'Lamia' chapter go. Michael then sent me letters demanding so many changes in the chapter that in effect, the story was eviscerated. On that major issue, however, I would not budge, even when I got a call from Moni Forman making the same demand.

I told Lisa how Jenny muttered that what I wrote was "fiction," yet in the end she only demanded about half a dozen corrections. A further assault would come via the mail. Jenny wanted references to Barbara Castle cut because they might hurt her family. At one point, Michael demanded I send back my tape recordings.[1] I did not even reply to that request. I made further cosmetic changes, but stood firm on the rest.

"We were sitting in the garden," I told Lisa about my last afternoon with Michael at Pilgrim's Lane "and he said, 'Well, Ken Morgan's doing my biography. That cuts you out.'" It was that quick and that curt. No preamble and nothing afterwards. "I think he's angry with you," Lisa said. I was certainly angry with him, I admitted.

[LP] Didn't you sort of know it would go like this?

[CR] How could it not? He's a politician. He wants to control everything.

I told Lisa Michael was angry about the house money-allowance issue. "He's angry about that? How small," she said. Jenny had objected to my writing that Jill had re-invented herself before she met Michael. "She just wanted to move on," Jenny said. How could Jenny know? I was writing about

---

[1] All of my recordings are available in my archive at McFarlin Library, The University of Tulsa. The archive also includes the full, unedited version of this book (close to 200,000 words, as well as several revised drafts).

a period thirty years before the two women had met. "Oh man," Lisa said.

129

On my last night at Pilgrim's Lane, Michael asked me to call him when I got home. He had no particular purpose in mind other than to be sure I got home safely. I think it was his effort to smooth things over. I didn't call him, but he phoned me and we had a short, awkward conversation. We spoke only one other time, when he called to say he was upset about the upcoming *Daily Mail* serialisation of my biography. He hated the tabloid, calling it "The Forger's Gazette." I told Michael I had no authority to stop the serialisation and I would not profit a penny from its publication. I had told the publisher that Michael would be upset, but the publisher could not resist the ten thousand pound payment the *Mail* offered. I was square with Michael: I did not object to the publisher's decision.

We never spoke again.

Cape May County, New Jersey
January 31, 2007

Index